Le Petit Jardin de L'âme:
Little Garden of the Soul,
more than a place,
it is a state grace in mind and heart.

Val J. Littman

Le Petit Jardin de L'âme: Little Garden of the Soul, more than a place, it is a state grace in mind and heart.

ISBN: Softcover 978-1725509818
Copyright © 2017 by Val J. Littman

All rights reserved. No part of this book may be reproduced or transmitted in any form or by any means, electronic or mechanical, including photocopying, recording, or by any information storage and retrieval system, without permission in writing from the publisher.

The author, has researched the quotations used in this book through individual online research and through a Publisher Licensing Service. If a copyright holder sees a failing to give proper credit or the use is not permitted under fair use practices, please contact the author at - vallittman@gmail.com - to discuss possible future corrections.

Cover Art Credit: Art work used in the cover design is by Derek Corke, commissioned by Le Petit Jardin de L'âme.

To order additional copies of this book, contact:

Parson's Porch Books
1-423-475-7308
www.parsonsporch.com

Parson's Porch Books is an imprint of **Parson's Porch & Book Publishers** in Cleveland, Tennessee, which has double focus. We focus on the needs of creative writers who need a professional publisher to get their work to market, **&** we also focus on the needs of others by sharing our profits with those who struggle in poverty to meet their basic needs of food, clothing, shelter and safety.

Le Petit Jardin de L'âme

Contents

Preface 7

Chapter 1 13
   A Bridge

Chapter 2 20
   2005 - Annus Horribilis - Annus Mirabilis

Chapter 3 26
   State of Depression and the State of France

Chapter 4 34
   Der Schrei der Natur

Chapter 5 37
   And then …? Et alors?

Chapter 6 42
   Sunday Morning B4 The Service

Chapter 7 48
   Little by little Can "Humpty Dumpty" be put back together, again?

Chapter 8 54
   Christmas 2005

Chapter 9 68
   Leaving 2005 behind Building a future in 2006 and 2007

Chapter 10 77
   An Overview of times ahead

Chapter 11 85
   In the Moonlight

Chapter 12
   There is always more than meets the eye. Behind the scenes 90

Chapter 13 104
   A brief hiatus, gentle reader

Chapter 14 105
   2008 and 2009, growth & growing pains

Chapter 15 125
    How does the garden grow?

Chapter 16 133
    Chim chimini Chim Chim Cherou ♪

Chapter 17 140
    Progress is a bumpy road

Chapter 18 156
    Rising up in 2010

Chapter 19 167
    A glimmer of inner-personal light and a new horizon

Chapter 20 177
    2011 - Disturb Us Lord

Chapter 21 196
    Moments of reflection and perspective

Chapter 22 204
    2012

Chapter 23 213
    In the New World Touch-down, Terra Firma, Panamá

Epilogue 220

An Introduction to the Appendices 224

Appendix I 226
Appendix II 227
Appendix III 230
Appendix IV 239
Appendix V 244
Appendix VI 249
Appendix VII 252
Appendix VIII 271
Appendix IX 278
Appendix X 284
Bibliography for Le Petit Jardin 286

Val J. Littman

Preface

Life in France (indeed, life anywhere) evolves, unfolds. Even the best of plans are not exempt from the unexpected. And sometimes those events are not only beyond our control but also often beyond our wildest imagination. In the first book, *A Bright Sun & Long Shadows* I gave an account of the glorious and the gruesome events of the first four years of establishing our new life in France.

Most popular works in the genres of international living, cross cultural adjustment, and life transitions seem to stop after an apparent success has been established in the story line, as if such an adjustment to life was now complete, the chapter closed and "they live happily ever after". I believe that, often, there is an unconscious need, on the part of author and reader alike, to establish this "Happy-Ever-After" ending as permanent; a static state once reached, forever achieved, much like childhood images in fairy tales, or a heaven of harps, angels on floating clouds and that final reunion with long lost loved ones. There's a part of me that believes this is necessary for our personal short-term satisfaction. Such myths make life more bearable than the inevitable uncertainties that, in fact, we experience as life rolls along past the end of the most recent "last" chapter and into the realities that come next. The future reveals itself, emerging from nearly indistinguishable forms illuminated by slivers of moonlight, hopes to rise with the dawn, then, at last seen more clearly in the starkness of a noonday sun only to advance to twilight, dusk, darkness and another dawn.

In the long-haul of life, and in the inevitability of growing older one learns that, while that Genesis myth is true, "in the beginning all was good"; if we also live long enough we know that life is not static, nor is this originally created goodness invulnerable to the many hard knocks that continue long after that first garden is created, then grows, as the future becomes present and many presents in turn pass by. In the Judeo-Christian context of my faith, I witness that part of our human nature is, after all, a myth of our beginnings over and over, book after book, chapter after chapter of the rise and fall of life.

This is the stuff of which life stories are made, and such it is with this volume as a sequel to the first book, *A Bright Sun and Long Shadows*.

Indeed, after the first four years, we thought that we had "made it" through the worst of times and looked forward with a Robert Browning attitude, of the best yet ahead of us.

Grow old along with me! The best is yet to be,

The last of life, for which the first was made:
Our times are in His hand who saith

"A whole I planned,
Youth shows but half;
trust God: see all, nor be afraid!"
-Robert Browning

This second book is titled, *Le petit Jardin de l'âme*. In fact, when writing the first book, which encompassed years 2000 through to 2004, that was the intended title of the first volume. But our life in those years was far from the garden we hoped for – and a reference to Goethe's *A Bright Sun & Long Shadows* seemed more appropriate to describe the discoveries of those early years. But one could argue that this little garden of the soul - a state of mind and heart as much as a place – is a theme throughout our life and retirement experience.

Certainly, four years into our life in France we thought we had arrived. The little corner of our world at *Le petit Jardin de L'âme* would be the reality we anticipated and life in France might start to look and feel like the France we envisioned. It seemed that after having met the initial challenges of adjusting to life in France we would, at last, begin to cultivate this little garden of the soul for ourselves, for our B&B guests, and friends yet to come into our garden. And indeed, the garden did grow to become something well beyond what we intended – for better or for worse.

Much like the first book, *A Bright Sun & Long Shadows*, I will continue our story of life in France in *Le petit Jardin de L'âme* from where the first book left off and follow it through the developments, which continued to unfold after our first four years in France. I hope, you find more in these pages than years of nostalgic remembrance. The book, *Le petit Jardin de L'âme* is more than a chronology of events in years 2004 and following. It is, in part, a journey of the soul; of my soul, the soul of our marriage, and the soul of a little congregation called Grace in the south of France.

As in the first book, *A Bright Sun & Long Shadows*, our Annual Christmas letters and correspondence form the skeleton for this book. But here, in *Le petit jardin de L'âme,* there is also much more, between letters to friends and family, in the years of 2004 to 2011, that was not said, or could not be said at the time, or I simply had not formed the words for what was happening.

Writing of this book began late in 2012, and continued into 2017. This delay allowed for a different perspective to settle in, from a very different place in mind and heart. In this different style of *Le petit jardin de L'âme*, given a little distance from the events that shaped our lives, some of the immediacy of events is softened by faded memory, some of it sharpened by reflective insight. And, with time, patterns of behavior are more noticeable from afar. I expect that you will see some character development in the two protagonists, as Linda and I live our lives in these pages for you. This life in France has changed us individually and our marriage forever.

The experiences that unfold in *Le petit jardin de L'âme*, tell of both the delightful and the demoralizing events of the seven years of life in France, 2005 to 2012, which is the time frame for this book. The success, of the first four years, of having claimed our personal space in our renovated *maison vigneronne* in the village, was in fact not the end of a story but the beginning of the most unexpected of adventures of our life in France.

Throughout this memoir there are many characters from our life in France in the years 2004 to 2012. At the time of the writing of this book, some have passed on through death, many are still living. Except for Linda and Myself, the names of people mentioned in the book are fictionalized to varying degrees. I found that in the telling of this story, the action, interactions and references must be true. Yet in some cases I felt that some persons, if they were to see themselves in the light that often comes with the passing of time, might well be embarrassed by what they once said or did. So, the names of persons, in some cases, may be disguised, or are a composite of personalities. The references to their actions are true and based on actual experience. What is told as happening, did indeed happen but perhaps not by one person identified by a specific name. In the writing of the book interpersonal relationships and group dynamics have taken precedence over any one individual's name. This "mystery" will become clear as you read on (I hope).

I found an earlier attempt at a completely fictional "cast of characters" a bit futile in writing this book. Perhaps that is just an indication of the limits of my writing skill. However, I believe that it is a decision made in the best interests of the story. It is a memoir, not fiction and gives the reader an honest look – sometimes a painfully honest look - into our life in France at the time.

I apologize to those who may not yet have read the first book – *A Bright Sun & Long Shadows*. Some of the events from our earlier years, such as the beginnings of a House Church (October 2003) and our first Lessons and

Carols Service in (2002), flow through this book. And the development of relationships in our village and the surrounding area are part of an on-going process. But, *Le petit Jardin de L'âme* can be read independent of the first book. Of course, you can still run right out and purchase your copy of what someday may become a trilogy or quartet, in leather-bound volumes with gold leaf edging on the pages, perhaps - yet to come! I still get encouragement to write the book about how Linda and I met. And as you will read in *Le Petit Jardin de l'âme*, there is room for yet another book beyond 2012.

As I begin telling of the events of 2005 to 2012 I am reminded of a story told by my favorite curmudgeon, Andy Rooney, in his book of his experiences during WWII, My War.

Andy Rooney's anecdote is from a time in the 1990's; a time when he was attending a conference of distinguished historians in Chicago. Each presentation at the symposium was professionally competent regarding WWII, technically accurate, and intellectually stimulating, but each lacked one crucial element. The presenters were all too young to have actually served in the war.

There was a significant difference between the professional presentations and Andy's actual experience of WWII. Recalling the facts, accurately, dispassionately, and objectively, is a form of truth but it is not the actual event, which, when experienced, is often messy, intense and somehow escapes an orderly presentation.

My experience as a psychotherapist and spiritual counselor also confirms that certainly competence is important, but it is the patient who has the most accurate, al-be-it subjective, view of the event at hand. The patient always knows, first-hand, just how much it hurts and what the personal cost has been.

So it is with the telling of this story. In this memoire, I have attempted to reference journals, documents and procedures to keep me in line with the facts. But in the telling of this story I have something to bring above and beyond conventional commentary about life in France and whatever might evolve as a more convenient recounting of the local church's history. I was there when it happened.

In some cases, you will find more documentation in this memoir, *Le Petit Jardin*, than the first book, *A Bright Sun & Long Shadows*. There is less reference to our personal journal entries because during this time we stopped journaling together. But in my search to understand what was happening to us, I turned more to sources outside myself for understanding and you will find them referenced throughout. And for the on-going story of the little congregation that grew up around us, I refer to church records kept from the beginning. These years called upon my social work and organizational development skills for documentation and observation. I will pull them out of the archives along the way to tell the story of our experience of these years in France. Such documentation serves not only to help me remember where I was and what I was doing. It also gives that credibility that only "being there" can give.

For context and continuity, we will now move forward by taking one brief step back.

The last entry in book one, *A Bright Sun & Long Shadows* is our Letter from Christmas of 2003. So, the story picks up, after a *petit pause*, where we left off. Here is a bridge between the two books, and a peek into our lives in the form of an "Update from France" – to our Friends - in the summer of 2004, and our Christmas Letter of 2004 at the end of that year.

Chapter 1
A BRIDGE: From *A Bright Sun & Long Shadows* - to - *Le Petit Jardin de L'âme*

An Update from France – Summer 2004

Our faithful readers have reminded us that it has been several months (Christmas 2003 I believe) since the last update. I can't say that "time flies" in the south of France, it just seems to evaporate, one day into the next and before you know it "Bientôt" turns into "Il était une fois".

Our "biggest" change of life since Christmas 2003 is the introduction of Bijou Bunné. Some time ago, to satisfy our initial curiosity, we purchased a book *Rabbits for Dummies*. After a thorough reading, and doing some internet research, we decided, that indeed, we were dumb enough to have a pet rabbit. We are now the proud "parents" of a Tricolor Netherland Dwarf Bunny. Bijou is a grand three pounds of one hoppy bunny. She adds French-country flare to our garden and she is a real charmer with our clients.

One set of guests recently asked if Bijou could "come out and play" and the next thing we knew she was taking a snooze atop their suitcase in their room. On the other hand, when we are not looking she can mow down my tulips, geraniums, solanum, basil, thyme, lobelia, nasturtiums and other seasonal garden treats in a blink of an eye!

It is true that our French neighbors' initial question was – "Are you going to eat it?" It is difficult for them to understand the usefulness of a rabbit that is too small to eat but, they now hang bags of carrot tops on our door handle for this curious little pet. Linda has successfully trained her to use the litter box – so there are none of those pesky little "rabbit pearls" or "calling cards" around the garden. She (Bijou) recently let herself out of her "minimum security" pen. When we got up from our nap, Linda discovered Bijou was on her way "to china" in one of the lower flowerbeds. So, just when you thought that stories from the south of France have come to an end, we have a whole new chapter of life with Bijou Bunné.

Alas, I have no stories about French workmen in this update. I am happy to say that – for the most part – French workmen have not crossed our threshold in the past year.

Well, there is one exception! Two years after construction, after endless back-and-forth with the pool man and then his insurance company, the expert opinion of three different specialists, and with the help of our friends whose French (and persistence) is better than ours, we have found the problem! It seems that the original pool-man did not consider that a pool built adjacent to our private terrace, on the third floor would need an outlet for water that would inevitably overflow or get behind the liner. It was also discovered that the original liner had a hole – a puncture - that in the opinion of at least one of the insurance experts was there at the point of installation. The problem is remedied for the summer and a permanent solution is scheduled for autumn. I am happy for the solution and most happy to have friends who are so helpful.

We are in mid-summer and mildly busy. Our client base, being mostly American (USA and Canada) is finding European travel more expensive this year. Linda and I remind ourselves that we did not come to France to be busy – so we enjoy the breaks between B&B guests for ourselves and casually search out promotion venues which match the style of comfort we offer at **petit jardin de l'âme**. Volume has not been our aim. We want to cultivate a clientele that fit what we have to offer. We are happy with the results so far.

As far as acculturation to France goes – and it goes on endlessly. Linda and I have settled into two different ways of life. Linda continues to try to assimilate, improve her French for social conversation, go for walks to meet the neighbors and in general become more a part of the local scene. This results in little surprises from the neighbors on our doorstep from time to time. Louis brings us fresh oreillette pastries. Henri brings us cherries. Yesterday we received a little clock that goes "cock-a doodle-do" on the hour! Are these ole French guys charmers or what? For me, I have settled into life realizing that I will forever be a foreigner in France; a bit of a curiosity for the locals. I discovered that my interest in French language is for assertive and defensive purposes. And, I find the beautiful world we have created in our courtyard often more enjoyable than forays with the French. I find that France is a lovely place to visit from time to time. I believe that this realist's perspective adds some balance to the super, hyper, over-the-top romanticism that surrounds all-things-French!

This said, we both have joined a French/English choral group in a village nearby and enjoy it. We will resume our French conversation classes in September. I am looking forward to, at last, being in the *intermediate* class! And we continue to meet people – some French, some English-speaking, who also have different views on why they live in France. This is the France beyond what you find in the tour books.

In the last year a small congregation who wish to worship in English has grown-up around us. About 20 people gather once a month for Eucharist. We recently had our first bi-lingual French/English worship service with the Eglise Réformée congregation in a nearby village, 33 attending! And, I will celebrate a wedding in September for a family at a private chateau nearby.

And so it goes; life in France – in the Midi - in retirement – in progress – "in eternum" AMEN.

During 2004 we expanded our social circle. Linda and I often cultivated our closest relationships among people outside the young and developing church group. In this aspect, developing a broad spectrum of friendships, we found that our lives and choice of closest friends followed a pattern we had unconsciously developed over many years, even before coming to France. One delightful example I include here. In September of 2004 and for several years thereafter was a celebration of "The Last Night of The Proms" (also known as "The Proms", "The BBC Proms" or "The Henry Wood Promenade Concerts"). This was a very English thing, celebrating the last of a summer's long concert series held at Royal Albert Hall in London since 1895. With a history going back as far as the 18th century and more recently expanded by popular demand, increased technology and the commercial market. The proms are a BIG cause of celebration not only in England but wherever English could tune in to the BBC live televised event.

Dear Friends, an English /Dutch couple decided to host a dinner evening and a big screen viewing of the proms concert. The second half of the last evening had a rather predictable format filled with fun and unabashed (slightly politically incorrect) songs from the days of British imperialism. It was an evening of great fun and high-quality entertainment!

As a part of this first year's celebration in France, one selection of the second half of the concert included the famed Gilbert and Sullivan, "As Some Day It May Happen" (I've got a little list) from the Mikado. The evening also included a nod to the USA with the guest conductor and a John Phillip Sousa march included in the program.

Val J. Littman

In sending our Thank You to our hosts after the party I felt inspired, though not nearly as clever as Gilbert and Sullivan, to frame my "Thank You lyrics" to the tune of "I've Got a Little List"
Put on your Gilbert & Sullivan hat and feel free to hum along with my little parody if you wish: ♪

Not one more day should pass without remembering "The Proms"
I've been a bit remiss -- But I've got a little list
Of many joys that evening brings to all the world around
A night not to be missed -- We've got it on our list
But none could be more happy than our closest little throng --
We drink fine wine and eat great meals while singing all along
We share this bit of revelry with faire England and her clans
Ev'n USA can chime in with great Sousa and his band
Thanks for your generosity - We wish to send our fond "merci's"
And glad we're on your list – And glad we're on your list
Chorus:
The last Night of the Proms, you see, we all enjoy whole-heartedly
A night not to be missed – We've got it on our list.

Happily, our relationships with some of the people from that evening developed and lasted many years.

Christmas 2004, le petit jardin de l'âme

Our fourth holiday season in our adopted home of France begins to truly feel like the holidays have arrived. Or perhaps, it is we who have arrived. The foreign and strange have become familiar and we now find that we have friends and "family" and some traditions of our own with which to celebrate the holidays à la Française. I count this year as our first real Thanksgiving in France. This year we had a table-full of dear friends - and a turkey!

The Turkey Hunt: As it turns out fresh whole turkeys in France are very much like French workmen. They become available about one month after you no longer need them. If the French are going to roast a turkey, it is for the end of December, not the fourth Thursday of November. Our request at area supermarkets was met with surprise. Indeed, our turkey was still grazing and gobbling to enjoy yet one more month before landing on the supermarket shelves. The local Florensac butcher did discover a fresh bird could be available for €6.60 kg (that translates into a "George Bush post-election-dollar" of about $3.90 per pound). At this we decided to reconsider our plans for our traditional a 20-lb. bird.

Turkey parts are plentiful year-round - wings, breasts, legs but the whole bird is rare indeed. One of our B&B guests suggested that we take the available parts and "build our own bird" but I could not bear the thought of the *Plat de Résistance* looking like a set of legos in the center of the table. Eventually we did find the rare bird, or should I say birds. It seems that French Turkeys are not like their American cousins. At this time of year, none are found any bigger than about 5-7 pounds. (Turkeys served at Christmas dinners are larger, but one month too late for an American Thanksgiving Day celebration) Anyway, Thanksgiving was a success complete with a *potiron (a pumpkin-like squash)* transformed into pumpkin pie and *griottes (tart cherries)* standing in for the cranberry compote. Our guests added to the celebration with sweets that I have not yet shared with anyone, a specially labeled bottle of champagne "*Le Péché du Pèlerins*" (sin of the pilgrims), and a bouquet of fresh parsley for our Bijou Bunné.

Bijou Bunné: Our bunny, Bijou, is now one year old and a real charmer. Our friends and we spoil her. While the French tolerate our eccentricities, it seems that they are genetically wired to think of rabbits only as dinner. Linda occasionally takes Bijou for a walk. That is, she puts Bijou in a basket and they go for a walk together around the old village walls. To some, this has become a conversation piece and is good practice for Linda's French. In one recent conversation, it became clear that we treat Bijou to herbs from the garden and celery grown in little pots just for her. Our French friend, knowing full well Bijou's privileged status, forgot herself, and with a glint in her eye said, "Oh she would be a tasty treat". Bijou is happy to live her pampered life in the protected environment of our courtyard.

Noël: The director of a local French/English Choral Group, recently retired from Eton College in England, is excellent and we have a whole new set of new French and English relationships. Linda sings alto and I am still able to sing tenor, but it is a stretch. *Our Concert de Noël* was a success and, at last, my high-school French was useful for singing Quittez, Pasteurs.

We also celebrated our third annual Traditional Festival of Lessons and Carols. About 150-170 people attend. Although most of the congregation is British, with a smattering of Americans, Canadians, some Dutch, and an Australian or two we are now translating the Bidding Prayer, Scriptures and my sermon into French as the French are showing more interest. This year we received newspaper publicity both before and after the service.

There is a bit more Christmas in the air this year. During the past three years we have seen more and more signs of Christmas. In the past, Christmas seemed to take place quietly behind French doors with little public display. This year we have a village competition for *Illuminations des Maison et Jardins* and the village merchants were given free *Sapin de Noël* for their storefronts.

There is a curious decoration item here in France called *Père Noël Grimpant (Father Christmas climbing)*. Around this time of year hundreds of little gnome-sized Santa Claus look-a-likes appear on ropes hanging from balconies. Since, in our village many people still actually use their fireplaces for heat Père Noël enters with his sack through balcony windows. To Linda and I, as long-time city-dwellers, a man with a sack, climbing onto balconies looks like a "Burglar Santa".

The New Year: Our long-standing tradition of a first of the year "retreat" and planning session continues with some variations. This year we will spend the first few days of January at Orange, a couple hours to the east. Here we will reflect on where we have been and what we hope for in the New Year. With our renovation complete we are on to planning the next chapter of our lives. Of course, we have home decorating projects ahead, a B&B to develop and our French to improve. We have a growing House Church group and Linda tutors a young man in English. We have plenty to "do" but we are now to settle in to what life-in-retirement will be for us.
This year's Christmas letter - and its availability on the web - is the product of my fledgling attempts to use our new computer. A new model has replaced the abacus we brought from the USA four years ago. With this new technology I now make my mistakes faster than ever before. And, in the New Year I expect to spend endless days, weeks and months locating, updating, creating and cursing this little time-saver. Look for a fresh new look to our B&B web site sometime.... oh... about Christmas next year!

And thus, dear reader, with this summary of Summer and the Holidays of 2004 you have a glimpse of what our life had become; what had grown out of the rubble of the first three or four years.

We were, in fact emotionally exhausted, frayed at the edges and had some psychological scars yet to heal, but we were set, again, with only four years delay, on our original road to enjoy France in retirement as we had envisioned. "And God saw that it was Good…" and they rested (read that collapsed) on the one thousand, four hundred, and sixtieth day.

In the south of France, things take a bit longer than the mythical seven days for creation of le petit jardin de l'âme.

Le Petit Jardin de L'âme

It is right it should be so;
Man was made for Joy & Woe;
And when this we rightly know
Thro' the World we safely go.
Joy & Woe are woven fine,
A clothing for the Soul divine;
Under every grief & pine
Runs a joy with silken twine.
-Auguries of Innocence, William Blake

Chapter 2
2005 - Annus Horribilis - Annus Mirabilis

As I anticipate writing the next couple chapters I think they will be most difficult. It is hard to describe the decent of years 2003 and 2004, into a most horrible year amid what many might see as admirable achievements of the life of retirement in France having, at last, arrived.

People more illustrious than I, have faced the two-sided coin of years that were both horrible and miraculous. It is in a biblical sense what makes up awe and wonder.

Some readers may remember Queen Elizabeth II referring to the year of 1992 as an "Annus Horribilis" in her Christmas Address that year, or the reference made by Kofi Annan in his United Nations address of December 2004. It seems that both these references to such combinations of the horrible and wondrous, go further back to a reference in 1666. It is John Dryden's reference that comes closest to my purposes for a title of this chapter. The poem composed by Dryden about the events of 1666. "*annus mirabilis*" seems to overlook the fact, that the year was beset by great calamities for England (including the Great Fire of London), but Dryden chose to interpret the absence of greater disaster as miraculous divine intervention. Strangely, this might be summed up in the present day colloquial expression," well, it could have been worse." I think this is the stuff for further reflection and it applies to our annus horribilis of 2005. I'll let you be the judge. Read on.

An Annus Horribilis does not happen overnight. One tends to "get over" Isolated, horrible events and "get on with it". An annus Horribilius is made from the accumulated stuff, repeated attacks, that erode personal resilience, attempts to navigate through difficulties repeatedly eventually shapes a hopeless feeling, facing one taunt after another, rising with determined (but flagging) resilience that tends to bring a bull in the ring to an inevitable end. It is a glimpse of light shining, in what seems unending night that draws the moth to the flame. So, I'll give you a little "run–up" to Annus Horribilis.

It became clear as early as March 2002 that I was suffering from a reactive depression – a normal adjustment to complex changes and unrelenting stresses of our first years in France with no end in sight. As was also normal, even as one trained in these matters, I resisted and thought I could handle this myself. But throughout 2002 and well into the summer of 2003

I received treatment for depression. (I refer to this in the chapter - *Of Dreams and Nightmares in 2002* in *A Bright Sun & Long Shadows*)

For all the benefits of an A+ health care plan that France has to offer, mental health treatment was, at the time, substandard. My treatment consisted of medication alone with a couple well-meaning but inadequate attempts at psychotherapy. This was in part due to lack of resources in English and a shortage of trained clinicians in private practice for psychotherapy. There were "Day Hospital" and inpatient resources for the more severe cases but not much available for the "walking wounded". Medication was the treatment of choice. I allowed myself to follow a medication regimen that, as a professional in my pre-retirement life, back in the USA, I would have cautioned against. But resources were limited and, symptomatically I didn't much care anymore. I followed the Prozac, and valium as needed, regimen from March 2002 to July 2004 with quarterly checkups that amounted to a 15-minute *pro forma* meeting and prescription renewal. There was a hiatus in medication for a short time thinking that the depression had lifted but this was followed by a return to the same treatment plan.

By July 2004 I was feeling marginally better; more resigned to life in France, would be a more accurate description than an actual cure of depression. I believe that Linda felt that there was some improvement in my coping and some relief. On the surface things were more tolerable.

I should say that in retrospect, I now suspect that a prevailing self-serving French attitude of "What could possibly be wrong with France" may have accompanied the French professional's assessment of my situation.

A few friends knew of the treatment, but in general I just kept on "getting on". However, unknown to me (perhaps sub-conscious is the better word) an arsenal of unused valium was accumulating in my bedside-table. This was not a conscious hoarding of medications. The valium was to be taken as needed and as time moved on I did not need it, but it was continued to be prescribed. And I, in a rather mechanical fashion, got the prescription filled.

The discovery of a means for suicide came as a surprise to me, and today is a reason for writing this chapter. Yes, this could be an embarrassment to my family and to me, but perhaps this story will help someone. Read on.

During the pharmacological approach to treating my depression, there was no cautionary monitoring of the use of the medication, nor was there a reassessment of the treatment plan, but rather a simple "if you are feeling better, then we just do more of the same". In retrospect treatment relied simply on an assumed accurate description from the patient rather than therapeutic inquiry from the psychiatrist. As the patient, with symptoms of a patient, it was not possible for me to apply the necessary therapeutic inquiry or "detective work" that I had for years applied in my practice with my own clients. In this case, with this psychiatrist, when my symptoms appeared to diminish it was an indication to stop. There was no gradual reduction nor was there a cautionary check on the drug supply. And it never occurred to me at prescription renewal time to say "Doctor, I have a lot of this valium lying around".

One day the "light went on". I can't say exactly when or why I noticed the boxes of unused valium next to the Prozac.

Thoughts of suicide had crossed my mind from time to time, but I discounted them for one reason or another. These were abstract notions and lacked a satisfactory means to an end. The thoughts now were precipitated by my depression, but, as part of my young adult life, I had considered, in an academic sort of way, the moral and ethical issues related to suicide. In some abstract way, these thoughts were not new. They were a part of my philosophical or theoretical, academic development. Long ago and apart from any clinical depression I had allowed for suicide in my own view of life as a possible end of life.

For many years, long before the move to France and the onset of depression, I knew that I was not afraid of dying. Philosophically and theologically I had for many years in my adult life known that it was not death I was afraid of, but rather suffering. As a part of a general philosophy of life, thoughts of suicide that involved a chance of suffering or violence passed quickly out of my mind, never a real possibility. Hypothetical thoughts of suicide that might inadvertently harm the lives of others by my actions were not real options - the drama of jumping in front of a train filled with unsuspecting passengers or an auto accident – came and went. My worst fear in this abstract thinking would be to attempt suicide and fail – so any attempt must be certain, painless, and not endanger others – and I had not found such a way. Nor, it must be said to this point; I had not been depressed or wanted to end my life. This was all - until now – academic, abstract and a way of understanding others. I had, as a pastor and in my clinical practice counselled people (rarely I should say) who expressed suicidal thoughts. Until now suicide, and my thoughts and feelings about it, were important pieces of self-knowledge of where I stood to keep my own ideas, assumptions and disposition separate while helping others in psychotherapy.

Then there was what I describe as that "Eureka moment" a surprise discovery when I realized I was looking at a means. Well over 100 tablets of Valium (I no longer actually remember the count, but it was about five or six boxes of 10 milligram pills of valium – probably 28 to a box) sitting before me. I now had a means of suicide. I could sleep my life away.

In a retrospective clinical fashion, I find it strange, the psychiatrist did not explore any of these ideas with me as his patient nor did he even ask except in the most general way in the initial interview if I had ever considered suicide. And my response was like the paragraphs above. Basically, I admitted generalized suicidal thoughts but had no clear method and had expressed a general desire to live and find enjoyment in my life in France.

Time went by. In general, I felt, if not better, at least less worse.

But a specter hovered overhead – over our heads – as this depression clearly influenced our life together. The cost of the previous four years of adjustment to France had left us as couple like strangers living in the same house. Our view to how to adjust to life in France was a tip of an iceberg. We generally had acquired a list of topics upon which we were bound not to agree – about life in France and how to cope. My choice for isolation – or selective exposure to things French, left Linda without her partner with whom she came to France to retire. Linda's outward sunny disposition, and search for the silver lining in each cloud, seemed not only to discount my feelings of despair but also covered her own loneliness and her personal struggles to cope. We were growing apart.

While the physical state of our home steadily improved and looked ever more like the garden we had hoped, our spirit, individually and as a couple, was in sad shape. Some sample journal entries paint a more accurate picture and show that what happened in 2005 has its roots in 2003.

A journal entry – From Val - October 2003:

It is 9:30 PM and my love has gone to bed – or more accurately – gone to the bedroom to sit in bed and read. This has occurred without much "feeling" or irritation between us but rather an ennui – a lack of connectedness that has become more prevalent.

This evening, for example we both returned home from our usual Monday shopping errands, we agreed that neither of us were hungry and perhaps later would have a snack instead of preparing dinner. Then I poured a glass of port (well, two) and sat on the terrace to watch the sun set. Later I worked at the computer while Linda sat and read a magazine. Around 8:45 PM she went to the kitchen (I don't remember her saying anything). When I went to the kitchen about 9:15 she was nearly finished with her snack and I prepared some tea, a pear and some cheese for myself. She then said she was tired and would be going to bed. I had set my place at the table across from her but after she announced she was leaving, I decided to take my snack up to the study where I am now – writing. And so, the day ends.

I will go to bed sometime around 10:30 or 11 PM and Linda will be sitting up in bed, asleep with the magazine on her lap. I will prepare for bed, turn out the light and if she shows signs of waking up, I'll say "good- night", with perhaps a token tap on her thigh. But my, oh my, our connection, our spirit, is gone. There is such "flatness" or at times a noticeable "disconnect" one from the other. We talk "about things" but we have ceased to communicate.

We have successfully completed – as much as any old house is completed – our renovation project. It is a lovely place, despite all the irritations along the way. I believe that in general we have even captured the spirit we intended – at least on the walls and in the furnishings. But in the process, we have lost our spirits. We are no longer together except we live in the same space. The renovation project finished makes our separateness more pronounced. Our shared interest and united front against a common construction enemy during the renovation project, no longer binds us together. We have grown apart.

It is a deep sadness for me on top of the generalized sadness / depression about life in France. We have lost our life together as we once knew it.

In the big picture of our plans for moving to France, our twenty-fifth wedding anniversary, December 2003, was to be a special event but as those days approached there was little enthusiasm to celebrate.

As I remember, we took ourselves to a nice dinner; a low-key celebration and didn't talk about the obvious; the disappointing life in France and its effect on our relationship.

In February 2004 another journal entry pointed to all the appearances of successfully adjusting to life in France: Our French had improved to carry us through an entire "French Evening" at neighboring village with a mix of French and English friends, but hidden in this apparent successful integration into French life there was the growing reality of a quality, a way of life that continued to be disturbing; something hovering overhead. Or as I later came to describe it "There was just something in the air we breathed, in the water we drink".

Journal entry of February 2004:

I find my life in France no longer as "desperate" as last year, nor as depressing as our first years. I have found ways to better tolerate this life in France, but happiness eludes me, and from four years of conditioning, I remain on the defensive. I find moments of calm within our sanctuary, a protected space, rather than leading the integrated life I had hoped for in France.

Do not misunderstand, I do venture out into the village and the area, but it is with necessity and a sense of determination that I will not be hemmed in. There is no joy. I find life outside our walls as harsh and boorish, not gentle. Of course, there are exceptions which my love will be quick to point out. A dynamic that works to further divide us.

I ask myself; what is it about "here" that I resist being drawn into? What is it about this way of life that I do not, cannot be a part of? Perhaps it is me. What is my fear about this way of life? How do I both critically look at myself and give my intuitive sense the credibility I have developed over years of study, reflection and helping others, to trust the invisible in their lives. I am not imagining this. There is something not right with life in France.

Chapter 3
State of Depression and the State of France

Coincidence or Corroboration?

> *The past has its afterlife in the present, and the future is not simply the unknown. Past, Present, and Future are not in isolation; one not only builds upon the other sequentially, but each infuses and informs the other. Such fluidity makes eternity.*
> -Val Littman, personal meditation

I had, by personal disposition and by professional experience come to realize that most depression is a combination of both "Nature" and "Nurture". Baring, the most severe diagnosis with an extreme biochemical imbalance, most depressions were a mix of personal disposition, biochemical change, and environmental factors. Sometimes reactive depression was, in fact, a normal reaction to abnormal circumstances.

In my current situation, I had passed the denial stages and sought help, taken the medications and still I felt that there was something beyond me influencing the quality of my life.

I became increasingly more alert to articles about life in France or the "European" state of mind. Earlier research prior to arriving in France had as its focus, lifestyle, customs, language and costs of living and property renovation. All our reading and research in advance of arriving in France was now at least five years old, and much of it from sources older than that, from our period of initial exploration.

My interest now included a search of a different kind, with my own, personal, experiences as a guide. For starters, I was now able to read some articles in French – it was a "slog" at times but I managed. Also, like knowing a language, I knew better what to look for – areas of mental health, attitudes, *"tendance profonde"*.

I turned to popular literature in English and some in French. First, I was trying to understand more about where I lived and the people with whom I lived. But nagging away at me was an attempt to understand an intangible reality, which I sensed in an environment that surrounded me. What was it in the air I breathed? Willing to "own-up" to my personal set of perceptions, and aspects of the depression, I still searched to understand something outside myself that was also truly a part of this depressed state; not my state of mind alone but the State of France and the French. I was convinced that this wasn't just about me.

I cannot say that my search was systematic in the sense of scientific research, it was random. I simply was more alert when an article came "knocking at my door" staring me in the face. I read it. Part of this randomness was that it was a common practice for friends to share their various magazine subscriptions both English and French, passing them on from one to another, therefore my choice of reading material was somewhat determined for me. At first, I simply read what came along. Later, I began doing some on-line research that took me a long way from the path that most ex-pats search as they adjust to life in France.

A picture and article in *L' Express*, caught my attention. It was a group of professionals seated, as if on the morning metro, commuting to work, looking at each other with guarded expressions – they were weary and wary. The bar graph above their heads represented 26 countries. The Title of the article: *Cette méfiance qui tue la croissance* (This mistrust which kills growth). The article elaborates on what the graphic indicated. Of twenty-six countries studied, when asked *"il est possible de faire confiance aux autres?"* (Is it possible to trust others?) France scored near the bottom of the list. The French score of "yes", 21%, was third from the bottom of the list. Only Portugal and Turkey had lower levels of trust in others.

In the USA by comparison, 46% answered "yes", it was possible to trust others. The UK and Germany found themselves in the middle of the pack (37.7%). Apparently, the Swedes, Norwegians, Danes and Finns were most trusting of each other in the 60% range.

The study goes on to explore cheating, as more or less tolerated in different countries. The *"pourcentage de personnes qui déclarent ' trouver injustifiable de réclamer indûment des aides publiques"* '- percentage of persons who find it unwarranted to claim public help unduly - that is, as the sub-title of the graph says; "on *n'hésite pas a frauder"*. They do not hesitate to cheat. France scored an embarrassing 38.6% - the lowest of 21 countries. In claiming public assistance, roughly 39% of the French found cheating unacceptable. Over 60% of the French found it OK - acceptable, justifiable.

By comparison 73% of people in the USA found it unacceptable to cheat in receiving public assistance, 70% in the UK, and once again the Northern European counties were found most honest, Denmark, Holland, Norway scoring in the top three. The study was conducted to measure these impacts on economic growth in France. I was interested in their impact on the quality of life in France.

Maybe there is something in the air that I breathe in France. It is not just my depression talking, the high levels of mistrust and high tolerance for cheating that I feel, is a part of the fabric of French life.

The life-style contradiction, which is my experience of France, raises its head in other ways. France, the champion of "quality of Life", "the art of living", the long lunch and sexual liberation, also seems to be a surprisingly miserable place.

Prompted by a series of suicides at France Telecom, companion articles from *The World*, and *The Economist*, asked "Why are the French so prone to suicide?". The title of the article, *Bonjour tristesse*, was a play on the words of is a novel by Françoise Sagan, published in 1954. The article not only revealed a high rate of suicide in France; the French suicide rate is 14.6 per 100,000 people, according to the OECD (**O**rganization for **E**conomic **C**o-operation and **D**evelopment). Men are particularly prone: 22.8, against 7.5 for women, the article goes on to say that one-in-ten French people are on anti-depressants. This is in addition to their already notorious levels of pill popping of every description for general ailments.

Here in the country of the 35-hour working week, with copious holidays to promote its joie de vivre and whose president extols the merits of measuring happiness, not just national income, the French suicide rate is over twice that in Britain and 40% higher than in Germany and America.

I researched a study from 2005. A long-term comparison of prevalence, risk factors and care for depression between 1991 and 2005 helped me to realize that my "sixth sense" was indeed picking up on something that was not only a part of my adjustment to life in France but was a part of the *aire de France* that I breathed.

Was it so unusual that my suicidal thoughts might also be a part of the depression in this environment? My reading brought me to a point of realization that the state of depression is the State of France.

Actually, I stumbled on this "State of France", as a more significant play on words than I could have imagined.

There was an aspect of daily French life, which troubled me. A form of secrecy, shame or repressive silence hovered over even every day

"neighborly relations". Little incivilities, which might ordinarily be handled with a straightforward faced to face request, were somehow filled with trepidation and a sense of foreboding.
We had come to learn that the French don't complain. Well, they complain all right, but not productively.

Like a caricature or cartoon, they complain to each other about someone, or something else. They mumble and grumble as many folks do around the world when they are unhappy or inconvenienced, but have trapped themselves in an ineffective dynamic without positive steps to fix what ails them. I've done it myself, we all do it on occasion, and so do the French but that is not the level of complaint I am talking about. In France there is a skeleton hanging in the closet, of which my neighbors would not speak, and which I had yet to discover.

At the surface of everyday life, it looks like this little cartoon (I must admit, an actual situation):

> I remember overhearing a conversation in the street between two neighbors – I am certain it was meant for me (and others) to overhear. The discussion was about the about the noise levels coming from the windows of another neighbor. Instead of asking the noisy neighbor to lower the volume, two other neighbors engaged in a conversation *about a* noisy neighbor. This, not-so-subtle, conversation took place directly under the noisy neighbor's open window. At the time I thought it a bit odd, then a bit funny – perhaps even clever. This "nudge-nudge, wink, wink" does seem funny at first but not as a way of life.

Witnessing a fellow citizen in violation of local laws may result in dysfunctional complaining but no real corrective action with authorities. People shake their heads, shrug their shoulders and perhaps complain ineffectively but loud enough to be heard, to no-one and especially not to anyone in authority - and I wondered why.

They seemed "blocked" by some socially imposed silence.

The "State of France", it turns out, refers not only to some mental state (as was my original intention) but to the deliberate change of term for France from Republic of France to State of France in the 1940s.
The "French State" (L'État Français), as it called itself in contrast to the "French Republic", in the period of July 1940 through October 1944. On

Val J. Littman

June 10, 1940, the National Assembly, faced with imminent military defeat by Germany, gave full power to Marshal Philippe Pétain. In 1940, Pétain was known mainly as a World War I hero, the winner of Verdun. As last President of the Council of the Third Republic, Pétain suppressed the parliament and immediately turned the regime into a non-democratic government collaborating with Germany. Vichy France was established after France surrendered to Germany on June 22, 1940, and took its name from the government's administrative center in Vichy, southeast of Paris.

While Pétain collaborated with the Germans, Charles de Gaulle claimed to incarnate the legitimacy and the continuity of France. Following the liberation of France after Operation Overlord, de Gaulle proclaimed the Provisional Government of the French Republic (GPRF) in June 1944. After the Liberation of Paris in August, the GPRF installed itself in Paris on August 31. The GPRF was recognized as the legitimate government of France by all the allies on October 23, 1944.

As historian Henry Rousso has named this in *The Vichy Syndrome* (1987), Vichy and the state collaboration of France remains a "past that does not pass." Historiography debates are, still today, passionate, opposing and conflicting views on the nature and legitimacy of Vichy's collaboration with Nazi Germany. The French as a people still live with fears of "collaboration". Report of neighborhood incivilities, as they are called, is low or non-existent for fear of the repercussions for "denouncing" their neighbors.

I make these references to the Vichy Regime from readings in several sources that eventually came together in my thinking and experience of Life in France. The above information relies on an on-line source; The Jewish Virtual Library – Vichy Regime.

Life in France gave me a greater appreciation of impact of World War II and the aftermath. There are a few common place reminders of the remnants of the Vichy Regime, and the French Resistance movement. It was not unusual to find in villages across France, plaques commemorating a stand of the resistance movement, usually a place of execution of a resistance fighter, there was also a creepy bit of "silence' about a government compound – largely abandoned but with token signs of activity – that was only a few kilometers from Florensac. It was a curiosity but more amazing no-one seemed to know anything about it. A friend and history buff concluded – which he recognized was speculative – but was based on limited sketchy information available and more importantly the difficulty in finding information, which lent credence to the story that this was a small government compound associated with Vichy government in the area in the early 1940's.

A regional newspaper *Nice Matin* revealed on February 28, 2007, that in more than 1,000 condominium properties on the Côte d'Azur, rules dating to Vichy were still in force. One of these rules, for example, stated that: "The contractors are to make the following statements: they are of French nationality, are not Jewish, nor married to Jewish in the sense of the laws and ordinances in force" [under Vichy, NDLR]" The president of the CRIF-Côte d'Azur, a Jewish association group, of course condemned what one of the inhabitants of such a condominium qualified as an "anachronism" with "no consequences."

There was a time when I often traveled from our home in the south of France to Clermont Ferrand. The train made a routine stop at Vichy, but it was often a time of reflection for me on one of France's darker moments, in recent history which may well have affected this spirit of mistrust and shame.

A lighter look at this same serious topic was found in an article in the Telegraph Review 21 June 2008 Sophie Marceau tells Benjamin Secher about her new role as a spy in an era that is still taboo in France. The film (In French: *Les Femmes de l'ombre*) is a 2008 French historical drama and adventure film, *Les Femmes de l'ombre / Female Agents* nevertheless prods at an uncomfortable question that continues to haunt the French, more than 60 years after war ended: Who resisted and who collaborated? In the interview regarding her role in the film Marceau comments; "It still hasn't been spoken about properly in France". "If people - or their families - collaborated, they don't tell you, they keep silent. And I think that has nourished a kind of complex. The French are weird sometimes: they can be a real pain in the ass."

Contrary to the public image of France and the French, the mood of the French is not very good. The number of people who see the future with pessimism has been consistently larger than the number of optimists. TNS-Sofres (*TNS Sofres*, **S**ociété **Fr**ançaise d'enquêtes par **s**ondages, a survey, polling and research company created in 1963 by Pierre Weill) has carried out the same poll since 1972 (source: Le Monde April 2008). It shows, globally, a negative trend with little recent improvement 1997-2002 (a slightly improved economic situation), a collapse 2002-2007 (the second term of Chirac) and a (momentary) improvement in 2007 (the hope generated by Sarkozy).

All this above, taken from periods that preceded and followed the time-frame of this chapter, and my state of mind in 2005, indicates that what I was experiencing in 2005 was the result of something much bigger than me and my individual depression. It also continues to be a part of French life.

I also sought out antidotes to this state of depression in my choice of readings.

The Happiness Hypothesis: Putting Ancient Wisdom and Philosophy to the Test of Modern Science by Jonathan Haidt, was one such attempt to rise above a negative thought pattern. After reacquainting myself with some of the ancient highways and byways of the quest for happiness, I came away from this reading, not with antidotes for negative thinking, but rather, with some new metaphors for my experience and reinforcement of my experience in what Haidt identifies as a "divided mind". He proposes there are two, sometimes competing dynamics that determine our future. Like a rider on the back of an elephant, the conscious, reasoning part of the mind has only limited control of what the elephant does. While there may be effective ways of getting the elephant and rider to work together, there remains a basic truth that happiness comes from both within and without.

The ancient's hypothesis that happiness comes from within and cannot be obtained by making the world conform to your desires; an idea widespread from Buddha in India and the Stoic philosophers in ancient Greece and Rome and many present-day psychotherapists and twelve-step recovery programs all counseled people to break their emotional attachments to people and events, which are unpredictable and uncontrollable, and to cultivate instead an attitude of acceptance. Haidt recommends that this dynamic need amendment (I do too).

This ancient idea deserves respect, and it is certainly true that changing your mind is usually a more effective response to frustration than is changing the world. However, this version of the happiness hypothesis is limited. There are some things worth striving for, and there are real external conditions of life that can make you lastingly happier (or not). There is relatedness - the bonds we form, and need to form, with others - in the world around us.

Haidt uses two similar metaphors to illustrate this interrelatedness "riding the elephant" and "riding the horse". The reality of the moment and the next moment are not solely dependent on what we do, or think, or interpret etc. Life is not simply just what we make of it – as some wisdom might suggest. Unless one thinks they have definitive control over the elephant which they are riding – we can nudge it, coax it and learn better ways of riding it but in each case, there is a divided self. And I would add that

Haidt's divided "self" is a microcosm for a divided social system, or divided world. Instead of limiting this analogy to an interior world within oneself I believe that it is representative – a metaphor - for the world in which we live.

For me this made sense in the social world in which I was living in France now. But it left me clear as ever that there was a French Pachyderm upon which I was riding through life in France. And for me in this on-going moment of four years I was as a rider, very exhausted by life and having tried every skill that I had – and the éléphant was going where it will and taking me with it.

Stop the world I want to get off.

Chapter 4
Der Schrei der Natur

In a page in his diary headed *Nice 22.01.1892,* Edvard Munch described his inspiration for *Der Schrei der Natur* (The Scream of Nature).

Most of us know this artist's work as The Scream:

Of this work, Edvard Munch is thought to have said; "I was walking along a path with two friends – the sun was setting – suddenly the sky turned blood red – I paused, feeling exhausted, and leaned on the fence – there was blood and tongues of fire above the blue-black fjord and the city – my friends walked on, and I stood there trembling with anxiety – and I sensed an infinite scream passing through nature."

And so, one day, I found myself in a hospital bed with bruises on my wrists, the signs of having been restrained, and of having wrestled against those restraints during a long dark night? I was now living the experience I had witnessed in others on occasion many years ago in two periods of work in on in-patient psychiatric units, one at a Veterans Hospital, a part of my training in clinical social work, and the second a part-time job while of my working my way through a second degree at Loyola University, Chicago.

It is difficult to tell this part of the story in the usual sequence of events because I, myself, must put it together from the other side of a nightmare. This next chapter is highly subjective, but then again, any suicide is highly subjective – it is built into the etymology – isn't it?

I have some remembrance of a precipitant, and some memory of intent, a realization that "now" was the moment for ultimate relief, that all was lost, and nothing mattered.

This day, in April 2005, was like most had become for us. Both Linda and I went about the continued reparations of shoddy workmanship and the details of finishing our home. After the workmen had taken their pay and left, our work began. Day after day we discovered things carelessly done and in need of our righting the consequences of their work. Today, mine was to repair cracks that appeared and re-appeared at the surface of the area surrounding the pool. It was important to get to this now that the weather was warm enough and finish before it became too hot to work in the full sun. The persistent cracks were not structural problems but rather something in the finishing layer that had not been executed properly, and my initial repair had not worked. So, I was to scrape off the finish coat (again) dig out the area of the fissure, and prepare to fill it, smooth it, and eventually cover it again with a new finish. This task since the pool was now filled with its liner and water was done on my hands and knees crawling around the edge of the pool inch by inch, head down, derrière smiling at the sun above.

After a few hours, thinking that I had now completed, the first step of scraping and cleaning out the cracks I asked Linda for a "consult". I had already done this work once before only to have the cracks re-appear and Linda maintained that I had not gone deep enough and that was the cause of the problem's return. Normally such tasks are her area of expertise but there was something about this task that had become mine. Perhaps it was because it was related to the pool which had already been identified Val's project, perhaps it was something that Linda, having no other remedy in mind felt should be left with its scaling layers and superficial cracks glaring back at us this summer. More probably, since Linda did not use the pool much, and I used it daily, it was I who had more invested in what it looked like. I remember an edginess in her tone even before I began the project as if to say that this was an exercise in futility. But, I had begun and now I asked for her opinion. She came to the terrace, looked and spotted a fleck – one fleck that she could flick off with her finger-nail. I had been working on my hands and knees for hours and this fleck seemed to indicate that the whole job needed to be done over!

The argument began familiarly enough, "Why did I ask her advice if I were not going to follow it ". We'd been here before but usually managed to work it out. But as the argument increased in tension I found myself holding the chisel in my hand and realized that I would have thrown it at her. The danger was unspoken but in the blink of an eye, it was very real to both of us. I grabbed her and shook her and then ran from the room, having frightened myself as well as her. It was a breaking point: The tension, the work, the gradual deterioration of our relationship, the day after day "I can barely get out of bed" feeling. I wanted it all to end.

In the courtyard garden I sat weeping. The pool quickly faded into the background. What came flooding to the forefront was the state of our marriage, and the worthless-ness of it all even if we could fix all the shoddy workmanship we would have nothing. I realized that now was the time. I needed a space and time to be alone – not to recover, but to put an end to this madness.

Linda urged that we go to friends and talk this through. Exposing the marital embarrassment to new found friends in a small ex-pat community was impossible for me and the attempts at therapy already were found to be of little help. I also was aware that Linda perceived this adjustment to life in France as my problem. Combine that with her own fear for her safety just moments ago and it is not exactly something you bring to discuss over "tea" with your new British friends. Eventually she decided to go, if I was not going with her, she would go to ask their help, adding embarrassment to my loss of control.

As Linda drove the car from the garage, the immanence of my life-falling apart intensified. I mentally planned my next few moments alone.

I remember writing a note saying that I "was going for a long walk – will be back late". I had no intention of going for a walk but wanted Linda, upon her return not to immediately search for me. I had, some months earlier in the gap between deciding to end my life and now, finding the opportunity, drafted a "suicide note" with instructions. I collected the valium, and some alcohol for extra measure. My plan was to go to one of the less often used guest rooms take the pills, wash them down with a drink and sit in the dark and sleep away. That is the last I remember.

I have a vague memory of going to turn off the light in the room, but in conversations after-the-fact I realize that the light did not get turned off. I must have "blacked out" somewhere along the way.

Eventually, late in the night, after realizing that I was not returning from my walk, Linda saw a thread of light under the door during her search. Emergency services were called.

For me, darkness followed until a time when, out of the darkness, a horror appeared; a half-conscious, long, painful, mind-numbing, scream of realization. My attempt at suicide had failed. I do not know if there was a scream, but the tree HAD fallen in the forest, the realization of failure was like thunder in a cavern echoing over and over – an infinite scream passing through nature. Is there anything that could be worse than the dream devastated, worse than the depression, worse than the sense of failure that preceded suicide?

Yes, Waking up.

Chapter 5
And then …? Et alors?

Strangely, it seems that the emergency psych-consult on-call the night of my admission was the very doctor who had prescribed my prozac and valium. In retrospect a curious question arises. My admission and subsequent treatment made me wonder just how this hospitalization would be recorded statistically. Perhaps the depression and suicide rate in France, mentioned in the chapter above, The State of Depression and The Sate of France, is under-estimated (under-recorded)?

I woke up in a hospital bed in the pulmonary unit. Apparently after the initial emergency, the concerns were for my respiratory system which had been compromised by inhaling my vomit. Although I was in a semi-private room, my roommate, another pulmonary patient, was discretely quiet and nurses went about their duties without mention of my suicide for a couple days. I was receiving some respiratory therapy. Later when the nursing staff did ask, they asked in a way that was to reassure all concerned that I knew why I was there. I wonder now, was I a part of the statistics for pulmonary patients, or psyche patients?

Linda visited, and we began to piece together the events and how we would deal with life after suicide. There were friends in France and acquaintances who would know that something happened, the neighbors on rue Molière must have seen the flashing lights from the arrival of the emergency medical team and there were those in the growing church congregation who would know that I was missing on Sunday, and substitute clergy to be found, because I was in the hospital.

My attempt at suicide left Linda to "hold the bag" of our social life with explanations phone calls and her own feelings about this. This too I needed to response to. In some ways this accumulation of "to-dos" after the fact made emotional recovery, mine, ours and Linda's, seem more like a public relations exercise than the therapy that was needed. The time for us should have been first on the list but we went about the planning of how to respond to others dutifully and with perfect aplomb. There was no attempt to hide this ugly part of life but how to say things and to who seemed more pressing than our needs. In some ways, telling the story had its own entry–level of therapy.

Sometime around day five or six in the hospital I was visited by a psychiatric consult. Was I ready to go home or should the treatment plan include a stay on the inpatient psychiatric unit – perhaps the day hospital for a few weeks? This was discussed primarily in French, enough for me to know that both inpatient and day hospital would be one grand French immersion lesson. Not exactly what I thought of as therapeutic. Since life in France and life with the French was a part of the problem we decided together that this might not work well. I agreed to reconnect with therapy – if only to attempt to get a different, more effective therapist.

The consultation prior to discharge was handled by a person I thought to be a psychologist or perhaps psychiatric nurse. She never completely introduced herself, but I had grown use to that I France. She was accompanied by an older woman who stayed benignly in the background. But in fact, I did not know who the players were. Was the person to whom I spoke a student? Was the woman in the background a student? Were they colleagues? Was she perhaps an English speaker? Did they always do these interviews in tandem? I never did find out. We began our conversation in French. Beyond the words of the conversation, to understand the situation I was translating in my head from my pre-retirement professional life experience. It was likely that she had some power to hold me in the hospital, transferred to a psych unit, or recommend discharge with a stated plan. She made that clear to me. I also made myself clear to her in French; our very conversation, struggling as I was to express psychological nuances in French, and she not speaking English indicated the limitations of therapy in French for me in the hospital or in any out-patient program with a group of French-speaking patients.

We then, after a little bit of "testy exchange" in which I figured I had nothing to lose, decided to cooperate. I spoke to her in English and she responded in French – it has its difficulties but - it was a sign we were working together. I was not averse to seeking help, was there help in English? She had none, but I agreed to search on my own – again. And "No", I was no longer suicidal, that is, I had given it my best shot and failed. I had no follow up plan and no longer any means to that end. I had exhausted my suicide plan and had no other. This was, I admit not a masterful discharge plan, but I could expect nothing more and she had some assurance from me that I was not coming back any time soon under similar conditions. Agreed – merci, au revoir!

At least for the moment I felt that I not she, was in control of my own life. Soon after returning home I contacted each of three couples considered closest friends, to explain what had happened. There was no sense in trying to euphemize or minimize or make some form of British understatement. They were supportive and understanding.

With other less intimate conversations and inquiries from casual acquaintances, with neighbors on the street, I simply relayed the facts: I had an emergency and spend the past week on the pulmonary unit of the hospital - true it was. No further questions asked.

But foremost on my list was a question for Linda: Why did you not just let me die?

We had over the course of our married life clearly told each other that neither of us wished for extraordinary means to keep us alive. This had not specifically included a conversation about a suicide attempt, but I felt that my wishes had been ignored. Linda's response to my question was: "I wasn't ready to let you go." I heard this as lovingly as I think she intended it, but she was angry with me for possibly leaving her alone, and I was angry with her for pulling me back into a life I truly wished were ended. No matter what was to come, our marriage could never be the same.

A glimpse into Linda's mind and heart is the note she wrote to me – on the night of 15 April 2005 while waiting at the hospital:

> Hello my love,
>
> Last night before I left I thought of leaving you a note, so that when you wake up and were able, you would have something from me telling you that I have been here from the start with you for the whole day, and that I love you beyond all measure. But I didn't leave it because I saw you would not be ready to read anything.
>
> This morning I come at 3:45 am. The nurses wouldn't allow me to sit with you. I tried very hard, but no. They were kind enough to have someone come to talk with me to explain. They didn't understand that I know what was best for you – for us, but I relented once I realized that you had been given heavy sedation to help you sleep and that you would not wake up until later this morning.
>
> Forgive me, my love for not being able to let you go. You are the

light of my life, my most precious flower. You enrich my life immeasurably. Please do not take your beauty away.

The nurses have been kind this morning. I said I would stay here and wait for you, I wouldn't be going home. They brought me a more comfortable chair in a more private space. I so want you to see me when you open your eyes to know that I love you. One of the nurses just asked what I would like for breakfast – so kind. I brought some fruit and can use the coffee machine, so I don't need anything, except to be with you.

I once again have that wonderful image of us; That image from the card, where (two children) are off together, holding hands. I know not where to, but together. Please take my hand.

Contrary to the 1970's song "Suicide is Painless," only successful suicide is painless. The pain after an unsuccessful attempt is endless. And the regret, not of having attempting suicide, but rather of having failed, lives on into a present for which the recently recovered expected to be a "no-show".

For those of "A certain age", the mere mention of the 1970's TV series or movie, M*A*S*H brings ring-tones to the brain of the song "Suicide Is Painless." Perhaps you are already humming the tune.

M*A*S*H was a unique, some might say bizarre, mix of the comedic adventures of the members of the Mobile Army Surgical Hospital set against the tragedies of war. The lyrics of Johnny Mandel's song, were written by the (then) 14 years old, Mike Altman, son of the director Robert Altman. This teen captured the dark comedy, the irony, and the tragedy of the Korean War.

And now it seemed an apt description of my life.

These early days post suicide had a bizarre quality to them. I was not feeling any better, but now had the embarrassment and humiliation to deal with from a failed suicide attempt. Surviving the suicide brought no relief, or joy to life. My approach was pragmatic.

I am not the most athletic of persons, have never been, so the analogy which follows, may "limp" a bit – sorry for the pun in advance.

Life for me was like being a runner in a marathon. You know at the beginning that only one person wins the marathon. Most people, I understand, run with their own goals of achieving their "personal best". In my depression, I had already concluded that, in France I was not going to "win" at anything. My getting through life had taken on a "do-my-personal-best" attitude. Now in this post suicide chapter of my life I had taken a serious fall in the race. It was time to re-adjust the goals - lower the bar – again. My approach was pragmatic: pick myself up and just get to the finish line, eventually, however best I could. I must make the best of a really bad situation when I would rather not be here at all. "Opting out" had not worked. In my life, before retirement, I had never been in this situation. Before France, I was accustomed to succeeding, personally and professionally; working hard and exceeding expectations. Dragging myself on through defeat was not in my repertoire of life experiences.

I am tempted to describe this time as a self-inflicted limbo, a purgatory where happiness was not even in the picture, but rather in the push/pull of life after suicide it was all about how best to get through another day. From a clinical professional perspective this is nightmare upon nightmare. But so, it was, and so while feeling no better now than before, I simply had a different task, responding to what others were thinking, asking feeling.

Sitting on my "pity pot" was not among the best of solutions, so I turned my attention to how to make the best of a bad situation. Frankly I remained convinced that the move to France was our, best researched, most anticipated and worst decision of our lives.

This personal challenge was the driver in the days, weeks, months, and as it turns out years after the suicide. I became my own crisis management manager. The first response after speaking to a few close friends, was time related because the next Sunday worship service of the little congregation that had grown up around Linda and me over the past two years, was just days away. How best to handle this situation? What would I advise someone in my situation?

Also, Linda, as my companion, partner and advisor in this chapter of our life together was still in need of some help in dealing with the mess that I had given us, and this key relationship was not working at its best now. I think we were both just picking ourselves up and dusting ourselves off but were not yet together as we had been in married life of years past and hoped someday to be again.

Chapter 6
Sunday Morning B4 The Service

The Sunday congregation which had started in October 2003 had been meeting for a Sunday Eucharist; first in our home and then in homes of other members. In less than two years we had grown from a casual 12 meeting in our living room to a regular 25 plus, meeting in homes across the region, once a month. Services were still informal and were organized by me as the clergy.

I had established a habit of creating an Order of Service with hymns and prayers, and rather than a formal sermon, I created a *B4 The Service Reflection* based on the scripture readings for the day. People could gather in a few moments of silence and reflect on the Scripture they were about to hear in the service. It had become popular and the accepted format. It also helped to make the transition to focused reflection and worship from the "Greetings" and "Good Morning, chit chat" that come normally when people gather. People eagerly volunteered to serve in various capacities once each month.

Although there was another retired clergy from the Church of England in the area, as he was approaching 80 years, in response to my request, he had indicated that he wished only to help on occasion, and the organization of this growing church community was something that he saw as clearly for me to do, not him. He wished to maintain his freedom to leave France and return to England for weeks at a time to be with his books and maintain tangential relations with the growing church community. Being that he was nearly twenty years my senior, this was understandable, and I appreciated his help on occasion. I felt that, as seasoned clergy, he had a sense of how a congregational life can make gentle, incremental and eventually substantial demands on its clergy's time. He wished to stay in the background.

One of these monthly Sunday services fell during the time of my hospitalization. The task fell to Linda to ask this clergy to take the April Sunday Service. Of course, this entailed some explanation. He was certain that this should all remain "hush – hush", so people knew of my absence in only the most general terms. A "get well soon" card came, signed by many of the congregation.

As it happens, the Sunday in May, after my suicide attempt, was Pentecost Sunday in the normal church year. It seemed to me that I had multiple challenges and responsibilities. As my own crisis manager, I looked at the situation in the following way:

I could not ignore my unexpected absence in April.

- In addition to my personal and professional belief that "hush - hush" is never really "hush hush" anyway, I am convinced that truth and transparency are often the better route to take when two roads diverge in the woods.

- I had a pastoral responsibility to be an example to this growing church on at least three fronts. Setting the example of how we would handle not only this personal embarrassing moment but also to use this moment as an example for this growing community. And this was a "teaching moment" for the community about depression and how we might as a church community respond to this, not only for me but for others.

- This day was also one of the most important days in the church year – Pentecost. Pentecost along with Easter and Christmas were major celebration days.

How would I do this? I could not ignore the realities around me, I keenly felt the pastoral responsibilities to this little church community and I did not want to overshadow this great day of the church year.

Some few knew the story of the recent weeks, some chose a diplomatic silence, and others, simply, had not a clue. Some of those who would attend on Sunday would be "regulars" with an established relationship to me and to Linda, and as is often the case, there would be a new-comer or two.

Here, in the text of the "B4 The Service Reflection" for Sunday, May 15th, 2005, was my best shot:

> Each of us in our lives is faced with a search for meaning; what is the significance of our individual experience. On this Pentecost Day I share with you an event of my past month. Perhaps it is disturbing (for this I apologize); perhaps it is stimulating (for this is what I hope). I share it with a feeling of humility and a hope that it brings us all to a deeper appreciation of our relationship to God.

As most of you now know, I was not here last month because I had a serious battle with depression. I tell you this before our Eucharist for several reasons: On a practical level, it answers some natural questions about my absence. On a professional level, I believe it is a way to de-stigmatize depression, a serious and common problem in our world.

This dark side of retirement to the sunny south has been a part of our life for most of our four years in France. This is not "just a bad day"; I chose not to go on living. After a grueling period of uncertainty for Linda, during my recovery, I asked her why she had ignored my wish - to let me die. Her response, "I was not ready to let you go."

Most importantly I tell you this before our Eucharist because it says something about our relationship to God and to one another.

In our hymns we sing of this relationship.

> *"And when human hearts are aching*
> *Under sorrow's iron rod*
> *Then we find that self same aching*
> *Deep within the Heart of God"*
> -Timothy Rees 1874 – 1939, Bishop of Llandaff - Music Abbot's Leigh

Pentecost is traditionally the "Birthday of the Church" when the gift of the Spirit transformed the horror of crucifixion and the awe of Resurrection into a community of Charity, Joy, Peace, Patience, Gentleness, Goodness, and Long Suffering. (Traditionally, known as the Fruits of the Holy Spirit) These qualities, which created the Early Church, are the same qualities that transform our lives today. And, sometimes in our darkest of nights, these are the gift of God saying, "But I'm not ready to let you go."

Our hymns for this Pentecost Day are the same as last month. I repeat them not simply because I like them, but because on this Pentecost Day they speak of the life of God's spirit among us. I am more aware of God's Spirit passed on to us, and through us, in the divine, and in the everyday touch of the Spirit of God we give to each other.

The response that day was a surprising spirit of support. I do not know what I expected, except to get through the morning without tears or feeling like a hypocrite or a fool. The congregation's response was – perhaps a "British understatement" – supportive. The conversations after the service included stories from others of how difficult it has been for them adjusting to new life in France, some others referred to members of family who experienced depression and how it affected their lives. All in all, I felt that a difficult day had gone well.

Mostly, I was relieved and felt that I could go on leading this congregation, my own experience respected and my leadership as clergy in prayer and faith confirmed and accepted by this group. I felt that this was one of those moments, a sign that we were growing as a community of faith. I felt energized to continue to lead the group. I was not aware that any other another word was mentioned by anyone in the congregation until more than four years later. (Ah, but I get ahead of myself).

My own pain that led to the suicide seemed to take a "back-seat" in the wake of a growing PR "to-do" list. After the Sunday worship, there was yet more "To-Do"; a responsible accounting to closest friends, some quieting of local rumors, my own recovery and our recovery as a couple, not to mention some plan for getting on with life.

My family was not to know of the suicide. They knew in general of my difficulties with life in France. I felt that a long-distance revelation, after the fact would bring my parents more anguish than benefit of knowing. Besides the imposition and interruption in their lives, in practice they could be of little help in France on any practical matters. It seemed that a partial truth was, in my estimation what they, specifically my aging parents, could bear. So, they knew that life in France was difficult but did not know specifically about the suicide attempt. It was for them I felt, protective.

I began a few selected calls to closest long-time friends who could help from a distance. This transparency to the church community and to friends was important, not only was it important because I wished with the congregation and with friends, not to live a lie either by withholding or minimizing information. This was for me a matter of integrity. It was an opportunity to live out an example which, professionally, I advocated as therapeutic and as one that grows mature relationships. By the same token I did not feel that I needed to make this act the center of a conversation when it would be a distraction. I needed to discern when this was an important part of my relationship to be discussed and when this may be something that I was more aware of than others.

A call to one friend took a more practical, straight-forward approach, since I was asking his help to locate an English-speaking psychiatrist and therapist in France. I had not thought of my friend as a resource earlier but since I did make an agreement to seek counseling I would try again. Through his international professional network in another area of medicine, a friend of a friend, helped to make a connection with an English-speaking psychiatrist in Montpellier as part of the university hospital faculty.

I established a relationship with this English-speaking psychiatrist. He was an improvement over the first psychiatrist I had found but was primarily concerned with dispensing and monitoring medication only. His psychotherapy skills were not much help for me, but he did speak English. He also was not much help in locating a psychotherapist. Eventually a member of the congregation came through with an internet link. She herself did not know the network of counselors but found it and thought it might be useful for me. I connected on my own and introduced myself to the therapist – about 45-minute drive, in the opposite direction of Montpellier.

The summer months were largely filled by this readjustment to life. Now the little church group was accustomed to taking a recess during July and August. So, my "work" for the summer was to connect to the psychiatrist, and psychotherapist.

During the summer of 2005, I received a call from the Bishop in Charge of the Convocation of Episcopal Churches in Europe, Pierre Whalon. It was a "call out of the blue"; I did not then nor do I now, believe that he knew at all the difficulties I was having in April. I surmised that in his professional network he had come into contact with some of my past professional and personal network in the church and someone probably told him he had a resource in the South of France that he could make better use of. The call to serve as mentor for a young priest in the convocation was an unexpected delight. This too led me into areas of life in the larger (diocese) Convocation of Episcopal Churches in Europe. This was to be the beginning of a relationship with the young cleric which began as mentor but continued as friend in years to come. It also was the beginning of a working relationship with the bishop which I found satisfying and mutually respected. This was a return to my personal sense of competency, professional respect and collegial support which I had enjoyed pre-retirement. I found my relationship with the Convocation one of the more rewarding experiences of life in Europe. It was indeed a gift at this time. I felt I was on a promising track

I first met Bishop Whalon when he was bishop-elect. We met briefly at his consecration as bishop of The Convocation in the autumn of 2001. I had since kept him informed of the activities of the informal church group developing in the south of France, but the relationship was formal and limited. Now In the summer of 2005, Bishop Whalon called to ask if I might consider a mentoring relationship with a priest new to the Episcopal Church in Europe as the younger clergy accepted his first call to a mission church in Clermont Ferrand France. I never really knew how my name had come to bishop Whalon's mind but assumed that my past professional network and the Presiding Bishop's contacts prompted Bishop Pierre to contact me. I imagine that somewhere in the informal network of bishops, Bishop Whalon had been made aware that he had a retired clergy resource in his diocese that was a perfect fit for what he was looking for. While I had retired to France with no ambitions to grow a church or an active ministry in the organized church, my past work with the church had caught up with me in a most pleasant way.

With the attempted suicide three months behind me, and my focus on getting on with life I did not mention it. Instead I saw this as an opportunity to move forward and find some meaning to life in France.

I was pleased to help. This would use some of my professional skills in consulting and counseling and give me an opportunity to be more involved in church life, a pleasant distraction from renovation woes, and the difficulties of integration with French life. It also gave me a chance to "start over" in an area where I felt competent after four years in France of feeling incompetent in so many ways.

Chapter 7
Little by little Can "Humpty Dumpty" be put back together, again?

Having established transparency with the little church congregation, I searched for a way to develop my own treatment plan with a psychiatrist for medication management and a psychotherapist and the re-connection with the larger church was a gift to my recovery. One critical area remained for recovery; our marriage.

Prior to suicide I made and attempt to explain "Why" for Linda in a letter, and to give her some help "post mortem". In hind sight it now seems strange, but I include it here because it helps to identify not only my breakdown but OUR break-down as a couple. Not only was life broken and my attempts to fix it were not working. I had not stopped loving Linda (though I believe that is how it must have felt to her) I could no longer live the life that had evolved in France. Death was a way and now that was past I could not build a new way myself. I thought perhaps we could build it together or could we find a new way together. Now, given the circumstances, these were still things that needed to be said as part of a recovery as a couple.

Instructions for Linda April 2005 – Suicide Attempt
Why, and what to say:

Inevitably you will be asked "Why?" What follows is intended to be some help to you. Of course; at this point I will no longer be a part of this life therefore what you say and do are completely up to you. l thought to offer the following suggestions as some last help to you. If they help, use them, if not, you will do what you think is best.

Why: Perhaps it is best summed up in the words I once wrote to you in a card – After four years; I have learned that our move to France was the best planned, most anticipated and worst decision of my life. This is compounded by the fact that financially it has also been disastrous: The fall of the American Dollar, rise in European inflation, cannot be compensated for by the development of our B&B. The B&B was never envisioned as necessary in that way. The necessary premature sale of our property at Rue General Fraisse all add up to limiting the financial resources we might have to pack up and leave France for another venue. I

Le Petit Jardin de L'âme

see no real way out that would allow for living a life we wished to live. However, in the end, there is no explanation that will truly be sufficient. For those who understand, no explanation will be necessary. For those who do not understand, no explanation can be sufficient.

Note: (In hind sight the sale of our property on General Fraisse turned out to be providential but at the time it seemed premature to recoup our investment)

There is no short answer that will be sufficient, but to try to answer, "Why?" I can only say that our life in France, the environment of France is unbearable.

Those initial disappointments and frustrations during the renovation I considered to be passing challenges at first, but I have come to realize that the way of life in France is more than disappointment. There is a basic deceit, dishonesty, denial … call it what you will; it gnaws at me. I know that you will counter by focusing on the positive. I do not discount the positive, but it is the exception to a general way of deception, "me first", "catch me if you can" way of life that I find intolerable. Some call it "the way of peasants" - the Paysanne, the country people. I was expecting a simpler honesty from these country folk, not daily treacheries. I know that you do not see this as I do.

Perhaps a reference to two examples, two similar life periods, that I know you do understand, will help you understand this one. Something similar – albeit less all pervasive - has happened to me twice before – once it led to my leaving the RC church because I could not live my life surrounded by what I saw as institutionalized daily deception and corruption of the life I had hoped to live. A second time it was what caused me to leave my position managing the Arthur Andersen & Co., Employee Assistance Program. In both cases I landed on my feet and had a better life. I came to France eager and hopeful. I found a daily battle between life as I hoped it would be and life as it is in the south of France. I am exhausted by the daily struggle and see that we are financially trapped. I have not the strength to continue indefinitely as if things might get better.

Life in France has been not only a grand disappointment for me, but an irretrievable financial loss has made a "way out" impossible.

Unfortunately, financially speaking, we put all our eggs into this French basket.

Even recovery from depression still leaves me in an environment that assaults me every day. I do not view my suicide as an act of depression. I cannot deny the depression, but my suicide is the way to finally surrender to an all-pervasive aggressor. I feel that we/I have been deceived; in little ways by individuals and on a grand scale by a cultural norm.

The life style that I envisioned was based on values that we shared, and one that assumed common values shared by the people and environment in which lived our life. That is not so, The France of our/my dream died, a dream turned nightmare. I cannot keep the appearances of the dream alive. I believe that it is impossible to create the environment we desired when surrounded by the life that is truly the "France" that I have come to know.

I now wish to rest from what has become a daily battle between a dream (our dream) of life in France and the day-to-day reality. I have neither the energy nor, realistically, do we have the financial resources to start over.

You seem to cope with this change; although I know it has taken a toll, you just will not surrender. But surely you see that you and I are no longer together on a view of life. So, a way forward is not a shared way forward and separation would be even more devastating personally and financially. I do not blame you for this difference, but it is there.

Some will see only that our life here appeared to be an idyllic life. In fact, despite many obstacles we have created a beautiful home and garden. It is beautiful; I regret that we planted it here. I have so appreciated some few new-found friends in France but in the end, they are oases in a dessert. Like our home, an island in a sea that is France.

Prior to life in France, I lived my life without regrets. Sure, I made mistakes but had no regrets. Life in France has many regrets:

I regret that I was not able to hold off this moment until my parents had passed on, so that they would not have to suffer this sorrow and I expect this embarrassment to them. I regret giving them this sadness but living my life waiting for them to die is no less regrettable.

> Lastly, and most important, please know that I have always thought that you were the best part of my life. Our decision to marry and our life in Chicago were the happiest for me. We had a dream together and I loved not only the dream but dreaming it with you. I continue to love you but our life in France has been unbearable for me and we no long live even this life together. I cannot go on living this way. I cannot continue to see what was once beautiful in our lives continue to disintegrate, strangled by everyday deceit from the outside and the dissolution of our common life and vision from within.
>
> You alone cannot make right what has brought me to this point. I know my depression has changed our lives. I regret so very much being the cloud over your France. But in the end, even depression can be an accurate reflection of the depressing situation. I believe that you have chosen to see the France you wish to see. Unfortunately, I see more than I wish to see. I would have wanted, if only for your sake to see the sunny side. But a bright sun casts long shadows.
>
> My love, I know that you will find a way to go on with your life. I believe that we have together made the necessary legal provisions so that everything that was ours is now yours….

I then go on to practical things of funeral arrangements, and such …

> How have I committed suicide? As you know, during the time I was on Prozac for Depression the Dr. also prescribed Xanax. I took both the Prozac and Xanax as prescribed. But the amount of Xanax was always more than I needed. The extras grew into a "stockpile" and eventually I realized that this was my opportunity. I do not know the exact amount necessary for a lethal dose, (Note: In retrospect I understand that I took 60+ 10mg tablets plus alcohol before passing out) but hope that the amount is sufficient to combine with alcohol to depress the central nervous system functioning and go to sleep without waking. This is intended to be a planned end of my life.

The above was used at the time of the attempted suicide of April 2005. Obviously, the attempt was unsuccessful. There have been recurring thoughts of suicide but without a means. And, having been unsuccessful once, a reluctance to be unsuccessful again serves as some deterrent. But in that Annus Horribilis of 2005 and all that lead up to it, I had come to a new frontier of life and death where death was an option. An option, not in an abstract way as it had been in my philosophical years as a student in my 20's, not in the way of my years as a professional therapist listening to a client, but in a very real way this gift of life, my life, was overcome by a willingness to give it all to death. And now, on the far side of that frontier I had to live.

We were each trying to make this experiment in France work. But I felt that we were each trying to make it work separately. And our marriage had been seriously affected, not only by the suicide attempt but by this entire four years of this experiment of living in France.

Putting on my clinical case management hat I looked to some couples counseling as a help. We had used couples counseling early in our marriage a couple times in the past to get through normal couples' issues. So, I assumed that we could try again. But the same problems in finding individual psychotherapy for me in France were present as I looked for a couple's counselor.

One attempt since I was at the early stages of a therapy relationship was to use the psychotherapist I had found, for some couples' sessions. We tried one. Not only did Linda not feel comfortable, it was clear that she saw this – recovering from the suicide attempt and living in France - was my problem. I made an attempt to say how I felt; that this had to affect us as a couple.

The therapist made an attempt, but Linda did not feel comfortable with the therapist. There was nothing improper about the therapist, but I knew from my past professional life that either there is a "therapy–fit", or no fit. The problem now was that we did not have an infinite number of therapists to choose from. Initially I had my own minor discomforts with this therapist, but I decided to "make it work" and also wondered internally if I had some internal resistance of my own to overcome. So I pressed on but without Linda. This left each of us to recover each in our own way. And from my perspective this has colored our married lives to this day. We had had a good marriage for 27 years, but growing together stopped somewhere in France in 2005. So, we were each on a road to somewhere. And perhaps, to use Linda's image, we were holding hands. But our heads and hearts and our most intimate selves were in different places. We were no longer together in the same way, and had not been for most of these years in

France, but we still walked in this garden, le petit jardin de l'âme, ever so tangentially connected to each other.

> *"A man may feel as if he had come to pieces,*
> *and at the same time is standing in the road inspecting the parts,*
> *and wondering what sort of machine it will make*
> *if he can put it back together again."*
> -T.S. Eliot on his life falling apart (as recounted by his friend Frank Morley in 1933)

Chapter 8
Christmas 2005

Our Christmas Letter of 2005 was the public image we shared with a larger group of friends and former B&B clients.

Christmas 2005 in France has become for us a busy time. We host an American style Thanksgiving dinner to begin the holiday season, with a few close friends. Having solved some of the logistical problems of years' past, we now have adapted to too-small turkeys (this year we roasted three, the size of "three French hens"), "potiron pumpkin pie", and a creative mix of berries to offset a scarcity of cranberries (eventually I found some). (It seems I cannot make enough of it). And on the second Sunday of December, the English Lessons and Carols Service has become (in its 4th year) a tradition for many. Over 200 attended this year with coverage in the local news and the event announced in a few churches by the local French clergy. Our past traditions have changed, and we spend Christmas and the New Year holidays with friends, who like ourselves, have adopted France as home. We will "get away" some time in the New Year to set our goals and make our plans for what's next in our lives – a modification of our New Year's tradition of many years past.

In answer to FAQs from our fans:

How is our French? We still think of ourselves as forever beginners. We do more than "get by" but we are spotted as foreigners even before we open our mouths. But now our efforts to learn the language have taken the form of immersion into local activities with French people rather than a formal course in language. We continue to read and attend cultural events in an attempt to understand the French people who only look like you and me. At times they seem, in deed, to be from another planet. The differences never end, and some remain unsettling, upsetting and depressing to Val. Linda is less bothered. In many ways, the adjustment to life in France for us is much different from anything we could have envisioned.

Adjustment to French ways for Val can best be characterized by a recent December "get away". To celebrate our 27th wedding anniversary we planned an over-night at a Relais Chateau in the Tarn Gorges. As we arrived, we quickly realized that the promotional photos were better than the real thing and the over-all décor was one for which Val has coined a phrase - "A touch of Faded Glory". We also sensed that it was going to be important to confirm that we had made reservations, at the time of booking, for dinner that evening. (The next possible restaurant was miles way on narrow hairpin-curved roads) Our host seemed surprised but recovered nicely and we were assured of dinner. Within two minutes of entering our B&B room at the chateau Val began to check: the shower, and the heat (one radiator worked the other, it seems, was for decoration), and the hot water to see if it was running (it was not), the toilet to see if it flushed (surprisingly, this one worked, it only had a broken handle). For Val there are two advantages of our living in France these four years. One is to know beyond a doubt, that at least one of the above will be out of order, and the second is that he is now able to telephone and make his complaint in French to remedy the problems. C'est la vie! All that said we were the only two for dinner by the fire in the 12th century monastery turned manor home. The scenery in the Tarn Gorges (about a two-hour drive into the mountains from our home in Florensac) was a beautiful mix of late autumnal color with a touch of light snow. And the brisk morning walk around the chateau grounds with the echo of cowbells from the fields was a pastoral masterpiece.

What about the latest riots? We live in an area of France left untouched by the fires and riots of October/November. They came as close as the large cities of Montpellier and Béziers but rural France "slept" through it all. Still to be addressed for France; the many years of badly managed immigration policy, which it seems brought this all about.

What do we do? We have settled into an everyday life that includes; A French /English Choral Group for Val and Ballroom Dance Class for the both of us. Being the more athletic type, Linda takes gymnastiques in nearby Pinet and a Sailing Class at Marseillan (Yes, even in the winter). Linda has also developed a Cours Anglais, to teach English to adults and privately tutors a growing number of adolescents and young adults. Once a month, Val travels to Clermont Ferrand (200 kms away) to mentor a new clergy. We find ourselves amazingly busy. In summer we have a pleasant flow of B&B guests. We could always take more, but the pace of life is what we enjoy. Day to day domestic chores seem to take longer when punctuated by leisurely lunches, time to play with Bijou Bunné, and an occasional siesta. The care we take and attention to the details of hospitality, we feel, keeps *Le petit Jardin de L'âme* in a class by itself. And it keeps Linda busy full time making sure that <u>our</u> hot water is working, and the plumbing is proper when guests arrive. Val shops and cooks for Table d'Hôtes, manages the small, but well cared for garden and the pool for our personal use. And there remain unending interior decorating projects. A small church community is developing, despite Val's insistence that he did not come to France to found a parish. The Home Eucharist Group, which meets on the third Sunday of each month, has grown, and beginning in the spring we will branch out into a traditional church setting. The Roman Catholic Archbishop, local Pézenas clergy, and a prosperous vigneron have offered the use of a lovely small church in a hamlet nearby. But mostly we enjoy having time to do what we want to do and to read or re-read that book we have had for years, to take the time to look up a piece of history or a factual detail in answer to a question, to develop a thoughtful sermon or reflection at a leisurely pace (We still choose not to have a TV).

But there remain many things for which there never seems to be enough time. We revisited the Loire Valley and Paris with Linda's family at the end of summer and took a short holiday for ourselves in Amsterdam. But in general, European travel, one of our reasons for moving to Europe, still seems to elude us. On Val's "to do" list for 2006 (again) is re-learning his guitar. He still looks at his guitar but can't seem to find the time to pick it up. Linda would like to do some solo sailing and always more walking. And we expect that in 2006 we will publish that book that people have encouraged us to write: *A candid reflection on the glorious and gruesome realities of creating a new life in France.* A Bright Sun & Long Shadows *takes you beyond "la vie en rose" in the south of France, to explore both the brilliance and the shadow side of life in the Midi.*

More and more, we enjoy receiving Christmas cards and letters at this time of year as a way to keep in touch with friends. We received our first Christmas cards just after thanksgiving. We frequently ask ourselves, how ever did we manage our lives before when we were so very busy and how is it that people in the hectic work-a-day world still get their Christmas cards out on time and we retired folks struggle to get them out before the three kings arrive.

Our Christmas Letters often took the form of a "Reader's Digest" / Cliff notes approach to our year. It was all true, but it was not ALL. There was no way we could put the full story out there, and there was more to our life than the despair that led to suicide in 2005. I remember three aspects of this letter for which I wished I could have found a way to say much more, but then the letter would have turned into an Epistle or even a book itself.

So here are three things that might have been between the lines of our Christmas letter: Tales of Bijou Bunné, forever improving our French, and The Life & Work of a Priest.

Bijou Bunné – a jewel at le petitjardin de lâme:

Until one has loved an animal, a part of one's soul remains unawakened.
-attributed to Anatole France

Having a pet, Bijou Bunné was more significant than either Linda or I imagined. Shortly after Bijou came to le petit jardin, we noticed some irregular breathing and discovered at the time she was neutered that she had some congenital respiratory problem. It was not immediately life threatening, seemed to cause her no pain and she developed normally.

Linda must be given full credit for her patience in successfully training Bijou to use the litter box. This made life (and clean up) so much more civilized. It also gave Bijou maximum freedom since she could be let out to roam in the courtyard and always returned to the litter box. Each night she was put in her hutch as a precaution against owls or other predators and by day she was a hoppy little part of our comings and goings through the courtyard.

Bijou Bunné, had indeed become a beloved companion. She graced the courtyard with a combination of French rustic ambiance and spritely mischief. The rabbit hutch, carved out under a large water trough was ample and dubbed "The Bunny Chateau". A print given to us by a friend, a rabbit detail from the unicorn tapestry at the Cluny Museum, Paris, was mounted and hung as an ancestral portrait. We were enjoying this bit of extravagance. Linda had successfully trained Bijou to always return to the litter box when necessary and she never had "an accident". Bijou had virtual free range in the large enclosed courtyard she had unlimited space to explore outside of her rabbit hutch, named Chateau Bunné.

Depending on our assessment of our various B&B guests we would let Bijou out "to play". She climbed the stairs to guests rooms, "puttered" in the potting shed under the stairs, lounged in the shade and when we were not looking, jumped into the raised garden beds. Bijou enjoyed following me as I went about trimming and weeding the courtyard garden. I enjoyed tossing her clippings from pruning of most plants. She would explore completely up to the deuxième étage (3rd floor) hopping up and down the external stairway from the ground level. Most evenings Linda and I would take some time to sit, have a drink, and watch our personal "Bunny Channel". In the colder months of winter, we would bring Bijou up to the study while we sat and read or worked at the computer. Bijou also had her own "central heating" (a low-wattage light bulb under a terra cotta pot) in her hutch in the courtyard to take the chill from the coldest nights in December and January. Bijou was a jewel at le petit jardin de l'âme. She helped us create lovely moments and memories of our life in France. This was a part of life in France as I had imagined it.

One time we hosted a couple who were particularly fond of animals. We took this as a hint to let Bijou have the run of the courtyard, perhaps more than usual. One day, I noticed, Bijou went missing. I searched the usual places; No, she had not taken up a cozy, comfy and cool spot under the staircase on one of the shelves for the potting materials. No, she was not to be found in the shaded corner next to the large planting trough at the foot of the stairs, No, she had not hidden herself in the raised flower bed happily devouring my geraniums. And I could not find her in the corner wine cave which served as storage – and was another favorite – though prohibited - cool dark place.

Time passed, and our B&B quests came to the courtyard from their room on the deuxieme etage (third floor). They sensed my concern, since I was mid-search and so far unsuccessful. Oh, not to worry, Bijou was in their room sitting atop their suitcase! She had climbed the stairs and made herself at home, so they decided to leave the door to their room open and she would come down eventually! This was exactly the serendipitous grace and charm that we had hoped to create at le petit jardin de lâme'.

Forever improving our French – even among the English.

I return, for a moment to the FAQ "How is your French?" It has varied answers:

Le Petit Jardin de L'âme

Well into our fourth and fifth year two basic things have evolved in our understanding of what it means to be fluent in speaking French and the nuance persists to this day.

Even now, after more than ten years, when someone, making conversation in English or in French, assumes that "You must be fluent in French by now? "(Yes, there is often a question mark at the end of that statement especially when spoken by someone from England)

My response in either French or English goes something like this: (I sigh a little, and say) "My French is functional, but often not very pretty. I can make myself understood in most situations but lack a finesse or nuance of speaking in my first language." (Roughly that goes like this : *Je parle français un peu, mais je ne parle pas bien., mais pas joli. Je parle français fonctionnellement (sometimes I refer to the French idom for speaking french poorly - Peut-être comme une vache espagnole – a little self deprecation often goes a long way to eliciting a compliment!) Je peux me faire comprendre pour la plupart. Mais je manque de finesse ou nuance de parler dans ma langue maternelle.*) You have to admit; the ability to convey that in French (even as it was, not perfect) is an accomplishment in itself and says a lot about how communicative I was - pretty or not!

And on occasions, happily, I receive a compliment. But I reserve "fluent" for the day when I can finish a sentence, and no one has the need to make a correction, well intended or not, even when some unsolicited corrections are blatantly wrong. Here's a little "for instance": At a cocktail party, while speaking in French to a woman I knew was English but was very proud of her French, I decided to go along, in French, as best I could.

I must admit, that I find something strange about a conversation between persons whose first language is English but choose to speak in French. And mind you, when necessary it is always possible to switch to include French if the situation requires. But to pursue a conversation in a language foreign to both persons seems unusual when they have a first language in common (Well, perhaps the English disagree on our common first language status). But I digress.

When two English speakers carry on a conversation in French, I suspect that communication is not the primary reason for this peculiar choice. Perhaps there was a wee touch of linguistic competition in the air at that moment, a bit of linguistic sword play. Some, it seems, find a lunge, parry, riposte and voila, "Touché!", an enjoyable accompaniment to their cocktail skewers.

Making conversation, my new acquaintance noticed that I had come that evening (at the request of the host) providing a bit of ambiance with my Orgue Barbarie. I had, as it seems many organ grinders do, adopted a "schtick ", borrowing costume accents from the French cabaret entertainer Aristide Bruant. Yes, I had the hat and red scarf reminiscent of the famous poster created by Henri Toulouse Lautrec. But I digress, again.

Back to my point, typical of conversations in French, the inevitable moment arrives for the linguistic expert to appear – usually in the form of the person with whom you have been, until now, having a passable, if not perfect, and sometimes enjoyable conversation. Someone, it seems always has the need to become the expert. In this case my French-speaking, English conversationalist found it necessary to correct the name. Switching to English, she asked, "Surely, you mean Aristide Bruand? "(Spelling it out for me – B-R-U-A-N–**D**).

Puzzled a moment as to why this distinction even becomes important in French where the final consonant in Bruan**d** and Bruan**t** must be imperceptible.

I retorted that I believe that the name on the traditional Toulouse Lautrec poster was B-R-U-A-N-**T**, since I had researched it for my costume and business card. "Oh, no", she was certain of her spelling. And so, I let it go, but it nagged at me until I got home. I discovered upon later research that my French was correct but had come away from the conversation being the one who had been corrected by an assumed - English, I might add - authority.

Such exchanges usually put a damper on conversation in any language. In my opinion, some French seem a bit more tolerant of those speaking in their second language, when they themselves are aware of their own disadvantage and often are ill-at-ease in speaking English. Oh indeed, corrections do come from the French (and with equal conviction and a certain amount of error based on local accents) but I take them more in the form of an attempt to help. But the English who think they have mastered French can be insufferable. With a hint of imperialism, they cannot let an opportunity pass to show self-perceived superiority- even when they are wrong. These moments are ever present in bi-lingual conversations where someone misses the point of communication in conversation and seizes on the opportunity to be the expert. It's a power and control dynamic.

Honestly, I expect never to be fluent in French since that would mean the conversation would ebb and flow without some necessary moment of instruction. What I describe above, takes the "union" out of communication. One gets to know another person much as one gets to know an opponent rather than a new friend.

By the way – for any budding English-speaking experts in French Language, my antagonist may have stumbled on a detail of interest, which my later research revealed. The entertainer known as Aristide Bruant (the basis for my costume), was born Louis Armand Aristide Bruand (yes, with a "d"). His stage name and the name on the famous poster is spelled with a "t", Aristide Bruant. Why? I do not know. C'est la vie.

I suppose I should thank my English, French-speaking, expert for driving me back to the books to discover this extraneous detail. After all, it may come in handy in some future conversation. My use of "Bruant" in conversation about my costume was correct. Her use of "Bruand" would have been correct had we been referring to his ancestry or his birth name. I am reasonably certain that she was simply in error, for if she had this little piece of trivia in her miscellany of conversation stoppers, she would not have hesitated to use it. En-gard, attaque, battement!

Things I've learned while learning French, may apply to any second language. There are four lessons, below, which come from my experience in France with the French but might just as well apply to any second language. And in this I include people in the English-speaking world who speak English with people from that island within the island of Great Britain called England. In retrospect I see the anecdote above and the lessons below more a reflection of interpersonal dynamics of power that some value more than joining together in mutual communication. Where one person has some need to show another who is superior, a game of linguistic, one-upmanship comes into play.

Languages, were never my forte. I have in my student-life had six years of Latin, two years of Greek, two years each of French and Spanish. In my adult-life I have taken courses and been tutored in conversational French in advance of our move to France. I have been known to say, "I can manage to make myself <u>mis</u>-understood in four languages"! Life in France has improved my French to the point that I am able to participate reasonably well, in a meeting to plan a bilingual worship service, or at the occasional all French dinner evening. I manage to understand and make myself understood in French, even if the conversation lacks any subtly, nuance or a spirited "play on words". I have given up the hope that my French will ever really be "pretty" but it is functional.

Here are some things that I wished Alliance Française had taught me in those early preparation classes:

1. The "comeback-line": When you make a request, or an observation, it is never enough to state your point and have a simple "Yes or No, "certainly", or "of course, gladly" as a response. You must anticipate the French comeback-line, usually in the form of a question. And have your own restatement for emphasis to show that your position is clear.

    EG.

    Me: (in French) Madame, please do not place your garbage on the street across from my house.

    Madame: (from her window ledge) But I have a small house and there is no place to put my garbage

    Me: Ah, but the conditions for using the (city provided) garbage bins state that you must keep them out of the public way until the night before garbage pick-up.

    Madame: The container is too big to fit in my little house.

    Me: Please Follow the "Conditions de Prêts". The front of my house is not a dump

    Madame: (pouts)

    Me: (walk away) after placing the offending container in front of her own door.

    P.S. Eventually, we managed a civil neighborly relationship of "Bonjours" and "Comment allez-vous".

2. An apology from a French man is in the traditional form of "apologetics", not in the sense of "I am sorry". In the traditional sense, apologetics is; "This is **why** I am doing what I am doing" (and I will continue to do it whether you like it or not). For an example see the dialogue above. The next time it happened – as it

inevitably would as a test – I physically placed her dumpsters in her own door way. End of conversation.)

Historical Note: The actual solution was that she placed one of her two garbage dumpsters in her house and the other one she placed next to her own front door on the street – still not following the rules of use but no longer in front of my house.

3. Speak slowly no matter how rapidly the pace of the other side of the conversation seems to be escalating. Speaking slowly may enhance your language ability by giving you brief nanoseconds between words or phrases to get the pronunciation correct, or the tenses right but the skill is not primarily about language ability, it is an important part of maintaining control of the conversation. A steady deliberate pace seems to drive the French crazy … ah, nice to have that shoe worn by some other foot… and they in turn will respond in Gatling-Gun fashion with a flurry of phrases. But if you take up their pace you are doomed, as the pace of the conversations escalates you will, inevitably be at a disadvantage. So, keep an even pace so as not to seem slowed down by your own language limitations. Start slow and keep the pace slow and even. It must be intelligible and not halting but it can be even-paced, and smooth. And a smile as you deliver your comeback line tells them that you are prepared for this cultural swordplay, it says "Touché".

4. Always speak in complete sentences – it forces you to practice all the forms of agreement; of tenses, of verbs and modifiers. And (something I still have difficulty with) placing those indirect objects where they belong. I still cheat by repeating the use of the noun to which I referred in the first place.

The Life and Work of a Priest

Church life was growing. In fact, as a church group, we all were surprise at the growth. Not only had I <u>not</u> come to France, in retirement, to start a church; this growth and increased local presence for ex-pats and among the French was something I had not planned as a part of life in France or the ex-pat community. I approached this growing life with interest and saw it as a chance to continue my work life experience and apply it to this unexpected opportunity. Developing the relationship between the growing congregation and the French was to become a full-time job. There were meetings and relationship development opportunities with local French clergy; requests for weddings in English, requests for baptisms, requests from the local French clergy for joint celebration of funerals. "Inch-by-inch" the group of 12 people was becoming a congregation with its own increasing need for "people management", rotation lists for certain activities, education events, management small group politics and occasional individual sentiments of "how things ought to be done", and "We've always done it this way" ... and a growing need to look ahead with foresight and vision.

Most of the little congregation were of retirement age" and a little older than Linda and me. Many were, by disposition and by age, ready to settle down. Linda and I by disposition and being a few years younger could see potential. Many came simply to worship but I was aware and could now envision future needs. I enjoyed this aspect of organizational development and public relations with local Roman Catholic Church of the Diocese of Montpellier, the Église Réformée, and eventually the seigniorial family at, Chateau de Conas. From the beginning, I had kept an informal record of church services, and later began to keep more formal records of church attendance and activities such as monthly meetings.

While I was often apologetic for my French language skills, developing these local relationships helped to improve my French and in some cases my opinion of "The French". At a professional level I was treated as a "brother - clergy" and I sensed their genuine interest in giving help to the fledgling group of fellow Christians. There is a fellow-ship among clergy; a sense of personal knowing and camaraderie that crosses denominational lines. This was, for me, the first time I had experienced this bonding-by-profession as clergy across international and linguistic lines. I had in my work-life experienced this internationally among professionals in my secular field of Psychotherapy, Employee Assistance and Addictions treatment but this was particularly enjoyable (and a relief) for me as clergy given our painful acculturation to France in the earlier years of 2001 to 2004.

I think that it may be important here to elaborate on some of the internal discipline that comes with being called as clergy. Education in seminary is more than book-learning. There begins a formation which lasts a lifetime and creates a view of the world and people that evolves sure enough but is a view of the world as a gift and of people as pilgrims on a journey. For me this formation began at age 14 as was the custom in the Roman Catholic church at the time. Yes, there certainly are academic requirements, but the process to ordination is a formation of one's spirit.

Most people measure a church and clergy by what they see on a given Sunday worship service. And in some basic sense this is a valid but very limited assessment. The Sunday worship is, at best, a microcosm of a larger vision of what a church is about – if this worship is understood in its fullest sense as the center from which all else expands. However, many casual observers see only the most obvious aspects of the hour long gathering and believe that is all there is. Other gentle readers, may take a broader look and realize that not only does the service itself need planning and coordination but such planning involves the development of talents from among the congregation, learning their likes and dislikes, the relationships, peculiarities and limitations of the congregation. It also requires leading people to places in their life where they might not otherwise go on their own; to develop a latent creative part, to question and change an assumption or bias, to "go-deeper" into some aspect of their life that has not been developed since childhood. In addition, pastoral leadership involves what I have come to call the "people - management" aspect of worship.

The careful management of interpersonal interactions, most of which you have little control over; the little "tiffs" and "snarky" comments and passive resistance that easily comes when people choose not to get along – Oh yes, Virginia, there is a Santa Claus in Church life! In most cases it falls to the pastoral leader to manage the sheep. When done well, people management is nearly invisible to the public. The worship service which seems to flow seamlessly from the beginning welcome at the church door to the follow through during the following week(s) is more than a one-day-a-week job. For me, planning a worship service that both fit where the congregation was as individuals also included subtle teaching moments to help grow their spiritual lives. As a priest, teaching takes on an every day, inner soul life, alert to, and searching for that five-minute moment for a chance to grow, personally, to help others grow, and to knit a community together.

> *The whole art of teaching is the art of awakening the natural curiosity of young minds for satisfying it afterwards."* -Anatole France

As this congregation grew up around us both Linda and I became increasingly aware of our change in role, our change in relationship to most everyone with whom we came in contact. People in good nature were pleased to, and playfully, identified me as the "The Vicar". But to me (to Linda and myself) this carried more significance and responsibility than most people consciously admitted. In time, we became painfully aware of what most people implicitly and unconsciously expected of us. Being the vicar is not a job, it is a way of life which draws on a level of consciousness not often acknowledged. We also began to see differences in perception of clergy roles between The Church of England and The Episcopal Church

(both members of the same World-wide Anglican Communion but with some differences in expression, some "American" and some "English")

The selection of the hymns, to take one example, is not simply picking from a list of the pastor's personal favorites (as was what one member candidly expressed in his opinion during our visit to his home) but rather, upon study and reflection, connects the content of hymns to the scriptures appointed by the larger church body for the day. And beyond that, it is important to select hymns that will be familiar enough to be "successfully sung" (in our case sung a cappella), at times easy enough to learn, and at other times expose the congregation to different genres or possibilities than the ones they have heard from childhood. Hymns, like poetry can awaken a different level of consciousness in the context of a worship service from the hearing of this hymn in their childhood. The hymn itself is a prayer not just a musical interlude between two pieces of something else. I must admit that many a Sunday worship falls short on this ideal, and for some clergy this is not their strong suit, but they try. But when successfully accomplished this marriage of liturgical music, scripture, poetry, traditional ritual and contemporary context feed the life of a congregation. It was my opinion and often reflected in people's comments, that I was particularly good at this aspect of liturgy.

The education of the congregation takes on these same necessary balances for enriching what people believe and believe they know, to stretching them to new knowledge and deepening spiritual consciousness.

And then there is the public or communal presence of the worshiping community in the larger community. Church XYZ has a corporate image and role in the larger community. Stereotypes of churches come from their corporate image as perceived by the larger community. It is the clergy's job not only to be that image, but to assure through training and encouragement that others in the congregation begin to take on this public sense, learning to be the church in the community at large. Developing this communal and individual identity is an ever-present and nearly invisible task that seeps into every conversation, meeting, and public event.

In this case, in this little growing congregation, there were a few who shared this vision. However, most were satisfied to see an increase in seats filled on Sunday, as if by magic. A typical Sunday church-goer comes primarily for their own moment with God and a bit of fellowship. For a few there was a sense of growing what had begun at the request of a few in 2003. And of course, even among the few with a sense developing the growth, not all agreed on how to go about it. So, managing that dynamic also becomes a part of the life and work of a priest.

Two references in the bibliography which came to me from two very different sources address these aspects from two very different periods of church-life in the Anglican Communion, in much more detail. I am grateful to a friend of mine, who describes himself as Atheist, for lending me his cherished copy of The English diarist Robert Francis Kilvert (1840–1879). These diaries reflect the rural life of a priest in the *1870s* (see the Kilvert Society). A more contemporary approach by John Pritchard, *The Life and Work of a Priest*, Society for the Promotion of Christian Knowledge (SPCK), was a gift from my bishop. Both, among many other sources, shed light on what many people casually see as "one-day-a-week job".

I was delighted to throw myself into this unexpected call. It came as a surprise, and I received it as a call. It was a joy for several years, though it later grew into two of the most miserable years of ministry in my (at that time) 37 years as a priest. You don't need to be Hercule Poirot to know that there is more to come in this story. But let me pull myself back to the chronology and end the year 2005 at le petit jardin de lâ'me before moving on to 2006.

Chapter 9
Leaving 2005 behind
Building a future in 2006 and 2007
"Cela est bien, repondit Candide, mais il faut cultiver notre jardin."
-Voltaire, *Candide*

During these years a personal relationship developed with the editor of a local ex-pat news magazine. He was known by some as a "difficult personality" but I found our conversations interesting and it became clear that we had a struggle with depression in common. At one point we discussed the possibility of my writing an article for the local monthly news magazine that took some of its current ex-pat help articles to a different level to address the important gap in services for ex-pats in the area of mental health resources. This was a good fit for me because of my background during my working life before retirement as a clinical social worker and drew on skills that I had developed to search out appropriate counseling resources for people.

I agreed to draft an article which went beyond the usual "How do you find a …plumber, electrician, contractor etc as an ex-pat in France. Using my personal experience to help others and expand the resources for Mental Health services seemed a way to turn my struggle into a benefit for others. It was also to be sure, a "coming out" regarding my own personal search.

The article printed below was Submitted as a two-part article written to identify the problem for expats and allow some time, between editions for people to respond perhaps with additional resources.

To your Health: The first of two parts

For most year-round foreign residents who have adopted the south of France as their home, and for those who live here several months of the year as a home away from home, the adjustment and acculturation to the local way of life is an expected change. It is necessary to go beyond the basic language skills of visiting tourists and familiarize oneself with the professional services necessary for everyday life in France. But there are some aspects of life in the south of France that are not easily translated or acculturated by foreigners. Even for those who have successfully met the challenges of communication with notorious French workmen, and the bureaucracy there remains an area of life, where the basic effectives of the service relies ones first language; mental health services. One may be willing to risk a linguistic "faux amis" when describing problems of their bodily functions, their heart, their aching back or their teeth. But when describing the more delicate, and sometimes intangible, matters of the psyche one often relies on nuance, euphemism, shades of meaning and cultural norms that were embedded in our consciousness long ago. Communication in the areas of our psychological well-being, and matters of marital and family life have a very personal vocabulary in any language.

Finding mental health services in a country where one is a foreigner can be difficult. Services in a second language are understandably few. In the case of psychiatry and psychology, providing service in English, in a French national health care system is a specialty within an already specialized health care field.

There is a significant additional impediment to finding psychotherapy and psychiatric services: our personal denial. People come to the south of France for the celebrated "la vie en France". The very image of the south is a picture of sunshine, sea breezes, and afternoon siestas. This popular image supports a system of personal denial. In such a paradise what could go wrong? Finding a mason, a plumber, an electrician, a doctor a dentist quickly rise to the top of the list when one arrives in their hew home in the south of France. But, tell me, did you have <u>psychotherapist</u> on your list?

Thankfully much of the social stigma of mental illness and the need for mental health services has diminished. But individual personal denial remains strong. After all, psychiatrists and psychotherapists are for other people, not me.

An anecdote of one person's search for English speaking mental health services is recounted in a soon to be published book A BRIGHT SUN AND LONG SHADOWS: A candid reflection on the glorious and gruesome realities of creating a new life in France, The chapter; <u>Dreams and Nightmares</u> describes the search. Here is an excerpt from a visit to the psychiatrist's office.

"… I began the conversation in French. I had prepared my opening lines to explain that I had a problem. I was living in France for about one year; I was seeking help for my depression and that I came for medication. I concluded by saying that I hoped he spoke English, since it would be easier for me to continue in English.

He responded simply, "No."

After a pause in which I was able to choke back my tears and frustration only partially, I said, in French, "Certainly you are making a little joke. I telephoned and asked for a psychiatrist who spoke English. And my appointment was made with you."

Again, he said, "No."

No explanation, no apology. ...

I remained in silence. Not only had I run out of script, I did not know what to do next, and I was afraid to open my mouth because the tears were so at the edge...."

Having raised the awareness of the need for Psychotherapy in your first language, this article will be continued in the next edition. Yet to be considered are comments from the professionals interviewed for this topic, estimated costs of mental health services and specific links to mental Health services in English.

And so, gentle readers, if not for yourself, for the sake of your friends, read and save this article, you never know when someone else might need the information. If you know of a professional who provides services in English, please contact Blablablah so that they can be interviewed before the next publication deadline.

Contact info and deadline info Here ----

End of part one

To your Health: The 2nd of two parts

In part one of To Your Health, the need for mental health services and the importance of receiving these services in a person's first language, was presented from the client's point of view.

From the professional's point of view, your general medical doctor may have many specialists at their disposal, but it is unlikely that they will fluent in English. It is in your own best interest that you come prepared with a suggestion to assist the GP with the referral to a specialist who speaks fluent English. Even with the best of intentions professionals who, in fact, speak some English as a second language, may not have the necessary fluency to provide services in English. In conversations with professionals in preparation for this article two clinical insights surfaced regarding the importance of finding mental health services in your primary language. The first, supported by studies over the years is that even in their primary language, general medical doctors often under diagnosis problems of depression and alcoholism. This does not make them bad doctors. It simply means they are not specialist in these areas. A second comment on clinical studies, indicated that in situations where an individual patient used their second language during the professional assessment, the impairment was diagnosed as less severe than when the patient used their primary language in describing their symptoms. In any language, accuracy in the diagnosis is the first step in determining what the next step should be. A mental health diagnostic consultation is best made in the context of the patient's first language. In one interview an interesting compromise was suggested. Perhaps the patient can speak in their first language (English) and I will respond in French since it is often the case that for both parties, comprehension of a language is more proficient than they then one's ability to speak it. I found it an interesting position to take if all else failed.

For maximum financial benefit, and the over-all coordination of your general medical care, it is best to obtain a referral to a specialist from the General Practitioner physician. But there are also sources of professional psychotherapy outside the national health system. Your out of pocket costs can vary from about 11€ per consultation if using your Carte Vitale to 50€ or more for a psychotherapy session with a private practitioner. These fees are significantly less than similar services provided by comparable professionals in the USA or UK the material in this article is intended to provide general information. It does not constitute legal or other professional advice. It is a starting point for information that may help you find a mental health care provider who provides psychotherapy or psychiatric service in English. Simply writing and publishing this article may bring yet undiscovered resources to the surface.

Here are some specific links to Services in English:

There is a very helpful website **Counselling in France.** The site itself has some helpful information related to counseling in general, domestic violence, marriage guidance, alcoholism etc and a list English speaking HELPLINES. Counselors and a brief history are listed by department. Seven counselors along with brief professional information are listed in the Department Languedoc-Rousillon www.counsellinginfrance.com

I have located a few therapists, with a variety of therapeutic approaches in addition to those listed at the Counselling in France website:

Here I listed an additional five therapists with contact information – the names have been removed in this book version of the article.

Now, clip this page, and save it along with your list of other important services for *la vie en France*. Finding good mental health services is at least as important as finding a good plumber, electrician, and a good restaurant. *A Votre Santé*

The two-part article was submitted but never published. Not rejected; it just went into a deep hole with no response. Perhaps it was "au fait, très franc", a bit too close to what many an expat experiences.

In another area of our life in France, we were soon to see our itinerant House Church attendance outgrow member's' living rooms. I began searching for alternatives. Eventually at Easter 2006 (with 35 people in attendance) we would make the leap to a more permanent worship space. At that time, we were fortunate to have two options for larger worship venues. It was time to establish a regular "home base", to have an identified location so that we could be "found" by the casual passer-by. It was time to break from small group, word-of-mouth communications between a dozen or two people, and publicize in the local news. As the clergy responsible for the worship service each month, I had already received several complements about the tone of worship. I chose what I considered the spot most conducive to the style of worship; informal but traditional, more reflective than grand, and one geared for the age group that was mostly retired with no small children at the time. The congregation responded enthusiastically to the space as very prayerful, picture-perfect. The 13th century gothic, limestone, chapel seated about 50-60 people, twice our current Sunday congregation, although growth of that size had not entered anyone mind including my own. The setting of the chapel, behind the chateau, down a narrow road, overlooking the vineyards and near the cemetery of the little hamlet all added to its charm. To a person, I cannot think of anyone who did not feel that we had found a treasure, and we ourselves were to become a part of the idyllic French rural landscape. It was known that, in its rustic beauty, it had no running water or toilet facilities, and everyone just planned accordingly. From my perspective the choice for space was also based on a larger vision of a need for resources available to us in the future from the Roman Catholic diocese. Nurturing this little group and growing it, was a part of my engagement with life in France in new ways that I had not previously considered.

Perhaps I should say something here since it will become an issue later. We did have another option for a place for worship. There was a church building, largely unused by the French protestant church, Église Réformée, in another village not much further away. It was also offered, and I declined with appreciation for their thoughtfulness. It did have toilets, and was said to have heat and water. As it turned out there was a problem with both heat and water. The heat required some repairs and a financial outlay for gas, and the water had been pirated by a neighbor and was subsequently disconnected. But more importantly, it was not an inspiring building. It had been up-dated (after a fashion) but was better suited to an all-purpose assembly hall than a place of inspiration. If we had no other option I would have accepted. But in addition to aesthetics and the non-tangibles that made the 13th century Chapel at Conas a prayerful place, the chapel at Conas gave us a connection with the local Roman Catholic Diocese and future resources. The Roman Catholic diocese made for a more fortuitous "marriage". And the village of Conas was well connected to the local tourist attraction of the village of Pezenas. At a practical level, basically I would forego toilets (everyone being aware of the fact) in favor of the aesthetics and the potential longer ranger advantage of building the relationship with the Roman Catholic Diocese and its resources.

Planning for each monthly worship now included scripture study and reflection, as part of the preparation of a "sermon". I preferred to use a "Reflection B4 The Service" to quiet the group from their happy "good morning" chatter, to a more prayerful reflection on what we were about to do rather than a traditional sermon. Preparation also meant, selection of appropriate hymns to compliment the scriptures, finding someone to lead the singing. More than capable of leading the singing, I enjoyed exercising my gift of voice and liturgical sensitivity that had not flourished since seminary. But I was also aware of step by step making this a communal worship not just my performance. The cultivation of the congregation's personal involvement was not only good organizational planning but good ecclesiology. Since we had no organ, hymn singing meant finding capable and confident voices from the congregation. It worked well and to a prayerful effect. After preparations for the worship itself, preparations meant anticipating all possible eventualities, including the rare but occasional incident of Madame Mas forgetting to unlock the church. Not only were supplies for the worship necessary (my own alb and stole, bread, wine, altar linens, chalice, communion plate, worship book, materials for congregation participation etc.), but provisions and ideas to include the occasional family who would come with child, materials to welcome new visitors, educational handouts for the general congregation, and materials to recruit volunteers to eventually assume some of the "schlepping" that Linda and I were doing. The space was lovely, but as part of appreciating its unadorned beauty also meant bringing everything that might be needed.

In addition to my evolution as "The Vicar", Linda was becoming "the vicar's wife", a role she had not sought and in our respective professional lives before retirement she did not have to assume. Eventually, Linda developed a prayer group, in part an expression of her own spirituality, and as a way to offer an intimate group experience of prayer as our original Sunday worship group expanded and took on different dynamics. Successful quiet days of reflection was added under her care.

A little anecdote helps to tell of our increased visibility as "the vicar and his wife" as well as our integration into village life.

Vicar's wife creates village scandal:

> As a part of her morning routine Linda would walk to the boulangerie at the center of town to pick up daily bread and breakfast pastries. The shortest and most frequent route for Linda took her past the door of an elderly man whom we affectionately called "Louis Quatorze". Louis was a fixture on the street in front

of his house with the usually "bon jour" to passers-by and a special "good morning" (one of his few English phrases) for Linda. As the friendship grew, the "good-morning" also grew into the familiar South of France triple-kiss, first on one cheek, then the other and back to the first cheek.

One morning after a short conversation, and as the "good-byes" were taking form, his kiss came to her lips. Keep in mind this is from an elderly gentleman of 90+ years. So Linda took it in stride as a new "normal". After all Louis would not do any harm and he was such an affable fellow. A few days passed with this kiss on the lips as a part of the new normal good bye.

A few more days passed, and Linda was having another morning conversation with two of the women with whom we had a pleasant association in the village. Getting breakfast bread was a village social event with short conversations along the way. One woman was Linda's age and the other a bit older – closer to Louis' age. Anne Marie, the women close in age to Linda had been told by Mado, the older woman, what Mado - madame with a watchful eye - had seen one morning as Louis and Linda exchanged this good-bye kiss. Both women warned Linda that this was not thought of as proper, saying that only husbands and wives or lovers kissed on the mouth. They allowed that perhaps in the United States this might be a family custom. But in France it had different connotations. They were giving her a friendly warning out of personal concern, that Louis had crossed a line that she should put a stop to it.

I guess that "hope springs eternal" even for a man of 90 + in France. Linda and I joked about the potential for scandal with this nonagenarian.

But, to Louis' dismay, she did put the kibosh on future good-bye kisses. We remained friends with Louis, Anne Marie and Mado. But we were aware that, subtly, even in the village, we were seen as the vicar and his wife with a reputation to protect.

For both of us our decision to follow the call of the evolving church mean putting ourselves "out there", taking the lead in sharing what was in our inner-most lives, and view of the world, fostering growth in spiritual life, and for me growing a congregation. It was the love of my life in this work to help shape a congregation, to help people grow in their spiritual lives. Growth for me did not have anything to do with increased attendance or bigger numbers. But in fact, the congregation did grow in size. We willingly placed ourselves at risk to observers. Our views were front and center while others in the congregation could choose whether to reveal their soul-searching or to be commentators. Some people grew and shared and expressed their gratitude for this leadership. Others preferred the safety of spectators or pundits.

A spirit of inclusion was consciously cultivated. Soon people were volunteering to organize readers for future worship service and coffee service after worship. Some took an active role in welcoming new-comers. We were as a group becoming a church congregation with a public presence in the extended community. There was a growing sense of pride in what we were. The local ex-pats news magazines were supportive of our growth and offered publicity. And the French took pride in supporting this "English" expression of faith which was so much like their own Roman Catholic heritage but without some of the uncomfortable limitations. Married clergy just made sense to most Frenchmen!

Personally, I was able to celebrate some of the most meaningful worship in this space over the next five years. This was a fitting spiritual home. Preparation of the liturgy had been a love of mine in Seminary and my eagerness returned. People freely expressed their appreciation, often noting the quality of the preparations and attention to details, and the reflective tone of the worship which fostered both prayer and participation. Part of my joy was in seeing how these prayerful moments were experienced by the congregation. My perception of their need and areas of growth informed my preparations. I enjoyed the ministry immensely. It was for me a first in France to have this life in retirement become something, totally un-envisioned but, very fulfilling – a real gift to me and a gift from me that I enjoyed giving.

Chapter 10
An Overview of times ahead

Our life in France in the years 2006 to 2010 included more and more church work. What began as a contribution of time and talent for a once a month worship service for a couple dozen people, grew into a full-time job with an average Sunday attendance of 35-40 people, and the intentional fostering of prayer life, charity outreach, and education among the congregation. The annual Lesson's & Carols service grew from its original 150 in attendance to 250 and 280 in attendance in years 2007 and 2008. Special Sunday's for major holidays were added to the worship schedule. Christmas, Holy Week and Easter services were added. Attendance at Christmas and Easter grew (Christmas of 2008 attendance was 57 people), filling our little chapel that we originally thought was bigger than we'd ever need. Families with children eventually came to attend Sunday services thus requiring Sunday school and preparations for introductions to the sacraments of Eucharist and Confirmation. These years were increasingly focused on the growing church and growing the responsibilities of the laity.

At this point one is tempted to "cut and paste" sections from the church records detailing our growth. But I will focus on general themes and a few pivotal events that filled our lives over the next four years. A record of dates and numbers, and business meeting minutes becomes tedious. More importantly, it is the human dynamics that are most colorful and tell a story richer than numbers could tell. Besides it was never about numbers. There are those who may voice "numbers are not important" but there is always some relationship between leadership and a growing congregation both in size and in spirit. And from the pew side, even those who voice "numbers are not important" there is not a one who could say they are not thrilled to see a church full rather and half empty.

Numbers actually do matter but not in the way most people think. For me as clergy, "getting bigger" was not a goal in itself. But we were getting bigger by simple attraction. People apparently liked what they saw and felt, and were drawn to the church. Numbers do certainly matter in terms of the style of leadership required – different for a small congregation than a larger one. The type of congregation interaction is different depending on the size of the congregation. So while growing a congregation is not simply a matter of bigger is better. It is often a challenge for church leadership to adjust leadership style to the size of the congregation. Personal interactions (relationship dynamics), communication styles and inevitably a budget must grow to support whatever size congregation there is and its mission (its raison d'être). For many people in the pews these growth challenges go unnoticed and is perhaps unnerving, yet for clergy leadership they are an ever-present part of on-going evaluation of ministry.

The life of the congregation expanded beyond the once a month worship in many ways. In 2009 Sunday worship services expanded into the summer months. Until that time the summer had been a hiatus for me as clergy in July and August.

Although, for me, summers were never completely "the vacation" intended. At first, summers were free, an hiatus from church affairs but as time passed summers evolved into a change from one type of church commitment to another, rather than the hiatus planned. Congregation life showed signs of increased demand as early as 2005 and 2006. For several summers a bilingual (French/ English) service with the Eglise Réformée was planned, which of course meant collaborative meetings and creating a bilingual booklet for the order of service. As our presence became more public, requests for weddings and funerals were made, a request for a baptism of new grandchildren visiting with their parents, and a request that children be confirmed. In 2006 additional services for Holy Week and Easter were added, then in 2007, a Christmas Eve service was added, Education evenings were organized and presented at our B&B, an informal group of lay leaders was formed. Eventually monthly meetings to cultivate a lay leadership base became the norm, and a nominal budget was created. Although we were not officially affiliated with any larger church at this time, it was clear that church polity of the Episcopal Church was what I followed and that my bishop in Paris was aware of the congregation's existence and my license to serve in Europe came from his office as Bishop of the Convocation. It was clear that we were worshiping according to the practice of the Anglican Tradition, but it was worship in the English language that was the common denominator for many rather than any one church affiliation.

As we were growing in size and in visibility in the local community, some connection to a larger Anglican Church would be necessary since there was no intention on my part to be a free-lance, non-denominational church. The connection to the Bishop in Paris was transparent in references to the larger church, my license to serve in The Convocation of Episcopal Churches in Europe was known by the congregation, and in worship I consciously used an order for worship that was familiar with both the Episcopal Church and the Church of England. I was clear that, at this point, I did not expect to be paid, my contribution of time and talent was to be an example to draw others into service. I had for the first three years resisted taking up the traditional "collection" during the service. But inevitably the question arose here and there – from a visitor or from members of the congregation. Why is there not a collection? It was for many a way to express their involvement and support.

After discussion with a couple of the lay leaders in the congregation, I offered to draw up a budget based on three priorities. A budget based on priorities, rather than the frequent approach of a budget based on covering immediate needs, was itself, and education and seen by some as forward thinking. In this creation of our first budget I set out three priorities for spending: On Worship (materials for worship, rent for the space, etc.) Education (for the group as a whole and for raising up individuals to positions of lay leadership), and Charity outreach (ideally this would involve financial contributions to a local French charity and some "hands-on" involvement in the community and one broader form of outreach. The creation of the budget was itself and education tool, attaching us to the larger Anglican Communion beyond our local community. At the end of 2006 our donation to charity was €300. This amount represented about one third of our annual budget. This along with some personal involvement with the local charity promised to set the example for our congregational life that I had hoped. I was pleased to see this embraced enthusiastically by the congregation. We began worshiping without a budget but since we were now in a place to create a budget, the budget itself should reflect that church life is more than just attending Sunday worship. I was pleased that the congregation did not resist this thinking. Whether they actually fully understood the connection was made clear in later years.

According to French law, in order to have a bank account we filed to become an "Association Loi" (a not-for-profit corporation) and accordingly set minimal "membership" requirements. We set a token amount for dues of €25.00 per year per person to be a voting member of the association. Thirty–nine persons joined *The Anglican Episcopal Church in the Hérault* as we were now named. We would accordingly have officers and an annual meeting. This step was approached in the simplest way possible but still it took two lay persons more than a year working with French bureaucracy to finalize this Association Loi. It was clear that administration was now a part of our church life. Our name as a French Association Loi reflected our dual – albeit informal at this time - affiliation with both the Episcopal Church (since I was Clergy and was receiving collegial support, advice, consultation, clergy retreats etc) from the Episcopal Church, and our world-wide connection to the larger Anglican Communion of which the Episcopal Church is a part along with others such as The Church of England, The Church of Ireland, Anglican Church of Canada, The Scottish Episcopal

Church – all of which represented churches from which members came. Now, I continued to offer my services free, but as time moved on and my time as the vicar increased I wished to find a way to include token compensation; not for me but so that we could eventually offer an honorarium, and attract clergy who might fill in for me on occasion for worship or education, and set the precedent for a long-range plan to replace me with other (partially paid) clergy. I made this an overt part of meetings, education events and conversations in an effort to stimulate and normalize this thinking among the congregation at large.

If we were to grow beyond limited once a month Sunday Worship into a church with additional services, lay leadership, a budget, educational programs and charity outreach, I realized that growing some clergy compensation would be key to the future development. I began to look at my ministry not only to the current congregation individually and for worship but also as a ministry to eventually replace myself with someone younger, and someone who would need some financial compensation. I was happy to have a goal of working myself out of a job. It was a sign of growth and it was all place right on the table.

By 2007 there were a couple key events that were to reveal the levels of awareness - or lack of awareness - that the members of the congregation held regarding their understanding of what a church is and how congregations develop, within the Anglican Tradition. Many in the congregation were English, or more accurately British (Scots, Welsh, English, Irish etc) but not all were Church of England. Some had been active in their local churches before moving to France and others, after many years away from church life, had a re-awaking, in their retirement years, and were attracted to this, informal, English speaking, congregation in the South of France.

In 2007 I was happy to see our first "nuclear family" begin to attend church. Members of the congregation, most of us "over 60", were also delighted. Soon the request that the children be confirmed came. This meant some education at several levels. First, there was a need for the children themselves so that they would make an informed decision, and grow in faith, but also for the congregation as a whole, and parents in particular.

Since the children were on the young side for confirmation (brother and sister, each plus or minus 10 years old), and they had not been active church members recently in any church, but they had been baptized as infants, I suggested that we pick up where they left off and have a short course about their baptism and bring them to receive communion. And then some day as they grow in their faith they could make the decision to be confirmed. This solution was acceptable since the parents were really interested their children receiving communion and in their mind that was only done as a part of confirmation. True this sometimes had been the practice in some parts of the church, but what I explained made sense to mom and dad so I set about creating a Sunday-school "home school" program tailored for two pre-teens and recruited some of the members of the congregation to share their faith with these children and the parents, through taking a part in teaching these Sunday-school lessons. After a few months of preparation, the children were received at the altar and received communion. Confirmation would be something for later in their lives and in the life of the congregation since we were not yet officially a part of the larger church and needed a relationship with the bishop to confer confirmation. This was received by all as a happy series of events and the first experience for this congregation of a church life that included children and families. For me, as clergy, it was an opportunity well received, to teach the congregation about the larger church, to update some of their own thinking about baptism and confirmation and to encourage a few members of the congregation to start expressing their own beliefs (through teaching) as they passed on their faith to the next generation. In research and choice of a curriculum for the children there was a need for a broader perspective. I searched for a program that would not only prepare the children, but one that would be compatible with the various levels of faith and expression of the belief shared by their teachers. I wanted also to choose from resources in the larger Anglican Communion to bring home the idea that we were one part of a world-wide expression of faith, not just in England, not just "American" of the Episcopal Church USA. There was a teaching opportunity here beyond that of preparing children, to awaken in the adults a greater awareness of the larger Anglican Communion. I was happy to find an education program from the Anglican Church of Canada that fit our situation. Few people understand the importance of what went into this little Sunday School program and few people realize that such moments mean much to clergy as they see the broader picture; of persons the sharing of faith, one to another, not just for the children but of the adults who are involved in a tradition of passing on the faith. There is for Clergy a bit of pride as a spiritual parent.

What I did not say or do at this time was perhaps as important as what I did do in this situation. The Parents, well-meaning, but apparently unaware, that within the Anglican Tradition their request that their children be confirmed required a Bishop. Priests, when ordained, function at the pleasure of their bishops. The Anglican Tradition is a hierarchical tradition.

I, for example, was licensed to serve in Europe because the Bishop of The Convocation of Episcopal Churches In Europe had licensed me to do so. Yet collectively as a congregation, the group wished to remain independent of any larger denomination. Some came from a "free Church" background and others, although having some history in Church of England congregations, were happy to be free of denominational ties (or restraints, as some alluded to; "we don't want anybody telling us what we have to do … or believe.").

Because of my growing personal relationship with the bishop I could have asked him to come and celebrate the sacrament of confirmation, but I felt that the congregation was not ready for this connection. Yet this family was asking for something that required this connection within the Anglican Tradition. I choose not to introduce this variable into our conversation since I felt it would not only be prematurely pressing a point, but it would also be, in my assessment, a distraction from the pastoral situation which was primary; that is, helping this family (and the congregation) grow in their appreciation of their faith. The question of larger church affiliation would come eventually as we grew as a church, they would, I felt, see the need for and benefits of connection to the larger Anglican Tradition. In many ways they were in fact receiving some of these benefits (myself as clergy, my time and pastoral care, and the tradition of worship, and the structure of our worship was freely and transparently drawn from the Episcopal Church and Anglican Tradition). For now, I was happy to work with them individually, as a family and as a congregation where they were in faith and in their implied understanding of the larger church.

I expect that the nuances of my approach now went completely over the heads of most people. But I offer it here as an indication of one of many levels of care, and "people management" that clergy must be aware of, and attempt to balance, in ministry, to a congregation. Every moment is an education moment. In retrospect, perhaps I should have capitalized more on this happy moment to introduce a formal connection with the Bishop, with The Episcopal Church and this congregation as the local Episcopal Church. I may have missed an opportunity to bring those who wished their congregational independence into an understanding of the need for connection with the larger church. What I felt would be "forcing the issue" of membership in the larger Anglican Tradition through the Episcopal Church. At the time made me aware of how this congregation had the proverbial "cart before the horse".

Just think of it, how many people first worship in a community and then decide what larger church tradition they are part of. On the contrary most

Le Petit Jardin de L'âme

people come to a "church" that already has established its identity. People generally arrive in a neighborhood and join, the Catholic Church, or The Episcopal or the Methodist or Lutheran: Church etc. etc. because they are drawn to some aspect of the church, but the church community already has it established identity, its affiliation with the larger tradition. If it is independent that is also known up front. I was beginning to see that perhaps we had it backwards. I was Episcopalian, an Anglican, it was clear, and our worship followed that tradition, but I could see that without an official connection to the larger communion, Individual members were free to imagine whatever they wished. Most people came to worship at the English Church – that is the church with worship services in English, not any denominational identity and certainly not a national identity. This sounds lovely and ecumenical, but it would eventually come to haunt us. I remain convinced, even more so after my experience with this congregation, that a church congregation indeed worships locally but needs a broader connection that not only reaches back through a spiritual tradition but also reaches out across the globe with a shared identity, not an identity separate from history, and future vision. The bigger picture is often lost to most local members. The connections with history and cultivating a shared vision of the future is a role for clergy leadership.

As the years passed Linda and I also increased our involvement in the broader life of the church within the Convocation of Episcopal Churches in Europe. My mentoring with the talented young clergy that began at the bishop's request in the summer of 2005, continued for a few years and then grew into a personal friendship. I was also drawn to be more active with fellow clergy within the convocation of Episcopal Churches; in their annual retreats, and professional meetings. These were generously supported by the Bishop and the annual budget of The Convocation. Eventually, I was elected to the Council of Advice, which functioned as a Standing Committee of advisors to the bishop and decision-making body in the event that the role of bishop was vacant. I was appointed as chair of the Committee for Mission Congregations and worked closely with other clergy and lay leaders in the Convocation. This level of involvement meant travel around Europe to various locations where The Convocation of Episcopal Churches in Europe had clergy and congregations. I enjoyed this work immensely and through it, enjoyed seeing parts of Europe in a way that I might not otherwise have visited as a tourist.

Apart from church-life, I became involved in an international choral group of about 25-30 members and enjoyed the direction and discipline of rehearsals and the active use of my voice once again. Though we often performed in churches, the repertoire was largely secular with some classic religious pieces performed for their aesthetic value rather than spiritual focus. I had a good voice, but my singing voice had been, "asleep" for many years and was now re-awakened. Tenors are always in demand for SATB choirs and being one of a few I enjoyed the added discipline to know my part well. In some years I was one of two tenors, in better years there were as many as six or seven Tenors in the group. This also gave me an overlap with relationships some from church in the choir and some in the choir outside of church life.

Linda immersed herself into local village life with a teaching role in the adult education program Foyer Rural. She acquired certification for teaching English as a second language and for many years during this time she volunteered teaching English as a second Language to French women in the village.

There were, during these years a few couples with whom we grew closer in relationships. In fact, our closest friends and most frequent social contacts, who refreshed out lives, were outside the church community. And there were also events where the two groups intermingled with as ex-pats in France.

And during these years, our B&B at le petit jardin de lâ'me established a level of business that we had hoped for. We were never truly "crazy, busy", that was not our goal. Rather, our client- base had been cultivated to fit our vision and we offered at *Le petit Jardin de L'âme* what we had dreamed. Our guests came and enjoyed what we offered. Income from the B&B was, as we planned simply supplemental, not essential. The ambiance of our home was described as: a rural elegance, a gentle environment where people could soothe their souls and re-awaken their own dreams.

The pain of the first five years did not disappear, but in the larger picture of our lives it would become a smaller part of our life in France; normalized or balanced with the life that evolved past those initial years. Perhaps we were still learning what "being older and wiser" was to mean.

Chapter 11
In the moonlight

There was a little bit of sadness among our happiness in the garden at le petit jardin de lâ'me. On a Tuesday night, 14 February, on the way home from choral rehearsal, I don't know why, but on the way home I saw three rabbits scurrying along the road in the light of the still full moon (technically, full moon was 13 Feb 2006). I was reminded of the story from one of our French Classes *LES LETTRES DE MON MOULIN*, by Alphonse Daudet.

Letters from My Windmill is a collection of short stories by Alphonse Daudet first published in its entirety in 1869. Daudet alludes to a windmill in Fontvieille, Provence, inhabited by rabbits. It is sometimes considered to be Daudet's most important work, cherished by many French, particularly in the South, for the picture it paints of the local culture.

An excerpt

La nuit de mon arrivée, il y en avait bien, sans mentir, une vingtaine assise en rond sur la plate-forme, en train de se chauffer les pattes à un rayon de lune... Le temps d'entr'ouvrir une lucarne, frrt ! voilà le bivouac en déroute, et tous ces petits derrières blancs qui détalent, la queue en l'air, dans le fourré. J'espère bien qu'ils reviendront.

The night I arrived, there were, I kid you not, about twenty sitting in a circle on the platform, warming their paws in a moonbeam.... In the time it took to crack open a window, frrt! the encampment broke up, and all these little white behinds with tails in the air were bolting into the thicket. I really hope they'll come back.

For a moment, I had a fleeting image of Bijou scampering into the woods to join her bunny friends. I had never thought of her really being restricted by the boundaries of our courtyard and I was aware that with her respiratory rattle she would not survive in the wild, but for a moment I "saw" her hopping along the road side and into the field. When I arrived home, Bijou had already been "tucked into Chateau Bunné" for the night. As I passed by on my way through the courtyard, I said, "good night", as I often did, expecting no response, just one of the many "conversations "we would have with our little friend.

Bijou Bunné died sometime during that night. Linda found her in the morning when Linda opened the grill to begin the daily clean and feed. She thought it unusual that Bijou was not already peeping out of her cage in anticipation of her every morning garden romp, maid service, and breakfast. Bijou was dead and already stiffened and cold.

Bijou was fine the day before and managed to snip off the first of my tulip buds. And she was her normal hop-itty self when Linda gave her a piece of carrot, her usual bedtime treat around 8pm.

Upon reflection, yesterday I noticed one "cough" more serious than usual, but in all other ways she was just her normal self. There was no sign that she was ill or suffered. We knew that her congenital respiratory problem would probably contribute to a shorter than normal life span, but she had a happy little life.

I comfort myself to think that perhaps my "premonition" last night on the drive home was her little spirit freed so recently from bodily limitations an enjoying that unbounded freedom which death brings to the body as surely as it brings the pain of loss to those left behind. It was that next morning that Linda discovered, in fact, Bijou had died during the night and perhaps (because the rigor mortis that had set in) she died in the late hours of that Valentine's day

So we are a little sad today. And already miss her mischief in the garden and the little inane "conversations" we would have with her each time we passed through the courtyard. Rex and Trudie offered their garden as a cemetery and we think that we'll take them up on the offer since it is a protected garden. We do not have deep enough spaces to dig here inside the village walls. Tony and Erna offered their field (they have the most space) but it is open to prowling dogs and wild animals. So, we chose the enclose garden of friends to bury Bijou. Rex dug a grave deep enough, and would put a flowering plant on top afterwards. Linda placed Bijou, in the grave wrapped in a linen dish towel and we all cried a bit at the loss of this unexpected little treasure.

Life had a bit of a hole in it without Bijou. She was a part of France that delighted us. At first, we decided not to get another pet. Parting with this one was painful. But by June we were sneaking a peak at pet store windows and going in for "just a look". We knew it was just a matter of time before we would succumb. One day it happened. We discovered just the charmer that won our hearts again. However, it seems that we each discovered a different charmer. Technically they were from the same litter – at least that is what the pet store told us. Technically they were both Netherland Dwarf Rabbits, more accurately, they were probably Jersey Woolies, a combined breed of Netherland Dwarf and French Angora. But they were like salt and pepper. One was long and hopped with graceful arches. Soft angora fur covered most of her body in colors of pale blue, silver grey with white and sand colored markings – a female. The other was short and "springy"; dark brown/black with white and whisky colored fur. He had a tête de lion head like a lion's main and the cutest bunny face. She was beautiful, he was sporty! We made the heart wrenching decision to buy the female, but before we got out of the parking lot we returned to purchase her companion. We fussed and prepared the bunny hutch, which was actually under our antique stone feeding trough. We charmed it up by adding a "family portrait" – actually a framed detail from the unicorn tapestry that featured one of the tapestry bunnies. We were unabashed in "cuteness" mode. It was fun.

Since we had purchased a male and female we had to do some research into a time for neutering. We loved having the bunnies but two was more than enough. Our correspondence to friend via email will give you a little insight into the bunny love affair.

We named them Champagne Bunné for a touch of elegance, and Whisky Wabbit for his springy little legs and whisky coloring. These were part of our joy in living in France, an innocent distraction and endless fascination that pushed troubles far way and made us aware the tenderness in life.

Val J. Littman

To: Ann

Subject: Bunnies - update

Well, the deed is done! We made the trip to the vet on Thursday - preceded by a preliminary check up to assure that Whisky and Champagne were indeed ready for their respective castration and ovario-hysterectome. So they went in Thursday morning and that afternoon we were able to pick them up - stressed and shocked - but otherwise OK. That refers to the bunny parents not the bunnies.

Bunnies are doing well. After a few days of serious recuperation, they have resumed their near normal behaviors (both bunnies and bunny parents) This was a more traumatic surgery for Champagne than Whiskey (and more traumatic for the bunny parent's pocketbook -- 110 Euros for Champagne and a bargain 59 Euros for Whiskey minus the 13 percent reduction for getting the two done at the same time) Now, we are on a twice a day AM/ PM Care: a routine antibacterial spray which they immediately lick off. This only proves that they are really French rabbits -- everything must be edible!

They are not yet reunited -- giving Champagne a little more recuperative time -- but will soon be back into the same cage. It is cute to see that Whisky comes out of his cage and sits next to the fence that divides the two cages, Champagne sitting next to him on the other side of the fence. They look like a pair of fluffy bunny bedroom slippers.

We have already had inquiries from friends as to when the darlings will be ready to eat fresh mint and carrot greens. We will be joining them (our friends, not the rabbits) for Lunch on Sunday to gather up a supply of "get well" goodies for the bunnies! By then, I am sure that both Whisky and Champagne will be enjoying the sexual freedom, they have rightfully earned!

And that's the way it is - from the south of France

We are in full summer mode and as we woke up this morning, we said to each other, almost simultaneously, "Too much fun" and rolled over for another 40 winks. In these longest days of summer, it is daylight until after 10 PM so it is easy to lose track of time and be out too late.

Guests arrive on Thursday and then we have a string of guests until mid July - then an unexpected empty spot but it will probably be a welcome break.

Having survived the adventure of bunny neutering, we are now experimenting with letting the Bunnies out to roam the courtyard. As Bijou grew older she was able to spend a considerable amount of time out free to roam while we were working or sitting in the garden. But the preliminary test is to see if Champagne and Whisky come back into their cage when called (or more likely tempted with some fresh mint). They two are just learning that. Linda lets them out first thing in the morning while she cleans the cage and we are reasonably certain that they will always return for their breakfast pellets. They are really cute hopping around in the courtyard -- a nice "rural, south of France" Touché!

Much Love,

Val & Linda

Chapter 12
There is always more than meets the eye. Behind the scenes

Our Christmas letter of 2006 was an attempt to give our friends and family some insight into the growing disparity between our public face and personal disappointments about life in France

> I tried to make our Christmas letter shorter this year but have been unsuccessful. In March of 2007 we will celebrate six years of *la vie en France*. There is still a lot to tell. Truly, it has not all been fun, but we are here and have survived to tell you about it. From our friends, there seem to be some Frequently Asked Questions (FAQs) about our life in France, the answers to which are never a quick "Yes" or "No" and sometimes change from year to year. So, in the interest of ending this Christmas letter sometime before Easter rolls around, here's the short(er) version.
>
> **Q: Now that you are settled in France, how do you like it? Are you happy?**
>
> **A: That depends on who you ask.** Ask Linda, and she will tell you she is happy (well, as happy as one person can be when the other is not) She enjoys the rural pleasures, the ample sunlight, and French acquaintances she meets during her daily walks. Et moi, now that the past three years have been relatively free from the hassles of renovation, I can give a qualified "No" to life among the French. Much of 2006 has been spent, in therapy, learning how to live with this reality. I have, it is true found that France has its beauty, but then there are "The French". Of course, there are a few exceptions, but most of these gentle people are over the age of 90 and are remnants a vanishing era. For me, retirement to France is not among my life choices that I would make again if I had it to do over. But hey, so far, I have not found a way to turn back the clock. And a change of our investment seems unwise. So, I keep a copy of the Serenity Prayer close at hand and I have achieved some equilibrium about France and my experience of life here. Linda and I both enjoy our home and courtyard for our own relaxation and for entertaining. We have met a few wonderful friends, and as a haven, our home is lovely and has become what we envisioned.

Q: What do you do in retirement?

A: Our B&B keeps us reasonably busy, as busy as we want to be. We still have time for: Linda to teach English classes to French adults and adolescents. Her classes focus on communication for French who have already studied English in school but have not learned to speak. This year she increased the number of sessions for more students. After capsizing too many times in the winter waters of the Mediterranean, she is looking into a more fair-weather sailing experience for 2007. We have an active church group which meets once a month for services in English, it has an outreach to a local French charity, organizes one or two education events a year, and this year the annual Lessons and Carols Service (now in its fifth year) had record attendance of 250 people. We did vacation to the USA this year (our return for the first time in three years) and we had an unexpected visit to Florence Italy this year (more on this surprise, later). I sing tenor in a French-English choral group, write an occasional article for a regional French-English Magazine, and serve as mentor to a young priest in Clermont Ferrand. My favorite bit of retirement is <u>time</u>: Time to look up that little obscurity, or historical fact that I have always wondered about, time to leisurely prepare a reflection on the Sunday scripture readings, and time to finish the book about our first three years of *la vie en France* (more on that later).

Q: How are the Bunnies?

A: Since last Christmas we lost one bunny and gained two. In February little Bijou Bunné died. She had a happy but short life due to her congenital respiratory problem (she had a little respiratory rattle from the day we got her) But Bijou was such a wonderful pet that after a month, we noticed we were still having inane conversations with a bunny spirit in our garden. So, we searched for a new bunny and found two. *Champagne Bunné* and *Whisky Wabbit* are very different but adorable additions to the spirit of le petit jardin de l'âme. They are tri-colored "Jersey Woolies", a mix of French Angora and Netherland Dwarf rabbits. Linda picks fresh dandelion greens and clover for them during her walks around the countryside. They have a hoppy time in the courtyard. They seem to understand "No" when they get in to the garden, but they remember for only about three seconds before they try again. The most frequently asked question from the French is, "When are you going to eat them?" But these bunnies are surely for bonne ambiance, not bon appétit.

Q: How is your French?

A: Again, it depends on who you ask. We have a little dissonance in our abilities to *parler française*. Linda continues to pursue improving her French one-on-one with one of her former students. Linda teaches her English in exchange. Linda can also be seen walking along the *digue*, mumbling to herself as she listens to and repeats the French news and interviews on *France Info*, a French radio station. I have stopped taking lessons for the time being. The irony is that Linda feels that my French is better than hers. More accurately, this may be that I have more of what the French call "courage" and have more fluid, but infrequent, conversations in French. Linda's use is more accurate and more frequent, but she feels that her French is more hesitant. I see my more fluid but infrequent conversations as one of the "benefits" of being frustrated so often by the French. I now just spout it out with the emphasis on communication rather than correctness! We both do rather well. We are no longer paralyzed when we pick up the telephone to enter into a French conversation. From day to day we still feel that we will never really "get it", but when we have B&B guests we realize how far we have come.

Q: Where's the Book?

A: The proof copy from the publisher is on my desk as I write this Christmas letter. I had hoped to be able to tell you to run out and buy (several thousand) copies. But alas, it now looks like it will be spring before it is on the book shelves. Yes, the book, <u>A Bright Sun & Long Shadows</u> is finished. But, as in many of life's projects, "finished" is a progressive state. It is written and submitted to the publisher and has been returned for a final proof and approval before printing. So it's on the way and that means that I will be doing a follow-up Easter letter to tell you all to run out and buy the book.

Q: What's new?

A: At last we have our *Carte de Résidence*, which allows us to live in France for 10 years without re-application. Linda says "hurrah" and

I am still trying to understand if this is a blessing or a curse. Getting the *Carte de Résidence* required an interview in French that tested our abilities to understand and speak the language as well as answering questions about our integration into French community life.

At the end of the summer, I had a call from the St James, Episcopal Church, Florence Italy. Their rector was away on a planned absence and his back up suddenly died. I was able to help them with their Sunday services and five "destination weddings" at beautiful locations in those Tuscan Hills around Florence. This also provided me with a lovely two weeks in Florence and Linda was able to join me for a week. In addition, we met some nice people at St James parish.

I now have a marvelous new toy. In my dotage I have become the village organ grinder with a casual likeness to Toulouse Lautrec's famous poster of Aristide Bruant. Actually, this picture is an ironic symbol of my life in France. It is a picture of an Old American Fool, playing his new English Street Organ at a local fair, creating that ambiance that seems "Oh, so French".

> *Life may not be the party we hoped for,*
> *but we might as well dance while we are here.*
> -Source unknown: I borrowed it from a long-time-friend, Ellie Nemeth

By 2007 the Annual Festival of Lessons and Carols had grown to more than 250 in attendance. It was a community-wide event participated in by many of the English speaking ex-pats. I should clarify that English-speaking ex-pats - is used here more broadly than "people from England". English-speaking ex-pats from the USA, Canada, Australia, Ireland, Scotland, as well as some for whom English was comfortable, though not their first language, such as those from Holland, or Germany or Denmark. This is an important distinction, frequently lost to The English, who are one part of the larger English-speaking world.

The Festival of Nine Lessons and Carols was supported enthusiastically by the local French Roman Catholics and the village of Fontès, where the church was loaned to us for the occasion. This Lessons and Carols of 2007 would be our fifth annual celebration. Members of a committee had by now fine tuned their organizing roles, each taking a share of the responsibility and working like "clock-work". I shared the primary responsibilities with a woman I will call Lourdes. Lourdes took on administration duties; keeping minutes, organizing lists, and was liaison with the local church and village of Fontès, which offered to print the 250 copies of the Order of Service. Lourdes, active in the local Roman Catholic churches, was also responsible for getting the key for opening and closing the church as we needed it. She was very organized and efficient. Other members of the team each had their jobs; to recruit readers for the service and prepare them, another organized publicity, and another organized the plans for refreshments after the service, another organized the welcoming of guests and taking up the collection on the day. This was a community wide activity that included the members of the growing Anglican/Episcopal Church in the Hèrault and people with no specific local church affiliation but enthusiastic in continuing this tradition.

As clergy I was responsible for the tone and content of the service, I prepared the sermon for the day, coordinated the music with the organist and choir director. Being a bit more technically adventurous, I had developed a few more computer skills than others on the planning team. Therefore, I prepared the master document which the village Mayor's office printed for us. Together Lourdes and I were the co-chairs of this group. Together we oversaw and followed up on all organizing aspects for a successful service on the day of Lessons and Carols. This meant much "back and forth" between Lourdes and I. We were an effective team with others each carrying out appointed tasks in preparation and on the day of the service. I enjoyed working with Lourdes.

I should note that informally when there were ruffled feathers to be smoothed, as happens in committee work, Lourdes came to me to smooth those ruffled feathers. After the Lessons and Carols of 2005 Lourdes and a couple others had reached a limit of tolerating one person's gruff personal demeanor. And while I had not experienced it personally I could see what they were talking about, having observed it from afar. And in the context of another group (the local church group) she was known to be little abrasive in her interactions on occasion. I also knew that Lourdes and this person had some friction bubbling up between them. So, in consultation with Lourdes I proposed a compromise and solution for the next year reducing that person's one-on-one personal contact but still keeping her in the work group. It turned out that while this change was accepted without difficulties, I later realized that (I will call her, "T") "T" resented this change but begrudgingly accepted it while assigning blame for the intervention entirely to me.

I found that I was often more aware of the value of including others even

Le Petit Jardin de L'âme

when it might be easier to do it all myself. Lourdes, for example was very capable but I actively sought out to involve others because I felt it helped to diversify the group and insure longevity. As was my preferred style of working, I actively consulted opinions from others as I put together the service, selecting carols and particular versions carols that would be successfully sung on the day by a large but diverse congregation who gathered but once a year, and had different versions of even the most familiar traditional Christmas carols. It is surprising to many who have not organized such events, just how many variations there are to songs that most of us consider have always been sung the same way by everybody; that is, to say always sung in the way that we remember from our childhood.

I'll digress for a few paragraphs to include just some examples for your increased appreciation of what things need to be considered in the preparation a worship service that most people think of as containing a familiar scripture story and Christmas carols that everybody knows. After all, just how difficult can it be, it's Christmas?

First, when people think of a Lessons and Carol service they usually think of it as a telling of the Christmas story. Yes, that is true. But not in the restricted sense as many remember, identifying only Jesus' birth in the Gospel stories. The format and choice of scripture readings for the Lessons and Carols does tell this story but in the context of a larger scriptural sense. And this larger context was envisioned from the original Lessons and Carols celebration in Cornwall in the 1880's and from a tradition carried by King's College Cambridge since 1918. Many people miss the larger connection and focus only on the nativity narratives of the Gospel. Many are unaware of the original plan or purpose of other readings from the Old Testament and prophets.

Of the nine lessons which make up the Lessons / Scripture parts of the Nine Lesson and Carols, the first four readings place Christmas in the context of a larger history and are from Old Testament readings. The next four readings, selections from the gospels of Luke and Matthew are what most people remember as the Christmas story, and the last ninth, reading is traditionally taken from the prologue of the Gospel of John; a poetic rendering of cosmic proportions. When we first introduced the Lessons and Carols service at our local celebration five years earlier, we had been selective – choosing most of the readings that most people identified with Christmas. By consensus we had agreed from the first year to follow the order of service of King's College Festival of Lessons and Carols – arguably the "gold standard" of this tradition. In early years we were timid and modified the traditional Nine Lessons to five, then in more confidence gradually grew to the full service of nine lessons and Carols. In recent years as a part of the growth, we incorporated with great success a couple selections by the choral group of which I and many people involved with the service were a part. Over the subsequent five years we progressively shaped the service to reflect the traditional Festival of nine Lessons and Carols, each year bringing us closer and closer the original and traditional service known throughout the world. For many people, they easily remember the "Christmas story as they knew it as a child" and forget the larger Christmas story which is intentionally told by the service.

Then, it is also important to consider that even Christmas Carols, known by everyone, are not known by everyone in the same way. Words are different for some verses, and in our specific context with a mix of English speaking peoples, even the spellings are different for certain words. In most cases I would defer to the "English" words and spellings that were particular to the Island of Great Britain rather than American, Canadian, Australian, other "English" versions. In some cases, a more contemporary wording might be better known than the 15th century version. Sometimes a new political correctness entered in, but as a group most people preferred "tradition" whatever that meant; it usually meant their tradition.

Melodies also differ. A familiar carol may be sung to different melodies as if it has always been sung that way – that is, the way the carol was sung in their childhood. For example, when "O Little Town of Bethlehem" is sung in the commonwealth of Great Britain the tune, called Forest Green (personally, my preference) is not the same as "O Little Town of Bethlehem" sung in the USA where the most frequently recorded tune is different and called, St Louis, except, in the Episcopal Church where it is often sung to the melody of Forest Green. Aside from getting these details right for the congregation to sing their familiar version it is also necessary to coordinate this choice with the Organist. Such differences in wording or in singing the melodies comes up in surprising places and I was pleased at taking them all into consideration for a smooth and flowing worship service, which added to the prayerfulness of the event, free from distractions   I prided myself in being ware of such differences and considering them in the preparation of the service. And more to my surprise, people noticed and commented.

The preaching of the sermon fell logically to the clergy, me. The occasion seemed to call for a more formal style than I personally preferred. I enjoyed reflecting and writing the sermon weeks in advance, in search for common current applications of an age-old tradition. I wrote the sermon, and re-wrote it in preparations for handing it over to the translator for our few

French visitors. Judging from comments over the years the sermon was enjoyed, and anticipated. Responses were often more specific than the perfunctory "Thank you, Vicar, for the kind words". People actually seemed to listen and make extended comments about something that they had heard, or some aspect of Christmas tradition that they had not known or a particular point that they appreciated. I often looked forward to the response of the editor of the regional ex-pat news magazine. He had a reputation for being critical. I thought of his comments as a sign that he was an astute listener. He was an enthusiastic critic; "How do you manage to top yourself year after year?", "had my attention the whole time" and that favorite English expletive, "Bloody good job!", then would he add some particular detail that he noticed.

I enjoyed the challenge of preparing and celebrating the Festival of Nine Lessons and Carols each year. Meetings began in late august (or early September) and included follow-up after the vent in early January.

But now, I return to the preparations for this year in 2007. There is a storm is brewing.

Preparations for the Festival of Nine Lessons and Carols, December 2007 began as early as August or early September. This was also about the time that the choral group re-united after a summer's break to prepare for the new concert season. The choral group, of which Lourdes and I were members (and many others who participated in the Festive of Lessons and Carols) was introducing in its concert repertoire a well-known and well-loved piece by the English composer, John Stainer. The selection taken from his 1887 Oratorio, The Crucifixion was a reflection on the scripture passage "God so loved the world that he gave his only begotten son…. (from John's Gospel chapter 3 verse 16)" It was perfectly suited for the service if the choral group were able to master it in their repertoire. This was not simply my opinion. In popular Christmas greetings it is not unusual to see this quote on religious themed Christmas cards; it had also been sung by the Kings College Choir in the 2005 Festival of Lessons and Carols, Kings College Cambridge being held in high esteem by all for the Lessons and Carols tradition.

I had successfully suggested a few years previous, that the choral group provide two selections from their Christmas repertoire as a part of the service. There was some initial resistance to this idea by Lourdes, but I convinced the planning team that the choral group would provide some respite from a marathon of congregational singing of Christmas Carols, and there was ample precedent for this variety in many versions of the festival of Lessons and Carols around the world. The introduction of the choral group was a success and by now their participation was not only a "given" part of the service, but the choral group itself looked forward to the opportunity.

Musically and in terms of scripture exegesis, the John Stainer selection for 2007 made sense to me as clergy in several ways. Therefore, at our first regular planning meeting I proposed the idea and indicated that it would also give me – as the preacher an additional touch point for expanding on the ninth scripture reading from the introduction to the Gospel of John. Response at the planning meeting was universal (or so I thought), with responses that ranged from quiet acceptance to a few positive nodding of heads. Since this was a part of the tone and content of the service it was for me to decide. One person voiced her opinion of how beautiful this selection was. More to my point, which will become clear later, there was no spoken objection. But, it turns out, Lourdes has some very strong (all-be-it misinformed) opinions about this musical selection.

I proceeded, outside the meeting to discuss this possibility with the director of the Choral group. So, at a subsequent rehearsal of the choral group a question was raised during a break from rehearsal. "Who in the choral group will be able to participate in the Lessons and Carols Service this Christmas?" Most were able, and the necessary complement of SATB voices was determined sufficient to make the commitment. OK, Did I as the leader of the service have any ideas of what two choral selections to consider? The question was directed to me, so I proposed one well known selection (an easy one for the choir and appropriate for the service) and I proposed the newer and more difficult selection by John Stainer, if possible.

To my surprise (and to all in the rehearsal room) Lourdes gave a resounding oppositional groan followed by a Gatling-gun series of short phrases about how inappropriate this choice would be. The initial responses from the assembled choral group varied from surprised disagreement, to some voicing objection, that decisions about what the group sang had never been determined by individual group members casting a vote but rather by the director. This short-term disarray caused by Lourdes' outbreak was called to a halt by the director and the founder of the Chorale. Having established order, they turned to me. I repeated my suggestions and rationale in a couple of sentences. Lourdes interrupted with an attempt to rally, "Let's take a vote!" This was so out-of-character for Lourdes and for the group itself. A series of comments, murmurs and general disbelief followed. The prevailing response was more a question from individuals and the group, "Shouldn't this be the decision of the Vicar?" Some voiced this, and others just looked to me. I agreed and took the opportunity to say that perhaps the director and founder and I should discuss this later.

My immediate concern was beyond what to sing at Lesson and Carols and beyond the John Stainer selection itself. Why would Lourdes embarrass herself and me in front of the group? Why did she not voice some concern at our planning meeting just days before? And less of a question, but a point of asserting my role, this was not something for her to decide. I planned to take Lourdes aside as soon as possible, which was at the end of our Choral rehearsal before she had a chance to exit.

We met briefly before the choral group dismissed for the evening. I could tell that people were "watching out of the corner of their eyes". My message to Lourdes was brief. I do not want this to happen again. And I will contact her in the next few days to set up a meeting to discuss this further.

What ensued was months of back and forth meetings, and emails with someone who was acting like an insubordinate teenager.

By way of explanation to those not familiar with the Stainer selection mentioned above; Stainer's Oratorio of 1887, has some structural and historical similarities to the more popularly known Handle's Messiah. For example, although Handel's Messiah was first performed during Eastertide in 1742 it has become a Christmas favorite. And even those Christmas favorites such as "For unto us a child is born" (from the Old Testament prophet Isaiah) and the Halleluiah chorus (occurring in the Handel's Oratorio as a resurrection piece) in their scriptural context do not refer specifically to Christmas but to a larger picture of the Christian Tradition. So, it is with Stainer's Oratorio, The Crucifixion. It was first performed in 1887 just after Ash Wednesday and, in general, has a Lenten reflective tone to it. However, the scriptural quote for this particular section "God So Loved the World" comes from the earlier Chapters of John's Gospel (Chapter 3 Verse 16 and following - not from the passion narrative much later in the Gospel). For the moment I will skip over the more nuanced scriptural exegesis that biblical scholars would attribute to this piece. However, this passage does provide the prospective preacher with lovely sermon opportunities. Instead, for the moment I favored a line of reasoning that would be evident to Lourdes and any follower of the tradition of The Festival of Lessons and Carols. This specific Stainer selection had been sung at the Festival of Nine Lessons and Carols at King's College in 2005. This service was not only a Christmas Tradition in England since 1918, but a source of English pride, and viewed by many around the world. A quick reference to Google and the 2005 Order of Service at Kings College on line would easily discover this. Many, including Lourdes, already knew this and needed only a casual reminder because, many British fans would have watched the live televised broadcast on BBC, so popular is this event among the British.

My initial approach to Lourdes, and as damage control to others who were puzzled by her behavior, was to take the explanatory and educational route. Offering information and education also reinforced my role as the one responsible for the content and tone of the service. I repeated the history notes from the paragraph above, I also alluded to the many Christmas greeting cards that use that exact same quotation. But to no avail. Email exchanges were not persuasive for Lourdes, so we met at a coffee shop for a discussion. Meanwhile it was clear that Lourdes was busy rallying support from outside the planning group itself. Some members of the choral group voiced their opinion via email to me, or by phone (I repeated my rationale). Lourdes told me that there were people (whose role was to prepare the refreshments after the service) were also upset with the use of this selection. It should be noted that these individuals remained anonymous and it should also be noted that members of the planning group became noticeably silent, but vigilant, I am sure, for the outcome.

My concerns were multi-faceted. I am so aware of the scandal that Christians cause the larger community when they cannot get along among themselves. "See how these Christians love one another"? To me there is no better way to discourage a person who is inquiring about how their spiritual life may be fostered, than to launder dirty linen of a church in destructive discord. Problems and differences well managed can be a positive dynamic and draw spiritual inquirers into a congregation but destructive conflicts and petty snipping is a scandal to the broader community. I also liked working with Lourdes and wished to continue this working relationship. And for my own reasons I wished that this event which had grown along with growing responsibilities of the little congregation, remain a pleasant work with joyful spirits. Personally, I did not wish this to become drudgery or an "up-hill-battle. I wanted it to remain fun and an energizing part of my Christmas preparations, not hard work.

I met with Lourdes at a local café. This discussion was civil but cool. We came to an agreement. If the Choral group was prepared – the term used was "concert ready" – to sing "God So Loved the World" then it would be sung. We both acknowledged that it was possible that as a new selection and a bit more difficult for the choral group, it might be that it would not be "concert ready". Only the Director would decide if the selection was ready to be performed. And we would have a back-up selection in the ready. As it turned out, that season, the Stainer piece proved a little too difficult for the choral group to be ready for concert performances and thus we did not use it that year at the Lessons and Carols Service. I was comfortable with that arrangement and Lourdes sensed a "victory". I felt that I had maintained my role as clergy determining the content and tone of the worship service, which, to me was the larger issue.

The public service, Festival of Nine Lessons and Carols was its usual success. We were able to give a generous donation of over €600. to St. Hippolyte parish in Fontès, for the use of the church for the day. And I felt that we had navigated the normal (but annoying) growing pains that come with success and group interpersonal interactions over time. Perhaps I was naïve, for this was not to be the end of the story. The financial success of Lessons and Carols raised another question which I was to introduce to the planning group in the next year. But I will come to that at a later time.

Little did I realize that in Lourdes outburst, I had just been introduced to two significant characteristics that were to surface again the next few years. I'll attempt some description of these personal styles here, because I will reference them later: "Staged Rage" is my name for one, and "The sinkhole" the name for the second. Once or twice before I had seen, outbursts of Staged Rage but could not put an identifier to a single, apparently isolated event, and, previously, these had not been directed at me personally. But in reflection based on observing a few experiences in different social contexts, one starts to allow for identification of common denominators and symptom characteristics.

I would describe *Staged Rage* as a "lose - lose proposition"- opposite of a "win-win" desired outcome from most productive conversations. I now know, based on observing this done to others and also being the recipient of this tactic that the person who regresses to this form has already abandoned productive attempts at negotiation. If one is at the receiving end of another's Staged Rage, realize that the stated topic for discussion has already been subordinated or completely lost. YOU are now the target and the intention is "make a scene" to embarrass you. Staged Rage is usually verbal expression. Though, it could be written (e.g. an email with BCC – the comments in the blogosphere are sometimes examples of written expressions of Staged Rage). As I write this in 2014, I am aware that some TV news or radio commentators, and "Reality TV" celebrities may provide us with contemporary examples of this Staged Rage. Staged Rage is "staged". It is always spoken with an audience in mind. It is therefore accompanied by a volume louder than needed for civil conversation, and staccato-like words, sharply punctuated; "How! Dare! You!". An angry, reddened-face, or distorted, grimacing facial expression enhances the delivery. Staged Rage is out of proportion to the event or topic at hand, and is primarily geared to elicit an immediate apology or placating expression from the person to whom it is directed. Most often, stunned silence is what is elicited from both by-standers, and the targeted person since one of its primary elements is the element of surprise. Staged Rage makes the outrage the center of attention – shifting attention from any reasoning or rationale that might have preceded it in the actual topic of conversation. Staged Rage uses exaggeration disguised as "facts", hyperbole and innuendo as its own special logic. Almost anything said by the person to whom Staged Rage is directed is futile and is used by the outraged person to add "fuel to the fire". In the end Staged Rage is an act designed to gain attention all-be-it in a most unflattering way, and to embarrass its target.

By contrast, where outrage is not staged, it is a legitimate, even if uncomfortable, feeling, there is an element of shock in the person themselves. The surprise is twofold; both the one who delivers the outrage and the recipient of the comment are caught off guard. Real outrage does indeed exist, but it is not a performance. Staged Rage is theatre. In the coming chapters you will see more examples of this demeaning tool.

The "Sinkhole" as a personal style is essentially an unseen activity bubbling and gurgling out of sight until it engulfs all that it has previously supported. The Sinkhole personal style may, at first, be an unconscious activity but at some point, there is a deliberate plan to undermine a position or person that it had previously supported.

Both Lourdes and "T" were prime candidates for employing this behavior. Their anger went underground. Initially supportive, not only of me but of a common group goal, they would little by little go underground with their agenda, gathering support using mis-information, and surface when they had gained momentum and numbers in their favor to stage a coup – to ambush an event – by "pulling the rug" out from under, not only a person (me) but by undermining the entire group esprit de corps.

We will see more of this later. The sinkhole needs some time to fester.

My experiences with both "T" and "Lourdes" was not only a personal challenge, and a part of group growth, but it was for me, a spiritual exercise in which I attempted to respond to in a way that would shape the local church community to which I had been called, despite myself, to serve. I saw these encounters with deception and the "little white lies" that are inherent in human interactions with the eye of a pastor.

If these were people in general society, I would not choose them as friends to spend time with. Being more selective is a possibility in general society in choosing friends. But these were people who had chosen to be part of a group for whom I was clergy leader. As the local clergy, there is a call to be pastor to all, even those with whom I would not choose to be friend. At this time, I continued to respond by trying to understand, to offer information and, education, to work with them taking incremental steps toward a bigger goal. It was a challenge that I felt up to and, received as appropriate for the role in which I had been cast.

> *"People cannot accept their own evil if they do not at the same time feel loved, respected and trusted."*
> -Jean Vanier, *Community And Growth*

Chapter 13
A brief hiatus, gentle reader

My apologies, as I depart from the flow of chronological events, once again. I do so wish that life would be more orderly. However, I pause here to let you know that after writing the above chapter I needed a break. I was not suffering from "writer's block" but rather fatigue that comes with reliving these moments, as some were painful. At the time they were a burden received when I could have just said "to hell with it all" but in remembering there is another form of re-living, no less real, just more distant.

I was aware of a growing sense of personal responsibility for what was developing. Warts and all, it was a part of a creative process. So, as I enter into the spirit of writing, there is a bit of interior wrestling match for me as I try to not only remember the events and the personalities, but to treat them as fairly as I can. Yes, this is a personal memoir, but I believe that it remains more credible to the extent that I can give some objective stance to very personal moments. Weighing my words and selecting a phrase is something that I am accustomed to by disposition and by training, but the good work of some objectivity takes a toll. So, you'll excuse me gentle reader, I needed a break. In fact, it has now been more than six months since the chapter above was written and I continue with a renewed sense purpose; to present the events as joyfully and as troubling as they were.

Even little gardens need a time to lay fallow before new growth.

I am aware of a subtle change as I move on to resume my writing. The chapters that follow will focus more on the life of the little church community and less on our over-all life in France. Indeed, there was a mix of the two areas. And Linda and I carefully cultivated a social life apart from the church community. But the intensity of time and feelings centered on the growing church community, my role as pastor and the larger church community in Europe. And so, the memoir will reflect this, skewed as it were, toward difficult times ahead. There were, it should be said also happy times. The larger Episcopal Church in Europe, its bishop and clergy and lay leadership offered enjoyable and supportive relationships. And there were a few close friends who were not "church-goers". They were members of a small expat community within a limited geographic area. These closest of friends were discrete enough not to inquire – or not to inquire too often. But they were not ignorant of the troubles as these troubles grew more and more public.

Chapter 14
2008 and 2009, growth & growing pains

Speaking of a hiatus from church stressors, we also had experienced an hiatus from the rigors of renovation. We, more or less, had had a reprieve from dealing with French workmen. Life had settled into a rhythm. Our B&B clients were sufficient, and we were happy to be able to be selective about just how busy we wished to be. But now we had to "bite the bullet " and have two large beams replaced in the courtyard. I would like to say that our experience made us more savvy and we would have better results. Perhaps we were savvier – but even if we knew more, and more selective, we still had to choose from available resources.

Even after seven years living in France it was necessary to select from among local French workmen.

We had a job to be done, we observed a local mason doing work for different neighbors - not once, not twice, but more than three or four times. He seemed reliable, he cleaned up after himself and his work seemed correct. In September 2007 we approached him (actually Linda approached him – I no longer trust myself front of French workmen).

In September we signed the devis – the estimate and description of the work to be done. We stipulated that it was to be done anytime during the winter months, and must be finished before the end of February. We made our first, one-third, deposit according to plan. (We do not object to the usual plan for payment: One-third deposit at the signing of the contract, one-third at the beginning of actual work and one third when the job is finished). It seems, if conversations with local French workmen are to be believed, that this is the proposed way of doing business.

On the other hand, if local French lore from a few boastful clients is to be believed, no one actually forks over any money until the job is completed. According to the "man on the street", one should never pay for anything until the work is finished. But we have not found any workman who is willing to even consider the project without the initial one-third payment. I think that this local "wisdom" about withholding payment until the work is finished, is nine parts braggadocios and one part wishful thinking.

The usual and expected delays were not a problem as long as there was time left to finish the project (estimated to be about one week's work). In mid-February – four months after our initial deposit- Linda approached the workman and made a salvo across his bow" ... work must begin soon or we want our deposit returned." The usual promise was made, and we were delighted to see that he actually did begin work on 25 February. Never mind that the estimated time to complete the job would take us into the first few days of March. We had learned that indeed this was close enough to the target date for the south of France.

And then came the reoccurrence of the French Workmen Nightmares that haunted us for the first four years. After four months delay followed by a false start only days before the absolute end of the agreement, a workman showed up. On 25 February he put up his scaffolding, tore out the necessary parts of the roof and the first decaying beam, "jacked up" the roof, took the second third of our payment for the job, and after a full day of "Laurel and Hardy" antics decided that he could not get the new beam into the courtyard. He left.

And here we sit for nine days after he said he would return, without a trace. We do have a lovely one-ton new wooden beam sitting half way between our garage and its targeted resting place. My untrained eye told me it would be a minor miracle to get a beam of the necessary length, and breadth into our courtyard. That is why we hired an expert. He measured, calculated and reflected, on how to get the beam into place, but he seems to have overlooked something. Meanwhile we are totally dependent on his scaffolding to hold up our roof. The spring has come, and the garden wants to be trimmed, watered and planted. The stone work needs to have the winter's grime cleaned off with pressure spray. The usual spring-cleaning needs to be done before our first quests arrive in a couple of weeks. All my conditioned reflexes, detesting French workmen have been reactivated.

The supporting scaffolding blocks the door way from the kitchen into the courtyard, the one we most often use. So we have been ducking in, out and around the supports. I have brushed off the layers of construction debris from our garden plants. I give them a "pep" talk each day encouraging their spring growth, and assuring them that they will not be trampled underfoot when the workmen return – well, my hope springs eternal. And of course, Linda and I have moved all outdoor furniture, and movable plants out of harm's way.

I am sure that there are more disastrous things going on in other parts of the world but here in this south of France paradise, it is life as usual - not the la vie en France of romance but rather unspoken chaos.

As the spring blossomed so too did many good things come in 2008, most notable of which was an eventual return to a sense of normality. Linda's and my French were now more relaxed, relationships in the village more integrated, my own expectations adjusted to reduce disappointments, and the development of happy routines and comfortable friendships.

Linda and I each developed our own interests and level of involvement with the locals. Linda's teaching French as a second language to women of her age was very rewarding for her and she also developed private tutoring with a select group of students preparing to take English Oral exams for the French *Grandes Écoles*. The International Choral group was, for me a challenge which I looked forward to; stretching my voice and my reading abilities through rehearsals. The growth of the church group was beyond what I had imaged but I saw the problems or challenges we faced as welcome signs of group growth and happily put my organizational skills to work. And I enjoyed the personal spiritual discipline that "being the vicar" awakened in me.

Not only had our French language skills improved but the French themselves were experiencing a change of heart as noted by news articles. In the Economist of 11 September 2008 – *Franglais Resurgent* – "Nicolas Sarkozy, who, although no linguist, rejects the atavistic anti-Americanism that underpins much hostility to English.

Appropriately, "Comme si de rien n'était", the new album by his wife, Carla Bruni, has a track in English—presumably not one his predecessor will listen to. And "The children of globalization are giving up writing in French," declared *Le Monde*, the bible of the French elite, 'without apparent regret".

It could not have pleased me more to see that locally there was – village by village – a war against dog poop and debris on the streets. Poster campaigns, and doggie bag dispensers to re-educate dog owners brought joy and relief to me and brought cleaner streets to the village. Even the noise pollution was lessening. Although not perfect, a curfew on highly amplified festival music was more often obeyed.

Happily, I continued the development of the church group. My time was increasingly spent on Church related projects, local administration, adult education and development of lay leadership. I also became more involved in the larger Episcopal Church in Europe, eventually in 2009 being elected to the Bishop's Council of Advice (called "Standing Committee" in most dioceses) and appointed chair of the Committee on Mission Congregations.

Collegial relationships in the Episcopal Church Europe were some of my most rewarding relationships and from them I received much support for work in the local church.

In February 2008 I began providing occasional Education Events and creating evening programs focused on our recent growth to "take the pulse" of the membership on plans for growth. The acting treasurer gave a written summary of the meeting and it was decided that we should at least look into being more formally organized as a church. The congregation began discussion about becoming more organized and became a French Association Loi 1901 (a not-for-profit organization). In April, I began research onto how we could affiliate with the larger worldwide Anglican Communion.

In November of 2008 we assembled after our Sunday Eucharist in the nave of the chapel in Conas for our first annual meeting of the newly created Association loi (required of all "not-for-profit" organizations in France). This was largely for financial purposes of obtaining a bank account and organizing our limited finances. In January 2009 I began to discuss some token clergy compensation with the Association Loi membership. Token clergy compensation was focused primarily on getting the congregation ready – personally and financially – for future clergy who might not be as financially independent as I was.

The prevailing voices of the congregation wished to remain "non-denominational". By that those who voiced their opinions meant that they did not wish to "be told what to do" by some higher jurisdiction, which was how they viewed belonging to a larger church organization. Clearly there was a need for some basic re-education around the areas of ecclesiology in the Anglican tradition, church leadership and authority in general. But I began to see that I was working with a group who saw church leadership as a burden not a benefit. Many in the congregation remained silent or had no opinion on this matter at the time.

Most people wanted a prayerful worship service and church life with which they were familiar. All the while we worshiped using a combined rite borrowed from both the Episcopal Church and the updated rites of the Church of England in "Common Worship". From time to time people would come to me and say something like, "In England we often did it this way." Little turns of phrase can mean a lot. As long as they were not substantive changes or contrary to the general framework I would listen and generally find a way to incorporate that practice into our worship. As clergy I attempted to steer to the middle ground between familiarity and freshness of worship. Our worship was traditional but not stuffy, informal but reverent. My personal style of celebration of the Eucharist seemed appreciated as reflective, simple and inspiring. It was also respectful of time being approximately one hour, no more. People not only seemed very happy with the style of worship, but word spread, and people came and stayed. This was a welcoming place and the worship was designed so that even a first timer could participate comfortably.

In the early years when we worshiped as a "house church" I attempted to stay singularly focused on worship and spiritual life. First this took the form of setting the tone and content of the worship. Intentionally I did not take up a collection and did not want to handle any money. As time went by the congregation's interest included charity outreach – mostly in the form of financial contributions, then education events. People encouraged establishing the time honored "church collection" as a way for them to contribute to this work. I resisted and then gave in realizing that this was a way for people to contribute to the life of the church. The position of treasurer was created. Still separating finances and spiritual life was my assumption. Over time, I was drawn into managing both of these intricately intertwined aspects of church life. The separation of these would only work if there was a common vision shared by both the spiritual leader and the keeper of finances.

There were structural or organizational issues which needed to be managed beyond simple attendance at Sunday worship. Our growth in size was accompanied by growth in enthusiasm for other areas of church life such as charity outreach, a need for adult education, administration and my personal favorite "People Management". These growing demands placed on me as volunteer clergy were either unseen or denied by the average person in the pew. While there was another retired clergy in the congregation he was nearly 20 years older and had expressed his wish early on to simple celebrate the Eucharist on occasion and leave the organization to me. The growth – planned or unplanned – inevitably would require some change from an informal gathering and ad hoc decisions to a more formalized organization and advanced planning. This change was being resisted. From my point of view, it seemed that many in the developing congregation saw the church only from the vantage point of their seat in the pew on Sunday. Not only was there was little awareness of the larger church, there was little vision of what being a church called its members to be in the larger community. As long as the Sunday services continued for them there was no need to change anything. But leaders are charged with seeing a bigger picture and growing a people.

I must at this point let you, gentle reader; know of my personal disposition at this time. Although I was a willing volunteer of my time and energy in my retirement, I saw not only the need for a connection with the larger organized church (The larger Anglican Communion and the Episcopal church specifically), I saw a benefit to acknowledging the Anglican Tradition that preceded us and of which we were but a small part. At heart, I was not a "freelancer". My license to serve (this congregation or any congregation) and my professional integrity were supported by this larger church structure. My training and continued education and professional life was connected to the larger church. My appreciation for history and the very tradition in which we all worshiped was a part of the larger Anglican tradition. I was not likely to start up an independent, non-denominational church.

This was also for me a living laboratory of church life. It suited me well with my background in psychodynamics, social work and organizational development. Spiritually it was for me to live out a call to priesthood as a shepherd-guide to a people to bring them to places in their spiritual life, perhaps deeper, broader, with new horizons on the meaning of their life. This excited me as an opportunity to build from the ground up a community of prayer, to help people grow in living out the gospel. Before me was a garden of souls to be cultivated with care, le petit jardin de l'âme, little garden of the soul was right here!

Simultaneous with the growth of the congregation, the annual Festival of Nine Lessons and Carols grew in attendance from 250 to 280 in December of 2008, in its sixth year. The lessons and carols service was a separate organization, separate work group (although there was much overlap of those involved from the congregation, the Lessons and Carols service had its own budget and included participation from the larger community from other churches and those who belonged to no particular church. In 2008 and 2009 Lourdes (you remember Lourdes from the 'Staged Rage" incident back in 2007) took a more reserved role at first participating but with a cold shoulder and eventually pulling back altogether in 2009 and 2010. Her husband remained active. He was helpful but there was always a tug and pull around power and control. His role was to be purely financial accounting. And he also served in the first years in the area of setting up the refreshments after the service, but his interests often spilled over into content for the service itself. By 2010 Lourdes, I speculate now, had convinced one by one all the members of the original planning committee to excuse themselves. I formed a new planning group from the members of our little congregation at Grace Church. They picked up the challenge admirably, and carried on the tradition. We continued to seek out volunteers from the broader community, but the organization of the event was carried by Grace Church. Both Lourdes and her husband were content to sit in the pew. Well, not really content but that is where they were physically, in the pew.

Church life in 2008 and 2009 was a major part of my retired life; it was increasingly more visible to the larger community both socially and spiritually. And it would undergo the stresses and strains of growth that any small group goes through. It was a stressful time, which I hoped I would manage carefully. I think I did.

We, as a congregation continued to explore how we might respond to our growing numbers. The series of meetings in February and March of 2008 were ostensibly to address how we might handle this growth. Less obvious to the congregation was my agenda to observe and assess how I might help them as a congregation grow and apply in their own way a dynamic gospel mandate that would take them as a group beyond sitting in the pews on Sunday to living out an active Christianity.

The bishop in charge of the Convocation of Episcopal Churches in Europe came to visit the congregation in May of 2008 as a part of our discussions on what it might mean to become a mission congregation. There were several misconceptions floating around and exposure and interpersonal contact might help correct erroneous thinking. The bishop had been kept informed of the growing congregation since its beginning but now we were growing by plan and no longer by accident and becoming a mission church was part of that plan. I was clear that we needed the benefits of belonging to a larger church community, many in the congregation could see that but some wished to remain an independent, nondenominational church, although in every way as we grew, we were operating as a member of the Anglican Communion and the Episcopal Church.

I felt that the congregation was ready to explore but not ready to commit to joining The Episcopal Church Europe. In my opinion the congregation was ready to enjoy the successes and share the pride of growth, but they did not trust themselves to on-going support financially or personally. They wished their autonomy, and most did not see the benefits of belonging to the larger church whether that be Church of England or The Episcopal Church Europe.

As clergy of this congregation licensed to serve by the bishop, I provided the structure for the organization as well the worship for spiritual life. I began to introduce adult education evenings. We had education events and guest speakers on such topics as Church History in our particular area of France, and an evening dedicated to better understanding of Islam. I created two adult education evenings focused on our church growth. These were to be a presentation of some figures about our growth in attendance at Sunday services, my time commitment to certain aspects of the congregation's life, and an opportunity for discussion which would give members a chance to make their contributions, ask questions, present their views, and to give me some reading of where individuals were regarding the issues that were on the horizon for us as a congregation. The bigger picture was to prepare the congregation to start thinking about our future.

What follows now are a few anecdotes that will help to flesh-out the group dynamics during this process.

In preparing for education events to discuss our growth, there was a rather clumsy exchange between myself, as chair of the Honorary Vestry and the president of the newly formed Association Loi.

A brief note here about church polity may be helpful here. Since we were not yet formally recognized as a part of the larger church but functioned according to established church policies, the leadership group was titled, "Honorary Vestry". They had no formal standing, but we operated as such and this was a form of governance with which many in the congregation were familiar (In England since about the mid-1950's, this is often referred to as the PCC – Parochial Church Council). When we became an Association Loi as required in France, there were certain minimal requirements for a leadership board of a "not for profit" organization in France that reflected a similar structure. The Association Loi managed our finances but the "Honorary Vestry" with the clergy as chair was to govern church life. For practical purposes these were the same group of people in lay leadership positions. The scope of the Association Loi was to be rather narrow and focused on management of finances and served the larger focus of the church congregation as a whole. By design The Association Loi met once a year (during the larger Annual General Meeting of the congregation) to give its financial report. The governance of the local church was the role of the Vestry (Or in our case at this time the "honorary Vestry" or eventually, as a mission congregation – the Bishop's Committee). This distinction was clear to me as clergy, and clearly spelled out for the Honorary Vestry as part of a learning process, and should have been clear to any active church member from Church of England or The Episcopal Church from their past membership in various congregations (a few had actually served in positions on PCCs in the UK).

However, what I was to discover was that while some members were familiar with this tradition of governance, some had experienced mutated forms of this governance (apparently bad experiences), others wanted no governance at all and a few simply ignored governance and did what they pleased. This later position was something like the arrogance of a bully in the school yard. I manage to stand up to bullies, but it does cost me something personally. It is not my preferred way.

As was my usual way, I sought advice from and then informed the lay leadership in advance by giving them drafts of my intentions for the first education evening on congregation growth. During this process in advance of the adult education evening in February, the president of the Association Loi sent me a curt email indicating that he, as president of the association would be taking charge of the evening. He was not asking or suggesting, he was telling me that he would arrive at my home (the location for this evening event) at the scheduled time and take charge. Since, in his mind this was a meeting and he was the president of the association, he went on to say, he would be in charge. We will, for the moment, over look the fact that I had chaired every meeting to this point including the recent first annual meeting of the association a few months earlier in November of 2008.

I responded at first diplomatically; clarifying that this was not a meeting of the Association Loi, it was an education event for the entire congregation. No decisions were to be made; only information exchanged and discussion that would inform what we would consider in future meetings of the Honorary Vestry. He was not happy with my response. I forwarded and copied the email exchange to the treasurer, which included a suggestion that the president and I sit down and talk (and the fact that the president had already declined this offer). As I hoped, the treasurer contacted the president, smoothed feathers, and convinced him that this was an education event not a meeting of the Association Loi. The outspoken president came to the education evening and seemed well behaved, but he offered no apologies.

Although I gave him the benefit of the doubt at the time (perhaps he misunderstood the role and relationship of the Association Loi and the larger congregation) I grew to see this event as the beginning of a struggle for power and control. Shortly after this evening, at another non-church related social event, he avoided my attempts to connect. His wife was cordial and said she could not understand why he would behave in such a way. The president remained in his role to the end of the term and gradually disappeared from church life, or so I thought. His complaint heard through the grapevine was that I was too autocratic and a "control freak". I found this amusing, coming from the man who told me, through an email, that he was going to take control of the education program that I had created and was hosting in my own house.

> *When someone shows you who they are – believe them, the first time*
> – Attributed to Maya Angelou, published source not found.

Two meetings on church growth were well attended, but the treasurer advised me that there were some people who wished another evening because they felt that their voice had not been heard. A third evening was scheduled at another member's home. Two members – the chair of our newly formed Charity Outreach and her husband - dominated the evening and set the tone with a scripted list of complaints. They were clearly unhappy. A few others had some questions, having had some time since our first two meetings to discuss among themselves but the evening was clearly the forum for the two who had attended the previous two meetings but did not speak out before now. Complaints were heard – factual errors attempted to be corrected but to no avail. There were moments that indicated there was a basic lack of knowledge about the Worldwide Anglican Communion and the Episcopal Church's role in it. Some understood the Church of England alone as Constituting the Worldwide Anglican Communion rather than being one among many. The Church of England is, to be sure, the mother church, but unlike a Roman Catholic design it is one among many national churches). A few people from the group did respond, more enlightened, they were able to inform their peers of other members of the world wide Anglican Communion even within Great Britain such as the Church in Wales, or the Church of Ireland, The Scottish Episcopal Church, to name a few and The Episcopal Church. These were members of the congregation who knew of or belonged to these various national churches.

But the uninformed were not to be dissuaded from their feelings, and took umbrage at being given more accurate information by me or their peers. Mistakenly, I thought I was dealing with reason and gave reasoned responses. I had a bias. I assumed that if people knew the facts they would respond differently. Perhaps they would not agree completely but we would have a forum based in fact from which we could move forward together. But I found inaccuracies repeated over and over without care to facts.

> *Reasoning will never make a man correct an ill opinion, which by reasoning he never acquired.*
> -Attributed to Jonathan Swift, 1721, subsequent variations claimed by many

Somewhere along the way a question was raised, "Why could we not join the Church of England rather than the Episcopal Church?". I agreed that technically all was possible. However, I understood that the concern expressed so far was about belonging to any larger church – they agreed. Also, I confessed, it is the Episcopal Church that licenses me to serve them now, it is the Episcopal church from whom I receive my collegial support, and it is the Episcopal church who has given time and resources to show an interest in the support and growth of this congregation. For me to change to the Church of England, which they showed no desire to be a part of, would require that I – without any compensation for my time and troubles - would have to apply for licensing, begin to network with a group of clergy not known to me, and seek financial support from a national church already known to give little or no financial support to churches outside of the UK. I had visited a few tiny C of E (Church of England) chaplaincies in other areas of France and known a few members from these chaplaincies.

The following was not discussed but had they sincerely wanted to become a C of E chaplaincy, I would have found a way to ease myself out of the leadership position and let them find their own way – recruit their own clergy and I would return to retirement. It was not discussed because it was clear what they were asking was for me to continue to provide what I had been providing in terms of worship, education, and leadership and organization, to do all the footwork to affiliate with a larger church organization, when they had clearly indicated that they did not see a value in belonging to a larger church that would tell them what to do or how to organize themselves, or, offer them resources for growth.

In addition to the above, I did say that Episcopal Church at this point in time had a few more flexible options that suited our congregation. Regarding worship we already increased options including the use of form from Common Worship of the Church of England. There was an openness to allowing both women clergy and gay clergy that increased our options for future clergy choice. Gay clergy in the C of E were still generally closeted and women clergy a relatively new phenomenon (1994 being the ordination of the first women in the C of E). People seemed satisfied with this and some, those with gay children or grandchildren, were openly pleased.

I did inquire of the group, were they asking me to become a "free-lance" clergy affiliated with no church in particular. This was not possible. It was not possible for me personally, but it also required some knowledge of the laws and customs in France. Perhaps there were some "free-lance" clergy but I did not know of any. As far as I knew it was not possible to just hang out your shingle and proclaim yourself "a Church". Even in a state which had taken great pains to separate church and state, there were laws that governed churches.

In the summer months leading up to annual convention 2008 of The Episcopal Church Europe, the bishop, in his enthusiasm had placed our little congregation on the agenda to be received as a mission congregation. When I read the agenda in advance of the convention I noticed this and was concerned. I thought that it was too soon, and that people might feel pushed into the Episcopal Church. But rather than make a unilateral decision, I took a poll via email. I explained what I thought was an error but described it as perhaps an over-enthusiastic welcome into the Episcopal Church. Before I responded to the bishop I asked the congregation should we allow this to remain on the agenda or should we slow down and follow a slower course in our decision making? The response to the poll was an interesting mix of comments such as, "Just go for it" – let it happen, and "wait, we are not ready". The numbers were nearly evenly split. I felt that it was important for the congregation to own whatever decision they were to make and choose for themselves rather than feel rushed. Therefore, I informed the bishop that I thought it was a bit premature to have this item on the agenda but thanked him for his enthusiasm. The agenda item of reception as a mission was taken from the agenda and we spent the next year forming our decision as a congregation. This email exchange was shared with the congregation using the group email list.

In the following months we were blessed with continued growth. Families with children were added to the earlier community of retirees. There was increased public presence much of it falling to the vicar with calls for weddings, and funerals, a baptism and an increase of worship services. We added worship services for Holy Week, Easter and Christmas services, and soon, in 2010 no longer took a break from worship during the summer months. There were requests for more time to serve growing administration, education and training needs. In 2008 Linda and I attended the annual convention of The Episcopal Church Europe in Waterloo, Belgium and gave a report to the congregation as a part of growing the relationship to the Episcopal Church.

In 2009 a lay representative from the congregation attended the annual convention with us in Geneva. And in 2010 another lay representative would attend the annual convention in Nice.
Now with an average of 37 people on Sundays, increased need for education and other budding programs such as charity outreach, and training, the budget of past years was insufficient, money was scarce and

demands on clergy time continued to grow. The task of building a budget to fit our growth was a difficult one.

From my past work with congregations in conflict and with committees I was aware of potential stumbling blocks where the organization is growing too fast or without design. In many congregations, people often first step forward to volunteer for projects based on their initial enthusiasm but lack structure or an overall commitment to a goal other than "the event" itself. It is such that many well intended church activities begin with a thrill of helping the less fortunate but never have a clear foundation how to fund the activity, or how to evaluate the activity or even how to end or develop this activity.

As pastor it was my role to provide oversight, to work with the leadership to form an over-all plan, to create guidelines to move forward with an expressed intention, guidelines for evaluation. Some people expressed appreciation and awareness of the value of this role, others, as I later found out resented it. In each case guidelines, drafted by me, were presented to the members of the Association Loi, who served also as a church vestry. The guidelines were revised according to discussions and approved at the meetings. They were, as it turns out, not necessarily followed.

In an effort to grow the congregation's expression of what they believed beyond the Sunday service, I had included three aspects of our church life: Worship, Education (education of ourselves in the ways of the Christian tradition), and Charity Outreach. Charity Outreach according to the guidelines would take the form of some local involvement (That is, in France allowing for some personal involvement in the charity work as well as financial aid, ideally both) and some support for a global initiative (most probably through a financial contribution and perhaps correspondence). Our financial supports must be sure to reach the intended group of recipients; therefore a choice of eligible organization which we would support financially were to have low administrative costs (15% expenses for administration as the target) and a maximum going to direct services (a target of 75% +) and a minimum spent on promotion (5%) We adopted these parameters based on larger organizations of which I was aware in both the USA and UK.

I organized our first Charity Outreach attempt was to a local French food pantry to which we could contribute food, and money, we could also have "hands-on" experience for those who wished to be trained as volunteers or simply collect food stuff in the organization's annual food drives at the local supermarkets twice a year. As it happened this was also the year of the tragic hurricane in Haiti, one of the largest and poorest diocese in the Episcopal Church and Anglican Communion. The Episcopal Church Europe responded to the crisis and it seemed a good connection for us to support this effort since overhead would not only be low, but we would have a direct accounting from the local diocese as well as, it was a chance to use this opportunity to work with other churches in Europe. Response was good, and out of that first year, someone volunteered to head-up future charity outreach initiatives for the congregation. The person was new to the congregation and full of energy. She created fund raising events that were well attended, and money was raised. However, she saw no need to build on what had been established and instead the charity of choice was changed to a favorite of hers, based in the UK. I did not want to stifle her enthusiasm. So, she had full rein. It was later that I discovered that although she was aware of the criteria and reasons for the choices of charity, she did not follow them.

A UK based charity would have been acceptable had her plan also included a local French initiative, but it did not. There was also a loss of personal involvement in the charity since the global initiative (al-be-it well intended) had no physical operations in France. When I investigated the organization, I discovered that it did not meet the financial targets for percents spent on administration, direct services and promotion. I allowed that these percentages were targets, and some slight variance was not a problem. Clearly, her work was appreciated; charity fund raisers provided socialization outside of the church proper and raised our visibility in the community. These aspects were noted. But at the end of the year when her annual report was due I raised the issues related to the guidelines which had not been followed. She took offense and left. At the time her husband was also suffering from a chronic mental health problem, so it was understandable that she might need to attend to him. But the reason she gave for leaving was that she had not been appreciated for all her work.

The lay leadership group acted much like a Vestry or Bishop's committee, familiar terms and structures to many in the congregation from general Church polity in the churches of The Anglican Communion, each a little different but all much the same. Under the leadership of the clergy chairman we discussed and made decisions relating to the congregation. We had very little finances. The current budget was about €1000. per year.

We were given a beautiful church space, to use for worship, at no cost by the Roman Catholic Diocese (we gave a token €100 at the time) as a thank you. There was no staff overhead – no clergy costs, no secretary, members of the lay leadership group donated their time and were pros at "getting something for nothing" when needed. Spouses who may not have been active "church-goers" offered their time for technical services when needed. Our home was used as office, our computer and printer were used for church work, our car was used for pastoral visits and funerals and other clergy travel, our living room was the common meeting place. In times past, other members of the congregation offered their homes as places for Sunday worship but as we grew into church space offered by the Diocese of Montpellier the occasions of meeting in other members homes diminished. Some homes were simply too small, other offers simply dried up. We had a large living room and common area and sufficient chairs, so it was only natural to meet in our home.

It was during an August meeting that I became aware of a significant obstacle. While discussing finances I proposed that we move from an "annual dues" system of establishing our limited budget. The budget, around one thousand Euros, collected as annual membership fees according to French Association Loi, was to cover all our expenses and the balance at the end of the year added to amounts raised for Charity outreach, so that each year we began with zero on the balance sheet. I proposed that we move to a system of church pledging from each member of the congregation and institute a stewardship campaign to encourage increased giving to support our increased growth in services, program, and charity outreach and most importantly to begin to prepare the congregation to consider supporting financially future clergy with some token financial support. As an interim measure I proposed that I as clergy be reimbursed for expenses – paper and ink for printing Sunday worship booklets, mileage for church related trips, and attendance at official meetings of clergy of The Episcopal Church Europe. The Bishop had graciously paid my expenses to attend a once a year clergy retreat and a meeting for professional development, but I thought it would be responsible for us as a congregation to start carrying some of this expense to the best of our ability rather than being 100% on the dole. It was a good exercise in fiscal responsibility and a way to stretch the fiscal responsibility of the congregation.

It was clear to all, that personally I was willing to continue for a time as volunteer clergy without pay. I was not asking this for myself. But to continue to make the worship life of the congregation dependent on free services was not in the best interest of the growing congregation. Perhaps in the future we could offer token compensation to some clergy and grow into part-time compensation to make this church attractive to some future clergy on a part time basis. A budget based on Congregational stewardship was a familiar form to all of the congregation. This particular budget at this time would increase from the past €1000 per year raised by membership fees ($25 per person per year x approximately 35 members) in the Association Loi, to a budget of about €1800 for 2009 raised by a Stewardship campaign. Although in promoting such a modest stewardship campaign you would have thought I was introducing the devil himself.

One member of the congregation said that no clergy compensation was necessary, since they do not pay their clergy in England. It was difficult for me to consider that this person might simply be in error since they had informed me that they been active in church life in the UK at several levels. The statement was – to put it mildly – so far from the truth I decided just to let it sit out there in mid-air for all to hear. I did not call her on it as a lie. It was a signal for me that I could not rely on things like common sense, or general good will to make some intervention by way of some adroit social comment. No-one made a corrective comment. It was a signal to me of the basic intentions of some in the congregation. It gave me the impetus to do some research, to find out how clergy are paid in England, and have some facts under my belt in future discussions. I discovered that in some very small congregations (who often share one clergy) the clergy is not directly paid by the congregation but rather paid from a larger fund to which all contribute; The Diocesan Board of Finance at the diocesan level or national level. The local church contributes its "Parish Share", using a formula for adjusted income, at a minimum (for the smallest parishes) of 25% of their income to the national church which in turn pays clergy salary and benefits. Clergy ARE paid.

This was just one of many opportunities that I had to do research into areas of Church Governance in the Church of England. It was time consuming but necessary in a situation where I was being quoted "the way things were done in England" often in contradiction to a plan that I was proposing. Research was also necessary so that I might "speak the same language". I did not want to ask people to do something so foreign to them, but I knew in a general way that many churches in the Anglican Communion operated in much the same way as in the Episcopal Church. I also wished to express my drafts using terms that were familiar to the Church of England folks who were having some difficulty accepting the "new "ideas. For good measure I often used the Anglican Church Canada as another point of comparison. Canada being a bit more acceptable than the USA since they were, after all, part of the commonwealth and their spellings more often coincided with the UK spellings for the same terms. The Anglican Church Canada was, in practice very similar to the Episcopal Church USA. What I found out was that, minor changes in terminology aside, what I was proposing were good churchmanship throughout the Anglican Communion. The fiercest opponents simply asserted some wished-for-truth and it was up to me to dig around to discover that it was pure fabrication. I spent much too much time in this type of research. Again, here I was seeking the facts, as if they might matter.

Many conflict resolution strategies begin with gathering facts, but my experience here was to confirm another most basic strategy; where facts do not matter. Facts have little persuasive value when dealing with innuendo and inflammatory comments. This type of conflict was not going to be one to be fought on a common ground.

One member of the lay leadership group at the meeting interpreted a stewardship campaign as being told how much to give to the church. We had not actually talked about amounts to give, but she knew that a stewardship campaign or a suggested tithe would mean increased giving beyond the current 25 Euros per year membership in the Association Loi.

I researched and prepared some financial scenarios for the next meeting. While the traditional "biblical tithe" is usually considered at 10% of personal "treasure". There are different ways of calculating that "treasure" – gross income, net income, 5% to the church and 5% to other charities etc. In my illustrations, I used a hypothetical 1% tithe of household income as a target that would yield a considerable increase of financial support for future growth.

For this I had researched average retirement income for British retirees. If our membership were able to retire to the south of France, many of the most vocal with property back home in England as well as here in France, it seemed reasonable to assume that they were at least average or above. I researched the average levels of giving for the Church of England and Churches in the USA. I have included some of this research as an appendix for those interested in the sources. While none of this came close to the Biblical Tithe of 10%, a 1% goal seemed reasonable for us - a great deal more than €25 but a great deal less than the average 3.5% on record at the time in the UK. As in most stewardship campaigns the goal is set but individual giving will vary according to an individual's means or temperament and the stewardship promotional materials made that clear.

As I presented this information at the next meeting, one member sitting next to me gave me a fierce look. (Remember "T" from the 2007 chapter where I was asked to find a way to remove her from direct people contact because she had limited people skills? Well Here is "T" again)

With a steely glare "T" says to me, "If I am told I must give more than 35

Euros a year I would leave the church". Where she came up with the number of 35, is a mystery to me, but it would be an increase from the current 25 Euros per year and far less than a 1% of the average British retiree's income. In any case "T" was not being told that she had to contribute a specific amount. I admit to seeing this as a dare, a challenge. I looked at her squarely while identifying what I thought were two important points: First, by setting a goal or a suggesting that each person considers their giving in terms of a target of 1%, she was not being told how much to give in any amount. Arriving at a specific amount in her household was a spiritual and practical exercise for her and her husband to consider. But a 1% goal for each household would help people to realize the possibilities that lie ahead for us if we were to reach that goal. My second point was not financial but rather in response to her threat that she would leave the congregation.

I remember "T's" look as I said, "It is not wise for clergy to be held hostage by threats to leave the congregation it sets a bad precedent". I expressed my hope that she and her husband would continue to be active church members contributing, as they had of their time and service. But the general welfare and future of the congregation would not be held hostage to the threat of her leaving. That decision was hers to make.

She was silent but there was fire in her eyes. The meeting group was uncomfortable.

I had learned the benefit of sitting with the silence to make my point, but the treasure made some remarks to transition away from the tension. After a silence, we moved on to other business. I could tell that a shot had been fired across the bow. Her phrase of being told how much to give to the church would remain her interpretation that she would continue to use and promote to others when she found the opportunity. It was incorrect. There were ample verbal and written examples of tithe, and averages of charitable giving used during the stewardship campaign. A proposed budget as well as setting forward a three-year plan to increase our budget could be made relying on general averages of incomes, and percentiles in giving. Our budget in all cases could use very conservative estimates and still meet our financial goals. All of which depended on volunteer giving. But no facts would change her interpretation of the day's events. "T's" "go to" slogan peddled to anyone who would listen was that she refused to be told how much to give the church. She continued to serve her term but by October she was no longer attending Sunday worship services.

I have attached in the Appendix a copy of some of the Stewardship campaign materials. It is a collection of the content from materials which were printed as handouts, content from group emails, and a sermon related to stewardship at the time. Most importantly it IS what was said rather than what people thought they heard.

There are more than the anecdotes above, but I fear that you will grow weary, if I give the impression that all was woeful.

I'll skip to some positives after one short tale and just share with you the amusing punch line that sticks with me to this day.

In the discussions over increasing a budget (a gradual increase year by year – over three years- to eventually cover some costs for part-time, new clergy) One person, still willfully confused that the income was for me, commented at a social event (to be heard by others), "I don't see why he (that is, me the current vicar) needs to be paid. He has a big house and fine antiques, and he's written a book you know. Why does he need more money?" I will ignore all the issues of social decency, justice, and the lack of a spirit of gratitude, generosity etc etc. The grand irony of her comment was in the fact that this came from a woman who (with her husband) had not one house as did I, but had houses; in England, in France, a condo in Cyprus and was building yet another house in France!

It is important to note these stories illustrate that the little congregation had now grown into the state of luxury to be able to complain. In years five and six of our life together as a congregation, I realized that the two most explosive areas of conflict – power and money had surfaced.

We as a group were like a married couple, finished with the honeymoon, and the "hum-drum" of life is now established. So there is a certain luxury to engage in conflict when all the basics seem accomplished. There is a popular notion in conflict management that conflict arises mostly from parish situations of decline. Some say that it is the stress of dealing with decline that forms the bed of conflict. I would disagree (or at least expand this notion) and present this congregation's history as evidence that conflict is born out of the luxury of success. The dynamics of power and control, typically expressed in the form of authority and finances are constant, even in successful situations. These essential dynamics must be addressed for the long-term health of the relationship. This approach takes the perspective that these dynamics are a normal part of any relationship (in decline or in success) and removes implications of pathology or failure and simply sees them as ever-present.

I believe that going forward, whatever was said from here on out, no matter what stories were told, and other symptoms uncovered, power and control, the challenge to authority and the power of the purse were what we were really dealing with.

> *The obscure we see eventually. The completely apparent takes a little longer*
> -- Edward R. Morrow

Chapter 15
How does the garden grow?

Not all was a stress in 2008, 2009 there were some lovely pastoral experiences. It is possible from reading the chapter above to conclude "Why would anyone want this job?". First and foremost, I have learned over many years that the gift one gives – in ministry it is often a gift of one's self, not only time and energy but in ministry your own spirituality and a gift of spiritual insight, is set out front and center on the stage of life. The exposure of one's self must be given for the joy of giving. Linda and I apply this same philosophy to our hospitality – our B&B has taught us this and we live it out still in retirement. What we offer is offered because we have a joy in giving it. It is not offered for whatever might be received in return. Certainly, a perception and acceptance of a call to such work helps, but the joy in giving is what determines continued giving. But there are some rewards along the way.

For me, personally the opportunity to create meaningful, simple and prayerful worship was a joy, I enjoyed studying the scripture and offering reflection which could – and did – stir the inner life of people. The most beautiful of liturgical celebrations is worthless without a congregation that responds, and liturgy is shaped and grows through that interaction. This is a form of creativity that goes to the soul of the people to whom I was pastor.

There are the obvious days of celebration; weddings and baptisms and confirmations that are the public displays of faith and in 2008 and 2009 we had them all. During this time, we also had a budding "Sunday School" with the patter of little feet racing to ring the church bell to call us to worship. There were also the unseen private moments which a priest is privileged to be a part, when called by individuals and couples young and old.

Because of our location in the South of France, we were a target for destination wedding seekers. I was averse to commercializing the church but wanted to stay open to serving people in a meaningful way. Sometimes weddings bring a couple into the life of the church and some are the result of people's history of life in the church; those occasions are precious moments. But many times, church weddings are merely a host location and the couple go on their way into their new life in new locations with or without the church; these weddings I have seen are more common than the church would like to realize. But each wedding is worth the risk; an opportunity to turn the common place into the precious.

Clergy and Weddings in the France have a different standing legally than they do in the USA or England. In France the clergy is not an authorized legal representative. The legal marriage must be officially performed and registered at the mayor's office. A church ceremony is possible – rather it is a blessing of the formal, legal, wedding that has just taken place at the mayor's office. It is the civil ceremony that is binding. The church ceremony is a personal choice. A bit of research into this is necessary because couples from the USA or the UK often do not know. So, beside any spiritual component there is this education as well so that the young couple does in fact end up with a legally recognized wedding. I did the research and drew up pamphlets and met with interested couples, and helped us all follow the rules. There are both state rules and church rules that need to be known and followed. These were largely joyful occasions. Weddings are fun, people are generally on their best behavior. I was privileged to gain access to some chateau, and private chapels in France that I would not have known, I met some very interesting people.

The arrival of one bride and groom to city hall was a grand staged event. The bride and her party, having processed through the picturesque narrow streets, walked down to the quay where her groom arrived by boat. In another wedding, the discovery of a private chapel behind a hidden door in one of the local chateau was just right for the small wedding. There was a garden wedding at a vineyard, for a California couple and their friends, some aging film stars as their witnesses. A young couple and their 18-month son celebrated their wedding day in a small mountain village. It had its own equally small chapel adjacent to a lovely courtyard. The sunlit sandstone of these villages and their churches lend themselves to scenes right out of the movies. And our own lovely chapel in the village of Conas was eventually able to be used for a wedding. The chapel was by design elegant in its simplicity, the bride and groom had put a lot of work into their ceremony and the day was perfect. It is also memorable because it led to contacts which continue to this day.

Funerals are not often associated with joyful occasions, but it brings joy to the giver in some ways, even in death. The first funeral I celebrated in France was for the husband of a lady I had met only once or twice in social events for Expats. I got lost in traveling to the mountain community where she lived and arrived at the Eglise Réformée church a little frustrated and a bit short on time for orientation to the space and coordination with the local French protestant pastor. And I was as bit inexperienced in the ways of French Funeral practices not to mention a cross cultural celebration for an English expat with many friends in France. But the connection to the local clergy and contacts made on that day were my reward. I was pleased to be a part of a bi-lingual service. The service was brief and the bagpipes playing Amazing Grace while the coffin was lead from the church by grandchildren was powerful. Due to distances and the age of the widow our contact was only occasional, but she was truly appreciative.

Another funeral, not so edifying, but no less memorable occasion was the bilingual funeral for someone who I did not know at all. A friend of a friend led the grieving family to telephone me and request my services. The family was clearly not familiar with church life, but the woman had recently visited their village church (Roman Catholic) and had asked her family that she be buried from there. It is hard to describe why some people with no connection to church life in their life-time, just appear on the church steps so to speak and wish to be buried from the church. But it happens, and this is not the time to question whatever might have brought them to this place in their life. The husband seemed a character of some curmudgeon out of Dickens. The joy for me was making further contact with the local Roman Catholic Clergy who had been so helpful to us in giving us the use of the lovely Chapel in Conas for Sunday worship. So, he and I led a bi-lingual service, neither of us knowing anyone in the congregation. After the church service it is customary to process to the grave site for a final internment. Since neither of us knew the family I offered to go to the grave site. Between us clergy this was my gift to him and a time-saver since it not only saved him time going to the grave but also excused him gracefully from the customary social niceties afterward, which would probably be in English. He was grateful.

On the way to the grave I was walking behind the casket with the widower and a handful of friends. The widower leans over to me in an "Irish whisper" to say, "You know I have no money to give you, so you can bugger off". Outwardly I remained calm, gave a non-committal half smile, and focused on the wooden box ahead of us. Inwardly, I was trying to process what he meant. Was he trying to tell me to "bugger off" - usually a rude way of telling someone "get lost", hey you are not welcome. Or, was he under the stress of the moment embarrassed that he had not thought to give an honorarium for the clergy's service and was giving me an opening – crude but nonetheless an opening – to leave? Or, was he insulting me thinking that I was in this for the money – which he was not going to give? Beyond his words, there was some indescribable unlikeable "something" that oozed from his pores. I had not expected a cent for funeral services but that was not the point. Upon reflection on the road to the grave, a question stuck in my mind. What was it about this man that convinced me that he was to be pitied and that his wife was probably, at last, happily at rest?

In the larger Worldwide Anglican Communion now, the ordination of gay clergy was front page news. It seems that the world press had at last realized that ordination of women would no longer sell papers and had moved on to something more exciting. This exposure at a public level made it possible for some, at a private level to come forward with their personal questions about homosexuality. In our little congregation, this took the form of parents with adult children who were gay. The sons were "out of the closet" but mom was not necessarily "out of the closet" about her son.

Two separate incidents came to me in this way. In both cases, separate from each other, mothers were trying to find a space in their social lives, where discussing the lives of their adult sons would find a normal place. How could they share with their friends the joys and pride of who their sons were? How could they get past telling oblique tales or being evasive in details which other families freely shared as parents and grandparents? People called, and since there was no church office, our home office was used for these conversations. To meet with them and help them find a place in this congregation for their joyful expression was touching and carried with it a responsibility for me that our congregation would in fact be a place for them to be at home. I could not control everyone's response but there were a good many people who would receive these women with care. I was proud for us all. It seemed that the homophobic quotient for this congregation was low.

There was also one couple who decided to maintain this "family secret". It was one of those secrets that everyone knows but no one talks about. They were in a position of influence, so they could have helped a great deal. But they kept the secret of their son's homosexuality out of church life, I think, because it would "out" not only their son but would call into question some of their own more conservative positions on life and practice. With them, I did the clumsy, oblique and unsatisfactory dance around the topic.

It is no surprise to people that many a congregation is unbalanced on the percentages of male and female members. Aside from the prevailing mortality rates among elderly males, in many homes it is the woman of the household who is the active church member and the men less involved or absent from church life. Our congregation was no different. We were blessed with a fair share of active male members, but we also had a noticeable number of households that sent their female representative to Sunday services. Among this group of absentee Christians, I found men who had been "turned off" by the politics of church life; cliques, gossip, and congregational conflict. They were not unbelievers; to the contrary they found too often that church politics had obscured the spiritual life for them, so they stayed at home. Others were happy to work in the wings, usually by themselves not in committee. It was rewarding to have these men start to come forward to volunteer their technical skills, to help in web design, and the printing of the Sunday service booklet, and gradually to accompany spouses to an occasional service. They made our church life better in many ways, but were often invisible.

On a Christmas Eve, one of these spouses attended the Christmas service with his wife. I will call him Simon Peter, since you will get to know him later in the course of events, he needs a name. Simon Peter had the stereotypical façade of an accountant, a little cool, and emotionally reserved. He could be brusque. He was often deep in thought. After the evening service, while sharing a glass of mulled wine in the winter chill, he said, "You have a good thing going here; if you need some financial support in the future let me know." Over time Simon Peter became a very influential member and you'll hear more about him later. Certainly, his offer of financial support was welcome, but it was the opening of his heart and knowing that he had been touched deeply that made this a moment of joy for me.

Beyond the life as a pastor to this little congregation I enjoyed collegial support from the larger Episcopal Church in Europe. Because clergy are geographically spread out across several European countries there is something like meeting long lost family when we got together for clergy retreat or for one professional development program each year. Not to mention that these were often held at interesting places monasteries on the Iles de Lerin, off the coast of Cannes, and Baden Baden, and Tutzing near Munich, an old English college in Italy turned retreat house on Lake Albano near the pope's summer residence, Castel Gandolfo. I also enjoyed working on the Bishop's Council of Advice when elected to a two-year term in 2009. Some of these collegial relationships continue to this day.

Not all events in 2008 and 2009 were church events. This was a time of a growth in affection and friendship with two couples who came to be our closest friends. We shared long Sunday Lunches, and holiday dinners at each other's homes and in the better restaurants of the area and many, many stimulating conversations thorough it all. Dining together was a pleasure. The menu may be forgotten but the conversations live on in my memories. These good friends not only gave us alternative experiences in France but alternative views on Europe (and an alternative view of the English) that in spite of trials in France and trials with "the English" we could always count on these good friends to keep our view more broad and open than the one that might have been formed by disappointments in other areas. They were a gift.

Personally, the years of 2008 and 2009 brought to me the death of my father after a long illness, the unexpected death of my younger brother, and a series of unexpected surgeries for my right eye. I had lived away from home in some way since I was 14 years old; First in minor seminary (a private boarding school preparing teenage boys for seminary) then in seminary itself for college and graduate work. For 25 years in Chicago Linda and I were 500 plus miles from either set of parents. And now we lived even further afield in France. I always had a more distant relationship with my family. My relationship was good but not geographically close-knit. Long ago I had expressed no need to race home only for tragedies, which they accepted. I visited occasionally and enjoyed my family while they were alive. I did not return home immediately after my father's death in 2008 but visited a few weeks after the funeral and the same for my brother's death in 2009. Besides the difficulties and expense of getting from Europe to the USA quickly, I did not want the extended family to wait for me and put the normal processes on "hold". I thought it best for everyone, especially when dealing with little grandchildren, to let things happen as they would in a normal time frame. Also at the time of my brother's death I was scheduled for one of a series of eye surgeries and returned home as soon as possible after the surgery. I was not immobilized by these deaths. I was saddened and concerned for my mother. For me, the distance, gave me a chance to reflect and appreciate the life that family had given me; a better appreciation for my dad in his aging and illness than perhaps I had in my youth. And a respect for my brother's life in which he did wonderful work with children and with his own family in a quiet way while I often got a bit more "show" as the eldest, living a romanticized life in a land far away land. Their deaths helped me appreciate their lives the quietness of a private life away from social rituals and greeting lines of well-wishers who, after years away, I barely knew.

Le Petit Jardin de L'âme

Reflections after Dad's death.

Dad's death was 07 April 2008. I visited Mom and family later that month.

During my visit, I stayed at my mother's home, in the spare bedroom and in the course of my visit used the bath room that Dad had normally used while he was alive. It was so soon after his death that although some of the recent medical equipment had been removed, and the room had been prepared for my arrival, his personal items in the medicine cabinet were still there.

Of course, I had traveled from Europe with my own toiletries. But one day I found myself using his shave cream (My travel-sized version was running low). Then there was an unopened lotion used for his skin (we had similar skin types). I tried it. Nice.

Then I noticed his Brut Fabergé, and splashed some on. It was essence of "Dad".

In my adult life I had long ago moved on to other men's grooming products but on this morning, I was transported back to the 1960's. I must have been about 14 when he gave me one of those distinctive green glass bottles with the silver medallion. Without a thought, I found myself making this sentimental connection with him, enjoying the memory and the fragrance.

Then a small sense of panic. What will mom think? Will this upset her to have me come to the breakfast table smelling all of dad? Oh, perhaps a big mistake.

Strange, she made no comment. Even though we later discussed my discovery of his face lotion and she encouraged me to use whatever I found in the medicine cabinet. There was no mention of the familiar scent. I decided it was best to let this pass.

I returned to Europe after my visit bringing with me a few small pieces of memorabilia: a set of cuff links and, most notably, a pocket watch in sad condition. The watch it seems had met with a traumatic collision, breaking the watch crystal and severing the crown and the watch chain had been crushed and bent in a few places.

I did some computer research and found that I could trace it to 1896 and that, in the right hands it was likely to be made whole once again. With further research I decided to have it repaired. It would make a lovely memorial and a restored family heirloom to pass on to the next generation. It seemed only right that a watch could – if at all possible work like a watch should. It was what watches were made for. The cost of repair, of over a thousand dollars, was steep but it brings me personal satisfaction to restore piece of history to its proper place in the world. And I now enjoy the watch for dress up occasions.

Several weeks after my return, when life had returned to normal, I was doing the routine grocery shopping at the local super market. While searching the aisle for other grooming products, I saw it there on the shelf. Brut Fabergé. I gave not a second thought. Reached to test it and put a bottle in my cart.

From time to time, I use the Brut as part of my grooming. It is a silent connection and reminder of the essence of Dad. Strange, there is no sadness in the reminder; more a comfort than sadness, a touchstone to a past life and a sober reminder that now I am the old man in the family.

My eye surgeries (four) during 2008 and 2009 – including one surgical error - eventually brought about a modicum of success with only a little diminished eyesight in the right eye. I have learned to live with it.

Chapter 16
Chim chimini Chim Chim Cherou ♪

November 2008

On the home front, by 2008 we were settled in, and the past years of painful renovation stories had nearly all succumbed to short term memory loss. In this our seventh year of our great French adventure, life at times, seemed normal, the irritations often ignored, and with scattered bits of happiness. But we were not without the haunting of the trials and tribulations brought to us by slipshod workmanship of the earlier years.

We have now lived at le petit jardin de l' âme for five years; Long enough to have corrected most of the original renovation flaws we inherited from the original French workmen and long enough to have discovered a few problems that we never knew were there. One example being, the support beam in the courtyard that was holding up absolutely nothing – ah, but I digress. There are even moments – a few - where I do not have to chant the mantra, which I acquired as a result of so many nightmares with French workmen: "Shoddy work is a 'joy' forever".

Our home is beautiful. And now thanks to years of "after-the-fact-corrections" most things work as you would expect – correctly.

But one there is one gift from our plumber that has resisted corrections over the years. The primary heating source for our house has not worked properly since day one!

I'll pass over the story of the original advice given us by the property manager, to say merely that when we purchased the property, we were told that we would not need such a thing as a central heating system. Winters were, it was said, mild enough so that an occasional log on the fireplace would be sufficient to take off the morning chill. We had a fireplace in the living room and a small one in the kitchen and one in the bedroom, so we thought we would "go native", with the occasional log on the fireplace.

As we became more familiar with the real winter climate, we made adjustments to our renovation plans. Although we decided at the time against a central hot water heating system under the floor tiles, as "over kill", so we avoided such an American convenience. We did install sufficient electrical outlets to accommodate electric wall units – just in case we were wrong. And when natural Gas was available in the village we piped it in, and installed gas-burning fireplaces with ventilated heating to the main living areas. This was by most village standards an extravagance. Still today the primary heat source for many village houses in rural France is a wood-burning fireplace; perhaps upgraded in recent years to more efficient enclosed wood burning stove. Visitors see truck loads and wheel barrels of old vines and chopped wood being carried to the homes and think "How charming". I now know that it is "Oh so necessary". Seven years into life in France, we now see that the newest homes are being built with heating units under the tile flooring and some limited central air conditioning and feature "American Kitchens".

Winter temperatures are mild. We have no snow and often no ice to speak of. But "mild' is a relative term depending on your point of comparison. We seldom get far below freezing. But, truth be told, nighttime temperatures in December and January and February hover close to the freezing mark. And those lovely stonewalls and tile floors that help to keep things cool in summer – remain cool all winter long. A damp autumnal cool begins to arrive during October evenings. Without additional heat sources, the early morning "freshness" of early September turns to "bracing" in October and then "bloody cold" by November.

When the noonday sun arrives all seems forgotten, sweaters are shed and that's when the pictures of the South of France in winter are taken. But no one seems to mention that we get most of our rain in later October and November. And though the tourist office boasts of 300 days of sun each year for the region, in my experience the cloudy days are gathered into the months of November, December January and February. Winter in the south of France comes, like most places in the northern hemisphere, with more gray sky than sun. And at the setting of the sun near 5:30 pm it is cold and damp. But this reality runs contrary to popular belief and the promotion of life in the south of France. Perhaps, to northern Europeans the south of France is sunny by comparison. But believe me without a proper heating system life is a bit more rustic than I care for. And I note that we live on the plain, near the sea with its moderating influence. Ask anyone who lives inland, and there is no doubt that winter is cold, and there is snow and ice here in the south of France.

Well, enough of the weather report. It is sufficient to say in the 21st century it would be good to have a central heating system for the months of October through April.

Our gas burning fire place inserted into the original large wood burning fireplace was to be the primary heat source, vented into our living and dining areas, up to our master bedroom & bathroom and further into the study. It was lovely to look at and appeared to burn "logs" all the time with a built-in thermostat to regulate the height and intensity of the flame as needed. Other small free-standing gas burning stoves were placed in other rooms of the house both where smaller fireplaces had existed. Each one was charming as well as practical and complemented the original design of the house. Judging by his disparaging comments at the time of installation, this was thought to be a troublesome extravagance by our plumber, François (By the way François took winter vacations to – above all places, Florida).

We discovered that in some ironic way that what seemed our own eccentricity – warmth in winter's cold - was in fact a necessity.

In year one, we expected some adjusting and fine-tuning until we got used to the system. After the installation Linda build a decorative surround to enclose the rough opening. She read the instruction manual being sure to leave the necessary breathing spaces required for the equipment to work properly. And then the fiddling began. The pilot light would not stay on. After several attempts and a couple momentary successes the fire lighted and all seemed to run properly – for about one hour. Then, inexplicably, it would turn itself off. More fiddling followed by flickering success.

When this type of frustration turns from hours to days, it is better for Linda to take over. My solutions at this point tend more toward force than finesse. Patiently she would eventually get the mechanism to work – or so it seemed. In the first year we were so happy to have it ignite, and stay lighted that we never questioned its effectiveness. It certainly looked nice, but the house was not all that warm. Perhaps it was an unusually cold winter?

Again, in the autumn of year two, the startup was much the same. The system was very temperamental. Perhaps the safety features were hypersensitive; perhaps there was too much draft, or too little draft. We called a heating expert. He did get it to running and it seemed that it needed a good cleaning. We had used it so little it seemed unnecessary but perhaps construction dirt had built up during its long idle period from installation to actual use. Within hours of the heating specialist's departure the heating unit was cold. Linda, fiddled and read and patiently adjusted and readjusted it again, with some success. But the house was still cold.

Val J. Littman

For special occasions and entertaining we would seal off the public areas and crank up the electric heat and achieve civil temperatures, but from day to day I was wearing long underwear inside the house, warming my hands while cooking lunch and dinner. Linda, attempting to adjust to this new way of life tried to believe that 15 degrees centigrade (59 Fahrenheit) was sufficient. Was it outrageous to hope that we would achieve something around 19 or 20 degrees (66 –68 degrees Fahrenheit) On those days when we achieved 17 degrees (62 degrees F) I was – well, briefly - happy.

Winter curtains went up to block off the stairwell, which Linda said was sucking all the heat up to the third floor (but the third floor was cold too). Well, then, the heavy cold air was creating a draft coming down the stairs and interfering with sensitive air currents that needed to go up the chimney. Over the years, we purchased chiminée aspirateurs, ventilateurs, and spinners to solve possible down draught and anti draught problems. Linda climbed to the roof-top to install them and later to uninstall some. Each theory had some validity but ultimately the fire did not stay on and the house did not get warm.

As a run up to winter number three, Linda researched the manufacturing company in Belgium. And to their credit a representative came out to inspect the system. What he had to tell Linda she already knew from two years of experiments. There was never a thought to look beyond the insert itself to the details of its installation. The machine was in working order. It should work. There seemed insufficient concern for the fact that it did not work. Again, Linda with days of persistence and numerous variables, too many to keep track of, got the machine to work - but the house remained cold.

During these years, various survival techniques were used; often, one against the other. In an effort to have the bathroom warmer than a 17th century out-house I would move in an electric heater, Eventually, I found a thermostat setting that met my needs. It could run on low during the night to achieve a civilized temperature by morning. Linda, with instincts to save money would turn it off during her mid-night waking or her trip to the bathroom. And the bathroom would be at a brisk 15 degrees to greet me in the morning. At other times, in attempts to warm up the kitchen before breakfast, Linda would turn on the little cast-iron stove which we had installed in the Kitchen as an auxiliary heat source. Or in other instances, the study could be heated by yet another cast iron stove. Our bedroom fireplace was working overtime but was reliable source for that room. The little cast iron gas burning stoves worked well but were not intended as a primary heating source and were manually operated. They were either on or off. In fact, in the absence of a properly working main heat source, this patchwork design of little gas burning stoves had the overall effect of constantly walking from one warmed room into a cold room turning on the heat and waiting for the cold room to warm up just in time to leave the warmed room and enter yet another cold room. Being warm – or rather not being cold - used up a lot of mental energy, since freedom of movement and a warm room did not necessarily go together. On another practical matter, my hands do not work well when they are cold. Picking up things and finer finger work was difficult. There are, I am convinced, aches and pains that come alive in the cold. I would find that I was unaware of a gradual body tension in an inadequately heated room. Eventually I wondered why I had a little muscle spasm in my back or neck, only to discover that I was shivering, chilled throughout little by little. It is also rather difficult to use the computer while sitting on one's hands to keep them warm. Linda would comment, "you are cold because you are sitting still – move about more", to which I would respond, "I am cold because IT IS COLD".

It is safe to say that as the winters wore on, most of the heat generated in our house was in the friction between us.

But spring came, and summer came and then it was, soon enough, year four. By year four, Linda had developed an intimate relationship with the gas fireplace in our living room. She could anticipate the direction of the draught, the wind outside, whether our windows should be opened or closed to facilitate the process of lighting the pilot, the sensitivity of the security shut off mechanism and all manner of details totally foreign to me – but more important less understood by the experts we had consulted. Linda was able to get the fire started and keep it burning by sheer determination – often several days of repeated efforts until voila! One day without apparent reason, it worked. But the house was still not warm.

By year five we had settled into the belief that lovely as the idea was of a burning fire place we had made a bad choice. This gas burning fire place was never going to be able to warm our home as we had planned. Even when Linda managed to wrestle it to the ground and ignite it, it would not stay on. In year five it predictably presented the same problems as in the past four years. Attempts to get the fire to work before our last B&B guest of season arrived in late October were unsuccessful. We made our excuses and warmed the house sufficiently by other (more expensive) means. October came and went, and we were still without a fireplace for Thanksgiving.

But now Linda had time for yet one more theory. Based on her intimate knowledge of the draughts, she determined that there must be some other source of cold air, which was interfering with the functioning of the heating unit and had not been captured by the chiminée aspirateurs and spinners at chimney top. With the equivalent of "key hole surgery" she determined that the space behind the fireplace insert was much larger than the insert itself. There was, in effect, a cold air room behind the fireplace box and excess space in the chimney that allowed a cold air down draft from the chimney that was interfering with the positive draughts. Cold air was being sucked up the chimney from inside the fireplace box as it should but there was another source of a cold down draught that was blowing out the pilot and holding the exhaust inside, thus activating the safety shut off mechanism. The fire place would work only when both this hidden chamber and the excess chimney space were warmed up in addition to the normal exhaust route and proper draught. This of course is not a problem when lighting a fire in August (when the original installation was made by our esteemed plumber, François).

In lieu of opening up the decorative façade of the living room fireplace, she decided to do some exploratory surgery from the top down. Cutting a large whole in the drywall on the third floor she was able to climb into the chimney seal off the excess chimney space and keep the return cold draught from getting to the fireplace insert below (effectively shrinking the space of this hidden chamber and interrupting the return flow of cold air). Lovely she looked, in her black tights, turtle neck, and a rag wrapped round her head. A sight to behold. With the dexterity of a chimney sweep (at age 60), she then went about making sure that the normal exhaust routes were working properly so that air was being drawn up from within the firebox. One other adjustment had to be made to protect the pilot for strong cross draughts in the room. The fireplace worked! Easy as One, Two Three … (Four Five, years)!

This amounted to correcting the original installation. On day one, the fireplace box should have been made to fit the insert. The oversized space created for the benefit of the François' easy installation actually created this hidden cold room, which surrounded the firebox and was the source of our mystery down draught problem.

Sometime in Early December the repairs were done, and the fire ignited. We soon discovered that we had more heat than ever before. Heat was actually coming out the ventilation ducts, enough to heat the living room and dining room, it was rising to the ventilation ducts in our bedroom and on to the study. There was no longer a need for auxiliary heating sources.

And aesthetically, the ever-burning gas fire in the living room sets that warm and cozy feeling that we hoped for our guests as they enter.

I was, for the first time in five years, comfortably warm in the rooms of our house that winter. For those interested, that means a moderate 20 degrees centigrade (68 Fahrenheit) though I now know that it could be warmer. I hesitate to add that sometimes the third-floor office gets a little too warm (Shh! – don't tell Linda). We no longer must strategize our movements from one room to the next, we are able to snuggle up next to each other by the fire rather have a heated debate over why it does not work. In short, we are able to live our lives rather than, fiddling about overcoming shoddy workmanship, but it took five winters, Linda's tenacity, and a bit of Chim Chimini from Ma Cherie!

Chapter 17
Progress is a bumpy road

When you hit that unexpected bump in the road,
remember that it is only a bump not a mountain.
Go over it or around it, but make sure you keep going.
Ed and Deb Shapiro

The tensions of 2008 and 2009 seemed to be with a few individual persons but the overall spirit of the group, judging from the atmosphere and attendance at Sunday Worship and social gatherings was positive. Meetings were productive and in largely without undue stress. Yet I was aware that I had acquired some "enemies". The President of the Association Loi remained distant. Eventually, he resigned and was replaced by the, then, treasurer, and a new Treasurer was found. I approached Simon Peter and he accepted. Remember him, from that Christmas Eve conversation? "T" was cool to me and began to parcel out tasks that she had volunteered for to others. I sensed that she had some long-standing anger with someone somewhere long before her anger found a target in me. To her credit I sensed that she was trying to find a way to disengage without actually having to say, "I quit". I actually encouraged this, and had encouraged it long before tensions arose. In my general approach to developing lay leadership, I encouraged leaders to bring others into leadership roles to cultivate potential successors as a general way of life. The chair of Charity Outreach started to skip some meetings and eventually, several months later, she would resign saying that she had not been properly thanked. And Lourdes, although not formally a member of this congregation had many overlapping contacts, many in the international choral group to which we both belonged. Lourdes, knew everything that went on in the ex-pat community and was like a ghostly observer of our congregation even if she officially worshipped in the Roman Catholic Church.

In retrospect there were a lot of "spectator" members who enjoyed participation in the good times and avoided tension when it did arise, often through silence.

The treasurer, now new president of the association, was a good work colleague and encouraged another new member of the congregation to start attending the honorary Vestry meetings as an observer; it was an overt attempt accepted by all to "train" this new member. He was a young family man with some aspirations to ministry of his own. I met with him and also encouraged the interest in ministry.

The atmosphere was positive, attendance at Christmas, nearly 60 people, filled our little chapel, and regular monthly attendance was near to 40 people. I continued to promote discussion of a three-year plan of stewardship, (planned giving) rather than the token €25 annual membership fee for the Association. In August, the new observer to our meetings volunteered to do a survey. It turned out that his skills in creating a tool to obtain objective data were limited. But when I tried to guide him, using my social work background in statistics and research, he began to be uneasy. My assistance, rather than being a search for objectivity, was looked at with suspicion, as an attempt to steer the results. I took a risk and gave him the independence he wanted and hoped that we would discover together –after the fact- that things could have been spelled out more clearly. It was a learning curve and I was OK with that.

More interesting to me was the larger dynamic that was becoming clear to me. My attempts to model a collaborative effort, presenting my ideas to the groups, hearing their discussion and revising materials until we had a consensus, was not catching on. There was little or no attempt to research other areas of church life for precedents or supportive data. When a member of the honorary Vestry took on a task – such as the charity outreach – and now again with a stewardship survey – there was a protective ownership of the task. There was no seeking of input in the public forums, no open discussions in meetings.

My recommendations for the wording of survey questions to be clear were not received well. What was developing was a two-tiered sense of accountability. As Pastor, I was expected to, document, collaborate, and seek the consensus of the group. I encouraged and fostered this approach. It fit my more collaborative style of leadership.

However, individual specialized tasks by lay leadership were accomplished in an autocratic style, and based on limited experience or based on how they as individuals remembered their experience. It was a version of "We have always done it this way", or This is how it is done in England".

In some areas such as antagonistic assertions about clergy compensation, local church governance in England, and levels of church giving, I was able to research more objective sources. But correction based on fact, no matter how delicately put, could not sway the most entrenched. My research did however impress a few. It was not so much the facts that impressed them; somehow, they already knew the truth, but they were impressed that I had put in the effort.

The results of the questionnaire regarding stewardship were a mixed bag of some helpful and some confusing comments. I present an excerpt below, not as an example of stellar research, but rather, as an example of the way things were at that time. This is a "copy and paste" from this vestry-man's analysis, not my words, and a bit of his editorializing on the data. This is a brief excerpt.

> Church in the Herault – Questionnaire Analysis
>
> Firstly, I have received 24 replies to the questionnaire. One reply was in the form of a letter from occasional visitors to the area (2nd home in Pezenas) and I have ignored this in the results, though they were supportive of the Church in both prayer and offer of funds. Another reply was in the form of resignation in terms of membership. The reply was concerned that the financial burden proposed for the Church was coming before worship considerations.
> Therefore, the statistics are based on a reply of 22 people, which is 59% of the membership and an excellent response.
>
> **GIVING**
>
> As I believe the crucial part of the questionnaire is funding I have put the analysis of this first. I have not analyzed point 2 at this time as 'other' fund raising activities can be decided once we have a clear way forward.
>
> 1. The membership level came out at an average of 70 euro per adult per annum. However markedly over a quarter were either unsure of a level or were against a membership fee in principle.
> 3. 2/3 would support a planned giving scheme and 1/3 against. This equates to 15 people who responded positively to planned giving, and of those only 9 were prepared to pledge an annual figure. No one was prepared to pledge a percentage of income.
> 4. The average level offered for planned giving was 220 euro per annum.
> Do these figures give us cause for concern or comfort? A little of both I think as there is definite financial support for an Anglican Church in the Herault, but there is some concern over the way funds are raised and some definite sitting on the fence.

My conclusion is that in the present economic climate congregation members will support the church financially but only to levels they feel comfortable with and not dictated too.

There was an indication that the response level was very good (a 59% response rate is very good but the sample is small). The interest in increased giving – al-be-it with some confusion of terms – was good, no matter how it was interpreted. With two thirds of the respondents in agreement about planned giving, I felt that I had some reason to move forward. The average level offered for planned giving (€220) was way beyond what I had imagined. Even the most conservative alternative route of €70 per person per year in Association membership was an increase nearly three-fold of the current 25 Euros. I agreed that association membership fees were not the route to go, but at this moment that was the route the first treasurer (current president) had chosen because the church bank account had been set up under association loi rules. I had no argument at the time but now would rather drop the fees, and move to traditional church stewardship as a practice. But more to the point at hand, the figure of €70 whether in association fees or not, was encouraging, and would be sufficient to meet our financial goal in the first year. Even this amount at the low end of the scale was double "T's" protest of a fee above €35 per year.

As I read the analysis and the editorial comment at the end I realized that the research I had done prior to the survey, and my presentations on levels of giving in the Church of England had been "spun" as my "dictating" how much people should give rather than objective data about the levels of actual giving. A few vocal people had been feeding me and each other a financial fantasy about what was customary in England – bollocks, I believe, is the English term here. They did not like being found out. But I came to understand that the facts of church giving did not actually matter to them?

Trying to take the results as objectively as possible, I was encouraged by the potential financial range that the survey showed. But I was disheartened by the attitude that was developing and the implication that I was not only a dictator but the identified enemy of the congregation. The few had begun to spin a tale to suit their power struggle.

Encouraged by the results of the survey, I moved forward on two aspects; a petition following church canons, for mission status and a three-year financial plan were created. By this time, I had become more active in the larger Episcopal Church Europe, and was eventually elected to a position on the Bishop's Council of Advice. Therefore, I was aware of possible grants for specific projects. A petition for a matching funds grant was drawn up. I saw matching funds as a way to encourage both a gradual increase in financial stewardship and growing the commitment of a part of the congregation for eventual clergy compensation. This plan was also to develop the relationship of the congregation to the diocese. The plan for a three-year matching funds grant allowed the congregation to increase contributions at a much lower rate than the survey indicated they would tolerate in the first and second year and we could grow together over three years to slightly more than they were considering at the moment. The end result would be a budget large enough to offer some limited financial support to part time clergy. I drafted my ideas to a skeptical lay leadership group. There was no dissenting opinion expressed at this meeting and the new treasurer thought it feasible and supported it. The plan was received enthusiastically by the Bishop's Council of Advice.

I have attached a shortened version of this plan in the appendix. Basically, we would request a matching funds grant of €2500 each year for three years for the purpose of increasing clergy compensation. Each year this grant would have a plan to match the grant at a different rate with increased effort placed on the congregation. The grant proposal assumed a Matching Funds formula. In year one, for every euro the congregation raised The Episcopal Church Europe would give us two Euros up to a max of €2500. That is, The Episcopal Church Europe would give a max of €2500 if the congregation raised €1250 for a total of €3750 total towards clergy compensation. This was an easily attainable goal. In year two the same grant of €2500 would be requested but the ratio different; a one to one ratio for a total of €5000 toward clergy compensation in that year. Attainable with the current number of congregants but required some increased giving or growth in the number of contributors. And in the third year of the grant request of €2500, the ratio would be, for every two Euros raised by the congregation, the larger church would offer us one Euro for a total of for a total of €7250 for clergy compensation. Such a plan offered the congregation time to grow in both size (as we had been growing) and in financial commitment to support clergy – still at a part time position, based on poverty level incomes in France.

By now gentle reader your eyes may have glossed over because of this financial planning but keep in mind both finances and authority were our two big stumbling blocks as a congregation. On the grand scale of things, financial planning for this congregation was still in infancy stages. We were talking about raising the overall church budget from about €1700 per year to still under €10,000, in increments and with grants from the larger church. We had been running a church – not on the proverbial shoestring – but on a thread. Even if our congregation grew by only five members over the next three years (an insanely low expectation at the time) the total amount pledged by each member to succeed in this budget would be less that the average offered in the stewardship questionnaire. This was very do-able!

> *There are two mistakes that can be made along the road to truth; not going all the way, and not starting*
> -Buddha

From the pastoral perspective, as clergy I realized that this is not about money. Unless there were cases of financial hardship – not likely among most of this group of ex-pats - I saw money as the symptom, a means to an end. In this situation the resistance to financial growth from a few is a sign of that more basic power and control issue. In the church and in volunteer organizations in general, financial struggles are most often evidence of some bigger spiritual deficit – a lack of personal investment.

I had done my research. It would be safe to say that most – if not all- of this group had at least the statistical average retirement income. Even when considering the financial difficulties of 2008 and 2009, the UK pension system suffered less than other progressive countries. And the same was true when considering the value of the pound to Euro. Based on that assumption the financial plan proposed was attainable given the average level of church giving in England.

However, the task for the pastor is not to raise money but to raise generous, grateful hearts and the rest will follow. My efforts we not to tell people how much they should give but to show them that the goal was achievable and well within their means. Apparently, there was a lot of work to do here with a few. But the general thrust of the congregation remained encouraging. If I led they would follow.

The immediate steps were three-fold:

Pass a working budget for year 2009 based on our current status. Prepare the petition for to be accepted by The Episcopal Church Europe as a mission congregation. Prepare the petition for a three-year matching funds grant.

In March and April petitions were drafted reviewed with the lay leadership. After a period of preparation and promotion we used Easter Sunday as our first date to gather signatures after the Sunday service. The period of time for Gathering signatures lasted three weeks and overlapped with both Church services and social events where the petition was placed in a visible location and people could sign (or not). In the end the petition to become a mission in The Episcopal Church Europe gathered 37 signatures (This was in the 90 percentile of total possible signatures) The petition to request a three-year matching funds grant garnered 33 signatures (again very high percentage of members) That a few people did not sign was not disappointing, it was a sign that people had used their discretion and exercised their choice.

We submitted the petitions to the larger church for their consideration. Each petition had its own time-line and administrative process, but I was reasonably certain that our petition for mission status would be accepted. The petition for the grant would be looked at favorably but was also in competition for limited funds with other congregations, so only time would tell. Without the grant we could continue to move along the road to better stewardship but perhaps at a much lower pace. But if the grant were approved the road ahead would be much clearer for both the congregation with specific goals and for the larger church to know that we were on the road to finding a replacement for me. There were some in the congregation that were concerned about making a commitment to raise X amount of Euros each year. Some did not understand the mechanics of a matching fund grant, that is, we have a target to reach and would be matched at the specified ration for each year. If were failed to reach our target, we would still be matched but only according to the amount we had raised and not the full amount. The matching funds concept was an example of a win-win approach, not an either / or, win-lose style of management.

As a part of this process the congregation was to select a name for itself. Our legal name for the French Association Loi was The Anglican Episcopal Church in the Hérault - not memorable and not very Anglican. Because we had begun our worship life at our home at *Le petit Jardin de L'âme* and meetings and social gatherings often happened at that site, some referred to the congregation by that name. It would have meant a lot to me to have the church named *le petit jardin de l'âme*. It was both personally meaningful and symbolic of how I saw this congregation. All congregations are from my perspective little gardens of the soul. A few in the congregation said, "I thought we already had a name – *le petit jardin de l'âme*." But upon further consideration naming an English-speaking congregation a French name seemed not practical. It was also a little wordy and not traditional. So we began to take nominations for names of the so-to-be-a-mission congregation. It was again a chance for member ownership of this church, to name it.

Normally, it is the practice of the bishop of the diocese to name church congregations, but Bishop Pierre allowed this to be a congregation decision, asking only that, whatever the name might be, it reflect church tradition in naming churches (that is nothing outlandish) and not be a duplicate of a church already named in The Episcopal Church Europe.

We took nominations. Names that came in were traditional but also duplicates of existing congregations – All Saints, Christ Church, among others. The name of St Martin was proposed. St Martin's was also the name of a small group of The Episcopal Church Europe, in another area of France, not yet a mission but I discouraged copping the name from them. It also was the name of the French church where we currently worshiped. I thought it might be confusing. I proposed Grace Church as a name. We had often used the hymn Amazing Grace in our worship, and had begun some of our more contentious meetings with this hymn. The lyrics seemed to fit us that "Grace had brought us safe thus far and Grace will lead us home".

A simple ballot was created, and a vote taken via email. Fifteen members responded in the vote. It was a low turnout (a little more than a third of eligible voters) and perhaps reflected that a particular name was not important to many. There was clear majority of eight votes for Grace Church with comments added such as "perfect". The remaining seven votes were spread between St Martin (3), and some write-ins which were all actually duplicates of existing churches, which had been explained in advance of the voting as not eligible. Given that I had not voted and neither had Linda, I selected Grace Church as the name of the mission congregation. The full legal title, in order to keep our bank account without making a change, was Grace, Anglican Episcopal Church in the Hérault.

During the summer months, I asked a friend who had many years as art director in large advertizing agencies to draft some logos for the church with the name. A few options were placed outside the church door on Sunday mornings and comments shaped the finished design.

We were, in the closing months of 2009, getting beyond the conflicts of 2008 and 2009. Yes, I had lost the support of a few, but with the significant numbers of the community that remained, I felt that we were moving ahead, and people were following – growing - amazing – An Amazing Grace.

In preparation for the October Annual Convention of The Episcopal Church Europe and in anticipation of our being received as a mission congregation we would attend and would, as a mission be permitted a lay delegate. I began to recruit a lay delegate to convention. The young man that was being groomed to fill a future spot on the lay governing board seemed a likely candidate. He agreed at first but nearer to the convention date he expressed reservations. They were not reservations about the Episcopal Church or attending convention itself. His reservation came in the form of (misunderstood) financial matters. Not attending convention was his way of saving some money. I explained that the money had already been budgeted and was available. He continued to decline.

In retrospect, I believe that his reluctance was a sign that there was something going on the background. But in real time I had yet to find out, so I was confused. With the benefits of hindsight – I can see that his reluctance was an early visible sign of a "resistance group" forming, meeting under the radar and without my knowledge. Things would become clear later.

I put out a renewed request for other interested parties and a response came – not necessarily eager but a dutiful response came from a delightful, elderly gentleman, who had attended worship regularly, and participated in social events but remained mostly silent during tense discussions. He clearly was attending out of a sense of duty and support because this is what the church required – a lay representative. He had expressed after a meeting with Bishop Pierre, that he was not particularly fond of the bishop but liked me - and was especially fond of Linda. So out of some sense of duty he would comply. He was as it turned out a most delightful traveling companion, an observant member of the convention and its people and gave a glowing report of his experience to the congregation back home after the convention. He prided himself as an English gentleman. He was the only person I've ever known who actually used the English suffix "Esquire" after his name; a hold-over from courtesy titles of a gentler era (he was not a lawyer). He had spent a few years in the USA (Virginia). And he openly expressed his surprised that Episcopalians, that is Americans, had an orderly meeting, dignified worship, and even when they had fun it was within the bounds of English respectability. (Yes, he actually wrote this in his report) I guess we were a pleasant departure from his stereotypes of Americans and the American Church. Most importantly his comments would carry weight in the congregation back home. His comments were respected.

In advance of my own attending the October convention and in anticipation of a celebration our reception as a mission, I began to prepare for our local annual general meeting which normally took place in

November. The past treasurer and now current President of the Association Loi felt that the decision to increase the budget (to €4750 (€2500 of that was a grant) needed some preliminary work so as to avoid difficulties at the annual meeting. I agreed. We aimed for a preliminary meeting on the budget issues at the end of October. Since this was to be limited solely to finances. It was proper this time around for him as president of the association that managed our finances, to conduct the meeting – as long as it remained explanatory and solely focused on the budget. What this turned into is difficult to explain – but I will try.

Just prior to my departure for convention, a Newsletter was sent to the entire congregation, from the President, received by me at the same time as everyone else. There was no preliminary draft and no consultation. This was another example of unilateral decision making by members of the vestry and a departure from the collaborative model that I had used, and encouraged to be used by others for a group our size. The newsletter went beyond the President's area of responsibility to propose two plans for the future of the congregation. Plan A was identified as "Val's Budget". Plan A assumed all that had recently transpired as a mission church, the grant of €2500 and the plan to begin limited clergy compensation. The total of this plan was €4750 in the first year growing incrementally over three years.

The president went on to suggest a Plan B, the proposed budget. The Proposed Budget had a line item of zero for clergy compensation and eliminated the grant of €2500. The proposed budget or Plan B was €2050.

The President's newsletter acknowledged that this would likely split the congregation. He went on to frame an upcoming meeting scheduled for 21 October as either a vote for "Val's Budget" or a vote of no-confidence. The newsletter was not too subtle in anticipating my resignation if the vote was no-confidence.

I had not given any previous indication that I would resign. (Although clearly some expected that is what would happen). The call was to either approve Plan A (identified as Val's Budget) or approve Plan B on 21 October – two days after my return from convention.

In addition, in a separate email, the treasurer reframed this proposal implying that the entire vestry was opposed to "Val's Budget"; saying that if people voted to approve "Val's Budget" the current Vestry would all resign.

Then, as if by "miracle", and still before my departure, another email went out from the president – canceling the meeting set for October 21. What did all this mean? There was very little time for me to respond to this.

On 19 October, upon returning home from convention, I had such a mix of possibilities in front of me. I felt like we had a new chapter ahead of us. The reception of the congregation as a mission church in The Episcopal Church Europe had been decided, but what was in the immediate horizon was a political insurrection, a coup and a sign that pastorally regardless of the outcome there was still a lot of work ahead in the area of formation of this congregation in their spiritual life. I had hoped to get past the tensions of the previous year and re-establishing an esprit de corps that had been wounded by strife. Some big surprises lay in wait.

The Newsletter from the President was an indication that there were several levels of dishonesty at work here. I learned that there had been secret meetings, hosted at the president's house and some others, and dinner parties at one or two other homes to further discuss (The social events were denied but the cast of characters present at both the secret meetings and the dinner parties were the same – you can figure it out.) The president and others in this group had been using the congregation group email (minus my listing and a few others) outside of the intended purposes. The group email list had been commandeered for subterfuge. I asked to meet with the president, but he was unavailable to meet for one reason or another, none of which I felt were completely honest.

I contacted the new treasurer, Simon Peter, who if the newsletter and subsequent email were to be believed, would be among the vestry members to resign, but he was more approachable. He agreed to meet.

I was not surprised to learn of some of the cohort. No doubt "T" and her anger had found a group for her to influence, the past president who had resigned, and the woman responsible for organizing charity outreach, these were expected. But the new member who had been recently encouraged to take a leadership position and did the stewardship survey, this was a surprise. The mild-mannered secretary, and the new treasurer, Simon Peter, were also a surprise. Not only had I prepared the budget along with Simon Peter's input he had "sold" the budget to the group at the last Honorary Vestry meeting. Most surprising of all was the current President of the Association Loi. Linda and I had become friends with him and his wife, including them n our social network outside church circles, and inviting them into our home. It was they to whom Linda had turned in 2005 during our deepest despair. I had valued his opinion. His change of heart was the most troubling – and most hypocritical.

I was able to meet with the secretary. In our courtyard garden I asked her as clearly and sympathetically as I could how it was that she was a part of this. I was clear that I was not asking her to change her mind. I just wanted to know how she got to this position. Without any hesitation she said "Well, I felt a bit bullied". I knew the secretary. She was a mild-mannered sort and had had an unfortunate marriage, a tough life and had many endearing traits. She would also be easy for others to intimidate. Knowing a bit of British understatement, I could well comprehend what "being a bit bullied" could mean for her.

When I met with the treasurer, Simon Peter, he was more remorseful and contrite, although I was not asking for contrition. I wished to understand, not change his stance. Simon Peter said he felt manipulated into this position by the group. Now I knew Simon Peter was a person to make an effort to see both sides of the fence, which I valued, but he maintained that his words had been exploited in doing so. It was in this meeting that Simon Peter and I analyzed the current situation. Within a few days he also sent a rather detailed confidential document (Appendix IX) to me of his own analysis which was very much as we discussed. He offered to stay on as treasurer, if I would have him, and seek the resignations of those other members leading the attempted coup.

I contacted the president. I intentionally did not try to mend this broken relationship. I saw it as lost, and continued to work merely on the professional plane for the two months until the end of his term. As it turned out he submitted his resignation along with the two others who were members of the Honorary Vestry. I was sad but saw little hope in overcoming secrecy and the loss of integrity. I never asked why he had first called and then cancelled the "vote of confidence" meeting for 21 October. I suspect that the group did some homework and discovered that they did not have a firm majority. Though decisions to this point had been made by consensus not a majority vote. We had not as a group established if in fact a simple majority could swing such a vote – perhaps it would need two thirds but none of this seemed to matter to the group leading the coup. So, a meeting held without these parameters clarified in advance would surely have been chaos. No meeting was held on 21 October, but it was the process of secrecy and deception that threatened the little congregation of Grace, Anglican Episcopal Church in the Hérault.

Val J. Littman

> *"Neither man nor angel can discern hypocrisy, the only evil that walks invisible except to God alone."*
> -*Paradise Lost*, John Milton – Book III-line 682ff.

Though the meeting of 21 October never happened. What did happen is that the expected members of the vestry (three) resigned. Simon Peter and the faithful secretary agreed to stay on in their post and we called for new recruits from a congregation that had been exposed, through unauthorized emails, to a lot of "dirty laundry". In the days after I received some emails to me, some not knowing that this was as much a surprise to me as it was to them. "What was happening to our lovely little congregation", wrote one. "This bickering is exactly why I stopped going to church" wrote another.

One Sunday during this time a woman came up to Linda and me, as the last of the people who had attended the fellowship / coffee hour made their way to their cars. This woman attended Sunday worship enough to be known to us but not one of the more noticeable members in the congregation. She was a cancer survivor, and lived a distance away but she had a depth of faith that radiated from her. Clearly, she had stayed behind this day to say something to us. Briefly she told us of her pre-retirement work as a parish secretary in England. She made it clear that she knew first had of the difficulties of parish work. She described how she had experienced her own vicar breaking down in tears at times at her desk. She wanted us to know that she understood first hand and said thank you. After expressing her gratitude that day, this woman was among the collateral causalities of congregation conflict, she attended less and less and then not at all as the conflict grew.

I must confess gentle reader, that I have nearly exhausted myself with these tales but there is much more to tell.

Inspired by memories of Andy Rooney and his insights; while writing this section I often found myself checking and re-checking original documents because life as documented was not always as I remembered it.

The events actually became more incredulous to me as I checked and re-checked documents of church attendance, minutes of meetings and signatures on the petitions. All of the members of the lay leadership at that time had signed both petitions requesting mission status in the Episcopal Church Europe and the petition for matching funds grant. What happened between the signing of these petitions in April and the attempted coup of October? What was happening in secret was an evil that walked among us, now no longer invisible to me.

My biggest challenge regarding accuracy was re-creating the time-line. I believe, in the end I presented it as it was and the events as they were. What may have been different is the intensity of feelings represented. Feelings have a way of oozing through the printed word and I hope that I have captured them closely. It felt much worse at the time in its freshness.

I was perhaps overly conscientious in record keeping. This comes from good social work case work training, writing of verbatim dialogues as a part of Clinical Pastoral Education, and documentation of mental health records and my general disposition for order. I had also become aware along the way that perhaps we were creating a template for growing an Episcopal church in Europe. I had hoped to set forward an example for growing a church in Europe. I used educational materials describe Anglican and Episcopal Church traditions to a people of mixed church (and no particular church) backgrounds, brochures which define the roles and duties of clergy and lay leadership, and the research into clergy compensation have all been re-worked into straight forward language, and adapted to the European setting. These church documents and my personal files that have been saved and backed up on computer are now several years old. The originals were backed up and given to my successor. Some things may have gotten lost or have been re-formatted in the various technical changes over the years involved in saving this data. But there is a well documented church life that has been passed on to church archives in Paris for future church detectives.

One more tale before leaving this section:

Somewhere during the heat of the attempted coup, I received an email from a member of the congregation. She was a frequent visitor to France from England and had her vacation home in a village nearby. She attended church events when she was in the area but had not yet completely moved to France until her retirement was finalized. Her email was among those that expressed concern about what had been openly aired on the internet. We set a time to meet in my home and I was fully expecting to relive the tales of the past months. It was one of those cold damp days in the South of France that the writers of tour books never seem to experience. It matched my weary, dreary mood. She came; we sat in front of the fireplace in the living room.

She sat quietly for a few moments while I began relaying the recent history. Then it dawned on me to check with her. "I'm sorry, perhaps I should begin with you, what was it you came for?" What did she want to know?

With calm reassurance that sank into my bones she said, "I want to know how you are." "How are you in all of this?"

I was so surprised, so touched, the tears rushed to my eyes. This gentle woman was the first person from the congregation to ask me in all this how I was. We talked afterward of facts and time line and hopes that Grace Church would get through it all, but her interest in how this had affected me was the first pastoral care that the pastor had received from the congregation in these months of betrayal. I have never forgotten. And she and her husband have become friends over the years.

There are a few more little tales of French country life that go beyond the church congregation. While at times it seemed that our entire life now revolved around the little church, in fact it did not. Emotionally the tensions of Church conflict seemed all embracing and exhausting, but there was more to our lives in France.

Linda took daily walks around the village and into the vineyards. These brought her in touch with people and animals and a certain rhythm to life and sensitivities to village life. She and I think of these as little moments of grace.

During her morning walk, Linda noticed Veronique, a neighbor, near a horse that often grazed at the edge of the village. But something told her not to call out with her usual cheerful "bonjour". She sensed that something was different. Later that same morning Linda discovered a large tarp covering a mound in the field and then noticed the hoof of the recently euthanized horse.

The neighbors were aware of Papillion's deterioration in old age and a recent illness. So a sign appeared on the gate to the coral.

Je m'appelais "Papillon". J'étais très gentil, un chef. Je suis parti au Paradis des Chevaux ...32 ans.

Often, I am tired from a day (many a day's) work wrestling with getting this little church up and running: even discussions with a supportive bishop mean many emails, discussion and documentation to set things in order and work through the details of French Law.

But then there are the times when I walk through the courtyard at the end of the day and along the way I encounter moments of grace: In our courtyard, walled around as if to protect us, I say hello to the bunnies who are already "half asleep" having received their "good night carrot treats". The darkened courtyard comes to light as if by magic (actually motion detectors) that lights my way. A little tree frog, that has lost its, way is sitting in "harm's way" and needs to be coached to a safer spot, damp, and protected from foot traffic. I see that two swallows have taken up a residence during the summer. They have made their home in a lovely (and expensive) straw floral arrangement positioned artistically in a long passage way neither outside nor inside but easily accessible to the swallows. The picture of two swallows resting for the night in the floral arrangement is a "still life" waiting to be painted.

How fortunate we are. Linda and I, each in our own ways, experienced such touching moments as these.

Chapter 18
Rising up in 2010

"Those who dance are considered insane by those who cannot hear the music."
-Friedrich Nietzsche

Somewhere during the height of tensions in 2009 I needed to do some personal evaluation of what I had gotten myself into. I had responded for the past six years to a call and had given freely and enthusiastically. A large part of the retirement that Linda and I had planned was now taken up with church life. Some of it was very fulfilling but there was a large part of the management of conflict and the people creating it that was changing our lives. Linda remained very supportive even though her role as vicar's wife was not something she had chosen. There were many times where she listened to me as I tried to figure out what had happened, or find a way forward in spite of obstacles, as I tried to sort out how to minister well to the congregation as a whole and not let the grumblings of a few color a generally healthy church life. I had my share of tearful dinner and breakfast conversations.

At one point I had a conversation with the bishop to evaluate how or whether I should continue. I was aware that I got into this because of my personal response to the call of a few, and this was in a very real way to me a fulfilling of a vocation that I had been called to many years ago. The congregation had grown under my guidance, but I believed, that unlike some clergy who had family to support or and a position in the community to protect, I always had the choice to continue or not. I knew I had much more freedom than many traditional clergy in many dioceses. In my conversation with Bishop Pierre I indicated that there was no need on my part to continue this role. While there were certain aspects that I enjoyed there was much that was ugly that had seeped into my life. I did not need the position in any way, I was not paid, so income was not a driving force and the joy of growing a congregation from scratch had faded under the pressures of the past two years. I asked the bishop to help me evaluate whether I should continue. It became clear that while I could let this all go, he now would like it to continue. He was pastoral enough to understand my position, but he also let me know that he saw this congregation as a good thing for the church in Europe and that he would like it to continue.

I did not share this conversation with the congregation, but internally I now had made a change. What had started as my response to a call and my choice, doing it for myself, was to change to doing it for someone else. This was a decision I made freely, but it was a change in internal motivation. Now, from this time forward, I was doing this because my bishop believed that this was good for the larger church. I did also encourage the bishop to think of an eventual replacement for me. I believe he seriously did, but it did not materialize.

A little explanation of church terms and church law of governance (Canon Law) might help before we move forward. Prior to October 2009 the congregation had no standing in the larger church community. We were not officially governed by any larger body, although under my direction we followed the general forms of governance of the Episcopal Church and used church terms that would be familiar to people from a variety of church disciplines. Now, as a mission congregation, we came under the jurisdiction of the Bishop in charge of the Episcopal Church Europe. As a mission congregation, that is, one that is not fully self supporting the clergy functioned as a representative of the bishop, our lay governing body was an extension of the bishop – therefore called Bishop's Committee – a committee belonging to the bishop (not a committee of bishops). We had a voice in larger church governance and we were eligible for support from the larger church – for resources and limited financial assistance, and most importantly in resolving local disputes that could not be solved on our own. All of this would not change our day to day operations because the congregation had been formed to be in keeping the traditions of the Anglican tradition and Episcopal Church from its beginning. So, most things remained the same and looked the same. But in fact, we now had some official standing, some voice, a vote at convention, some support and some responsibility to conform to the larger church.

Resignations from the disaffected vestry members were received around 21 October 2009 and by 30 October we had a new group of lay leaders. We also had a chance to begin again. Grace Anglican Episcopal Church in the Hérault had a new life as a new mission of the Episcopal Church Europe. We could now properly address this lay leadership group as the Bishop's Committee – leaving the informal and unofficial title of Honorary Vestry aside. Generous people stepped forward. I used the opportunity to draft new, clearer descriptions of the various positions including my own as vicar. With Simon Peter we made revisions to the Association by-laws according to French Law, and drafted Church Bylaws to conform to the Canons and constitution of the Episcopal Church. We were dotting all our dots and crossing all our "Ts".
With Simon Peter we also were closing some of the loop holes and clarified terms that had, until the conflict, seemed clear enough. Any that had been

used by those who had tried the coup of October 2009 were examined and re-examined. We were more explicit about the use of the group email list, contacts and phone numbers, the resolution of disputes, if there were any in the future we could not resolve on our own. The roles of president of the association loi and the chair of the Bishop's Committee were now held by the vicar, hopefully removing future division. The revisions were a tedious task, but necessary. The new Bishop's Committee approved our work when we finished, and it was submitted to the larger church for approval.

The November 2009 annual meeting for the Association Loi reflected these changes (Appendix II and Appendix III). It also reflected our new life as a mission congregation. The bulk of the annual meeting was dedicated to church affairs and church growth and followed church canons and by laws. The annual meeting was open to all members of the congregation. Having experienced the conflict of the past two years I was interested in this as a sorting out process. Those who would attend (or expressed their wish to attend) would help determine who were members of the congregation after the attempted coup of October 2009. The congregation, as might be expected, was diminished by four couples. This was no surprise since these were the leaders of the earlier "vote of no confidence" movement. Of concern to me was the fact that I knew there were others who had been a part of the secret meetings but had decided after the fall-out to stay with Grace Church. One of those characters was the aged Church of England clergy and his wife. They had been a part of the congregation from very early on, and had by their own choosing taken only an occasional role in the congregation. The retired clergy made it known to me that he clearly did not want a leadership role and would be happy for occasional celebration of the Sunday Eucharist and perhaps a lecture or two in the form of Adult Education. It was in this way that he contributed to the congregation life and I appreciated the help.

The annual Festival of Lessons and Carols 2009 was its usual success, although "Lourdes" had resigned from the committee and encouraged some other members to not be available that year. The event maintained its broad appeal. More and more, key roles in planning were now taken up by members of Grace Church congregation. I passed over an opportunity to propose that the financial proceeds be shared by both the Parish of the Roman Catholic Diocese who had given us the use of the church space, and Grace Church as a major contributor to the event in terms of manpower and time. I had informally proposed this in the previous year, when our donation to the local Roman Catholic Church reached nearly €500. I saw that my proposal of capping our donation to the diocese at €500 and begin donating the surplus in future years to Grace Church might not be politic.

In 2008 Lourdes opposed it vigorously, making her imprecations were heard even if she was not longer on the planning committee, so I dropped it. In 2009, given the opportunity to make the revision with a supportive planning group, it seemed bad timing to raise it again, and frankly, I was not up for another possible battle or backlash even if the planning group approved such a move. Politically it seemed best just to continue this single donation. In 2009 these decisions took care of themselves. Attendance and donations were slightly lower. But 200 in attendance, and a donation to the Roman Catholic Church of €466. it was still successful. Perhaps I should wait for another year, for things to settle down before proposing a change.

The year 2010 would prove to be a prosperous year. It was not free of bumps along the way, as you will soon see, but I was optimistic that we had successfully navigated through the treacherous waters in a sea of conflict and were one our way. Now that we had agreed to strive toward funding part time clergy in the future, the goal and the process was open to long term planning discussions.

In meetings with the newly formed Bishop's Committee it was clear that a goal of finding my successor was hand in hand with the continued growth of the congregation. A project to find new - larger- church space was given to the new Church Warden. I drew up the guidelines for worship space, the Bishop's Committee reviewed them, and the warden did an analysis of the congregation to inform the choice of some future church space. We were still heavily dependent upon free church space – with a token annual donation raised from €100 to €200 allotted in the budget. A space that was geographically central, with space for Sunday school and meetings in addition to worship - Oh yes, modern toilets and heat in the winter would be would be greatly appreciated. There was a monastery geographically central that would be ideal and the Prayer Group – organized and initiated by Linda - had already been holding some of their meetings at that location so we had the beginnings of a relationship.

Other projects, a part of our church life, continued. The Charity outreach programs were under new leadership, and this time the chair was following the guidelines. I continued to organize adult education events, and expanded our number of worship service to fit special occasions in the church year. We also openly discussed the possibilities of expanding Sunday worship service to twice each month on a regular basis.

Over all, church attendance, in spite of the loss of four couples, was stable. During 2010 we would re-coup our losses through attraction of new members. We also celebrated our first Confirmations of two teens in

October with a visit of Bishop Pierre. And he would also be our guest at the annual festival of Lessons and Carols in December of that year. During this most optimistic of years an obvious recruitment of new clergy took place. After consulting with Bishop Pierre in February I worked with two clergy from the Episcopal Church Europe to expose the congregation to other clergy – one, an older retired clergy who was born in the UK, grew up in New Zealand, and a priest in The Episcopal Church and the other a younger clergy from England who preferred church polity in the Episcopal Church rather than the Church of England. Each of these clergy came for Sunday services to help the congregation adjust to my eventual replacement. Each gave the congregation a view of what life in the Episcopal Church Europe could be as a part of the larger world-wide Anglican Church. The younger clergy was prepared to search for a part time teaching position in the larger city of Montpellier to support himself while gradually growing the congregation to part-time compensation and eventually full-time support for clergy. I believed this was going to happen!

The year 2010 was still young – early February - and I was planning for worship services. A normal part of my planning was to include the retired Church of England clergy in the March or April worship schedule. As had been my practice in the past years, I sent him an email. If he were interested, I asked, I would like to include him as celebrant of one of the worship services in March or April, which would be best for him?

His response was a surprise. Briefly, he said, "… perhaps I should meet with you and let you know what has been going on". Curious, I responded, "Shall we meet at your place or mine, or go out for coffee?" He chose to come to meet at my home. We set a time to meet within a few days.

As we met in front of our fireplace in the living room, he began to tell me that some members of the congregation (those who had led the attempted coup of October 2009) had approached him a few months ago and asked that he lead worship for them as a separate group. He explained that they felt excluded from the Grace Church. While he first declined their request, he was now going to honor it since – in his thinking – "… it would be a shame to deny them the sacraments".

As he elaborated it became clear, using his terms, that he was aware of political dynamics involved and technical jurisdictional issues which as our conversation continued he would later say he knew nothing about. I think he was not lying. He may have been initially unaware but someone, probably the Arch-Deacon from Nice had made him aware and had given him key terms to use. He said that he clearly did not want to start a "rival"

Le Petit Jardin de L'âme

congregation and the new congregation would only be "loosely affiliated" with the C of E Diocese in Europe and the chaplaincy in the Gard. The Gard was the neighboring department - far enough away to camouflage the real breech of a long-standing agreement between the four church members of the Worldwide Anglican Communion with over-lapping jurisdictions in Europe. The "loose" affiliation with the C of E was an interesting development since this group had not wanted any affiliation with a larger church organization – But he himself would need some affiliation in order to be licensed to serve just as I did.

My response was measured, trying to respect a clergy colleague, and aware that, if he chose to effectively start a second church in the area, not only would it be a workload more than he ever indicated he wished to undertake but it would be difficult for the area to successfully support two congregations. I did not mention at that time the scandal to the larger community of a visible breech that this Christian community was apparently unwilling to heal. See how these Christians love one another?

As I began to support his initial instincts to decline their request, I sensed that a different decision had already been made. Since he and I both knew that the better approach in terms of living out the Christian message and financial success was for conflicts to be resolved, they should be resolved not divide the congregation. It was important to me to clarify the thinking that they were being "denied the sacraments". I had reached out to some in the group and they had declined to meet (those two who I had met with were back and active in the congregation at Grace Church). I spoke candidly as I would with a colleague. I made the distinction; that those who feel that they are denied the sacrament are welcome to come to worship – at that time, they were still receiving the regular email announcements about worship and church activities. I speculated with him, perhaps a ministry he could offer to the local church was as clergy to encourage those who wished to separate from the church to return; not to start a second church competing for people of the same demographic. If they were deprived of the sacrament, it was because they were choosing not to attend the church, they were depriving themselves of the sacraments. To this comment my colleague gave piercing stare and gritted his teeth, seemingly in great exasperation.

It was at this point in our conversation I mentioned the agreement between the Church of England, Diocese in Europe, and the Episcopal Church ratified at Lambeth1968 (resolution 63 at the worldwide meeting of Anglican churches in Lambeth 1968) and informally referred to as "The Concordat". Commitment to this document was renewed in letters and meetings 1997 to 2004 by a group COABICE – College of Anglican Bishops in Continental Europe. I had come across the concordat in my earlier research when considering application as a mission. One of the requirements from the Episcopal Church was to determine if the establishment of any new mission might pose a threat to any nearby previously established congregation in either the Episcopal Church or the C of E Diocese in Europe. This concordat acknowledged the long-term harm when two church jurisdictions within the same communion compete for the same people. The Concordat was an agreement not to establish competing churches in the same communion in the same geographic areas, serving the same populations. In fact, a bit of research into this concordat acknowledged that the worldwide church had been aware of this problem since the 1870's but had finally taken positive action in 1968 through resolution 63 at Lambeth. My colleague appeared not to know of this agreement although I knew that his advisor, the Arch-Deacon in Nice would be well aware of such a document. I did further research after our meeting and sent him links to the documents. I also advised my bishop that we now had a bigger problem on our hands.

> *Only the guy who isn't rowing has time to rock the boat.*
> -Jean-Paul Sartre

At this time, I felt confident that this problem had now been "bumped-up" to a higher level, to the bishops of the respective jurisdictions Church of England Diocese in Europe and the Episcopal Church Europe. My role it seemed was to continue the work pastorally with the existing congregation of Grace Church to build on our successes and let the bishops handle this. As a jurisdictional or political matter, it was much bigger than me, and Grace Church. It was something to be resolved at the level of bishops and perhaps there had been some other precedents in other parts of Europe where both the C of E and The Episcopal Church had churches. I felt confident that at the level of bishops there would be an agreement that would respect the Concordat since most of those who had signed the most recent COABICE letters of agreement were still in authority. The establishment of a competing church within ten minutes drive from us, drawing on the same demographic base was clearly in violation of the concordat.

It seemed my colleague was to follow the same pattern of the separatist group absenting themselves from worship that was offered to all who would come as it had been for the past seven years. I discovered after the fact, that this group had contacted the Arch-Deacon of the C of E in Nice (five hours drive away) to plead their cause. The arch-deacon, without

Le Petit Jardin de L'âme

acknowledging the existing church, or without contact of my bishop, advised the separatist group how to proceed.

I was again experiencing the tactic favored by this group; a unilateral decision made in secret; an "end-run". There was no attempt at collaboration, no discussion and no basis in fact.

I should acknowledge here that months after the fact an investigation into official correspondence revealed a bit of chicanery on the part of the arch-deacon. He had a reputation for "lost mail" blaming it on the Nice Post Office. This was an inside joke among church administrators who realized that correspondence of important documents were notoriously selectively received or not received by the Arch-deacon. Some which were sent to him he "did not receive" were blamed on the Nice Post Office or those to which required his response were also "lost" or never sent. So, it was in this case where the archdeacon claimed to have sent a letter to my bishop. Letters of notice (and copies to the respective bishops) were received by two bishops of the C of E Diocese in Europe but the same letter sent to the Bishop of The Episcopal Church Europe had been pronounced "lost" by the Nice Postal System. The letter was a "no show" on my bishop's desk. The bishop of the Episcopal Church Europe was to discover, at a meeting of his C of E peers that they were moving ahead to establish a congregation in competition with Grace Church based on accusations that my leadership style was autocratic, that they had been coerced into signing the petition to become a mission, and that they were being denied the sacraments.

Although we were ostensibly in the 21st century, it seemed that old fashioned medieval church politics were alive and well. The bishops were maneuvering on the chess board over a new little fiefdom in the south of France for England.

At this early stage it would have been possible to correct supposed failings of The Nice Post Office. And because of my routine documentation, the misunderstandings and accusations could easily be corrected to establish a new ground for discussion. But the archdeacon in Nice and bishop of the Church of England did not ask for information and there was no discussion. The C of E simply moved forward as if Grace Church did not exist. There was never a back-down from this breech of the concordat. However, that was not the end of ecclesiastical sniping and ambush.

My clergy colleague, had come out of retirement to attend to the neighboring church separated from Grace Church and did not take the offer to be celebrant at the Grace's Sunday worship in March or April. However, that did not stop him from occasionally attending church services at Grace Church. Indeed, there were a few people from Grace Church who would attend both churches. The core leaders of the separation did not return to Grace Church but the average person in the pews was now caught in a social – if not ecclesiastical – bind.

Some duped themselves with the thought that they would support both churches. How nice it was - some expressed - that a few years ago we had no Anglican Church in this area of France and now we have two! With a touch of magical thinking, the basic math of allotment of time and finances seemed not to cross their minds. Those who had been most concerned about how to expand the budget of one church were now deluding themselves into support for two churches. Eventually I was to see that some of the newest members actually came to Grace Church, and attended the other congregation to "hedge their bets" on which one would survive. Eventually it became clear that a few actually used their attendance at Grace Church as an opportunity to recruit the unsuspecting to attend the separatist group.

In most cases I opted to turn my eyes away and did not want to enter the fray of confronting this embarrassing activity. But I must confess to actually confronting the retired C of E clergy during the social fellowship (coffee hour) that routinely followed the Sunday service. I noticed that he was in a rather animated conversation with some newcomers. It was unusual that he actually was prepared with pen and paper and was taking some notes. Being that efficient was not his strong point. In fact, in times past if he were to do anything by way of engaging newcomers he would make it a point to direct them to me, but not today. Having contact and welcome information for visitors was routine. I always made sure that it was visible and handy, and members of the congregation knew where to find it. But this is not what was happening. I walked up to him as he was handing his contact information to the new couple. At the time I simply pointed out that there was information on the table nearby to help the newcomers take information they desired for future contacts. But his deed was done. I knew by his reaction, that he knew, that I had just caught him "stealing sheep" – a professional faux pas that he was well aware was unacceptable.

I discussed this development of this second congregation openly with the new Bishop's Committee. The consensus was that we would continue to welcome everyone to the church, and we would strive, through excellence in worship, and education and social programs to attract more members. Some expressed what I also felt personally, that a church founded on deception, and fabrication of lies was destined to fall. The consensus of the group was to let the work of Grace Church would speak for itself. And let the bishops figure out how best to deal with the breech.

We continued the plans to seek better church facilities, we would continue to develop the Charity outreach, and education programs and would continue to consider the viability of adding and additional Sunday service. I established and adult Education program for training lay leaders of Morning Prayer as a way to expand the Sunday worship services. Developed a home study program for preparation for confirmation, and in October of 2010 we celebrated our first confirmation of two teens. I was enthusiastic about the church's future and the "high road" that this new group of lay leaders was taking.

During this time my bishop continued to work with me through this maze. Though I had moments of personal self doubt over how I might have handled things better and I am sure that there were times when he wished my emails to him were shorter, he remained supportive. Two short stories of his support come to mind in addition to his many visits to our home and to the congregation.

The gift of a book titled *When Sheep Attack* by Dennis Maynard was particularly well suited to me. So much so that at the time, I thought it was specifically given to me. I later discovered that the bishop had thought it valuable for all clergy and it was a gift to each of the clergy in his care. The book, the result of practical and qualitative research of clergy and congregations, is based on 25 case studies where clergy were attacked by a small group of antagonists in their congregations. While depressing in many ways, most clergy targeted in this way do not recover. It is also supportive, in that one common denominator is that the book dispelled the notion that this happened only to congregation in decline or through clergy mismanagement. The book pointed out that the toxic characteristics of the antagonists were experienced in successful well managed congregations and that every parish is vulnerable to this phenomenon. Strangely that was reassuring.

During this time bishop made many visits to our home. We looked forward to visits from him and his wife and sometimes other members of the lay leadership from the larger church. Our home being first a B&B lent itself well to quick and convenient accommodations. Most often these visits had an agenda of sorting through the conflict with the congregation established by the C of E in violation of the concordat. Often, I was present at these meetings, but at the time I reference here, I was not. On this visit the bishop was to meet with the separated group in an attempt to hear their side of the story. They had had earlier opportunities one of which was overtly sabotaged by the informal leader of the group who sent messages explicitly advising that people not attend. This time there was some implication that such a meeting had the support of the C of E bishop, though he personally did not attend. After my bishop's return from the meeting, he and I were standing in the kitchen, sorting through the various complaints and accusations raised his meeting. Not much was new – nor was it credible – except one new piece of information. The group had now added to their list my attempted suicide in 2005. The bishop said he was not surprise, though I had not personally told him of the events of 2005. He did ask in a pastoral way why I had not come to him at that time. I explained that at that time I had very little contact with him and I did not have the relationship that had now developed over that past five years. He was not accusatory, and the new information was no more a credible reason for separation than the other reasons which had been fabricated. I felt no recrimination from him. My singular concern was this; that he had been caught off guard, because I had failed to anticipate that this event would now be dug up. I had inadvertently left him vulnerable to surprise. The event was already five years past, I felt it had been dealt with well at the time, and it preceded my pastoral relationship with many in the current parish. It was not a secret; it simply was no longer part of the current equation. However, with these people in their desperation to succeed in and their attempt to rationalize the unreasonable this had now become "fair-game". I believe that its use by the group was seen as a "low-blow" by my bishop.

> *It disturbs me no more to find men base, unjust, or selfish*
> *than to see apes mischievous, wolves savage, or the vulture ravenous.*
> -Jean-Paul Sartre

Chapter 19
A glimmer of inner-personal light and a new horizon

Meanwhile during 2010, Linda and I began to look to our future; evaluating our life in France. Taking the long view, we realized that when we first moved to France our intention was that France was to be home "for the rest of our lives". After ten years of life in France we realized, that "the rest of our lives" could be a rather long time. Something we had not counted on – besides the troubles of adjusting to France, which were plentiful – was that we had underestimated just how resilient we were. Having successfully navigated this cultural adjustment once, we found that we were more ready to try it again!

Somewhere along the way in late 2009 Linda and I had discussed our life in France and decided that a change was in order. Yes, the on-going conflict in the church had some impact on this decision but quite apart from the Church in conflict, we had grown tired of France and Europe in general. When we moved to France in early 2001 we intended to call France home, forever. We had invested in the area and in our home as if this was where we would live out the rest of our days. But over the years we grew to experienced Europe, and France in particular, as "stuck" politically and economically.

Linda found herself reading one of the regular issues of The Economist magazine to which we have subscribed for many years. In the section on international living, The Republic of Panamá was highlighted. She read the article and said to me "I think I could live there". I read the article, and found that, at least in the article, Panamá held out some intrigue for me. There was energy, there was optimism. Panamá, was "going places" and Europe was "stuck". The allure of France had long ago worn off for me and I had no place that held out a new horizon for me. Building the congregation and activity in the Episcopal Church Europe had become very rewarding for me until recently. I was not "itching" to leave France. Nor was I enamored to stay. No viable option came to mind, until now. In 2010 we made our first research vacation to the Republic of Panamá to see, first hand, just how true that article in the Economist was. Ah, but I get ahead of myself!

I was still, in 2010, fully engaged planning the future of the Grace Church. I was active in fulfilling my two-year term on the Bishop's Council of Advice.

(titled Standing Committee in most dioceses) I was, by plan, winding down my activities with Grace Church. Linda and I had no specific plan as yet, but we were clearly ready to be free of the responsibilities of the congregation, and ready for a new adventure.

It is difficult to explain – and therefore I am often misunderstood – about what it was like to live in France. This is especially important in conversations between Linda, and myself but also with those ex-pats and curious French, who inevitably ask, "How do you like life in France?" - or- in the periodic conversation with visitors, many of whom have their own dreams of life abroad. "Do you like it … No regrets?"

Now, being among the veteran members in the ex-pat community, I had come to learn that, rather than an informal interview seeking my response to my life experience which may be a few years in advance of their own time of adjustment, this question, coming from other ex-pats, or soon-to-be expats, in whatever form it comes, is often a search for validation of their future or of their own uncertainties. People search for an emotional companion on their journey, which has had its own share of frustrations and disappointments. I am now more likely to give a considered response rather than the perfunctory and politically correct "Oh, it is lovely, the weather is great, and the wine wonderful who could ask for more."

But it is difficult to find a satisfactory illustration of what it means to me to live in France, and why we would leave.

I had some considerable success in adjusting to life in France, nearly 10 years down the road from our first experiences I found positive personal pursuits, looking past the day to day incivilities, or in some instances confronting them. I found ways to distract myself from these things which have, in the past, driven me crazy and which detract from the quality of life for which France is known.

In this success there is a strange contradiction. The more successful I am at this life task, the more difficult it is for people to see just how much life in France is not a good fit for me. After all it looks like I might even be enjoying myself at times! And at times I do. But this enjoyment has little to do with France and does not erase the experience of life in France which I still find intolerable. I just cope better. It does not mean that France is any better the place for me to live.

For a moment let's take a little diversion.

I offer an experience in which an example and opportunity for clarity came together for us as a couple. This tale includes many of the things that make those romantic picturesque evenings in the south of France and somewhere at its heart it also includes what I found intolerable.

We made plans to attend a lovely evening of wine tasting and a meal at one of the local wine domaines. We had done this several times before with friends and enjoyed the meal and the wine pairings with the food and the ambiance at this particular domaine, so we were looking forward to a pleasant evening.

Also, we had B&B guests, previous clients who had stayed at *Le petit Jardin de L'âme* before and become friends. They decided to make this evening part of their French vacation experience. We often gave our B&B guests the benefit of our local knowledge of events that might give them a taste of life in France that they might otherwise miss on the normal tourist information guides. Ah, but this is an aside.

We attended the degustation and wine pairing dinner. The hostess placed us at a table with several English-speakers who have made the area their regular vacation destination and some who live in the area part time. I believe that our hostess thought she was doing us a kindness by placing us at the same table.

The evening was insufferable. Rather, our tablemates were insufferable. Linda and I, along with our B&B guests made the best of it. The wines were of good quality and variety, the food was up to its usual good standard and the setting in the courtyard of the Domaine was picturesque. But the conversation ranged from polite discrete tolerance for the outrageous and inane comments made at the table to an occasional diplomatic attempt to ground their statements in reality, "Really, are you sure of - x,y,z - that sounds unusual!", "I've never heard it described quite that way!".

"Isn't that interesting, I never heard that the letters of the Hebrew alphabet were based on the shape of an apple core…!"

The more confrontational approach to topics of discussion were generally avoided with my superego well in charge; Oh, this will pass, it's only one evening. But the evening conversation was a charade. I enjoyed the food, the wine and the ambiance; a picture postcard of the dream of life in France. However, the experience, beyond the scenery and stage setting, was intolerable.

Actually, it was Linda who made the overture, as quickly after dessert as socially permissible (but before coffee was served) to make our excuses and exit. Our B&B quests, quick studies as they were, picked up on the opportunity. Though we had arrived separately and could leave separately as well, they saw this as a moment for escape.

It was the next morning, only two minutes into their breakfast that one of our guests, no longer being able to contain himself, started to "debrief" on the evening in a most humorous way. And as a comic sketch, a vignette of a dinner party gone awry, we all shared in the amusement of an evening that we would not be likely to endure again.

Life in France for me had become that diner party, every day. Yes, the food is good, the wine is wonderful, and the weather can be delightful compared to some places. Our home, some have told us, should be submitted to Architectural Digest or Décor de Provence, French Country Living. But then there are these people and their behaviors – regardless of language – this was our experience of France. I can successfully get through the evening – and even find ways to savor some tasty morsels in the experience – but do I want to repeat this "dinner party" as a way of life? No. I have managed, sometimes better, sometimes not so well and at times I find some fellow travelers like me. But I found that France was a charade in place of la joie de vivre.

It is always tempting to equate a reduction in pain as a cure for the disease, to equate successful navigation through treachery as a victory. It is tempting to just "get through It" or "get to the other side" however, health and happiness implies a wholeness; that all fits together well. And that is what was missing in our life in France. I had managed to put Humpty Dumpty back together again from the terrible years of 2005 and found a successful life in growing the congregation. We survived the coup of 2009 and had the satisfaction of being once again on a positive trajectory. But life in Europe (and in particular France) just was not satisfying to my soul. Our life as a couple had also survived but was calling out for more. Perhaps a new journey would put us, again, on a common trajectory. Now we were discovering a new horizon to reach for, perhaps it would be Panamá. But the destination and location was not as important as journeying together. Linda had coaxed a creative genie out of the bottle. We were dreaming again.

Le Petit Jardin de L'âme

La vérité vaut bien qu'on passe quelques années sans la trouver.
Truth is more valuable if it takes you a few years to find it.
- Renard

The year 2010 came to an end with all the signs of success. Fittingly, my bishop was the guest celebrant at the annual Festival of Lesson and Carols. This event helped to increase his visibility in the area and I thought was a good transition from me, as the celebrant for the previous seven years to whomever would succeed me. Although plans for my successor were still uncertain this was an opportunity to place the local church clearly in his hands in the minds of the general public, even those beyond the Grace Church congregation. The event was a success with a record attendance of 280 persons and our monetary contribution to the local Roman Catholic parish reached a new high, over €600.

Over the course of the years 2009 and 2010 Grace Church had become Planning Committee for this event. One by one original members of the planning committee offered various reasons for not being available. The organist, with whom I had had a good rapport, had inexplicably decided that he was not able to accompany the carols this year at lessons and Carols. So, I searched for another. There were murmurs that the director for the choral group would not be in town this year for the date of the service. I negotiated with him for an alternative. I sensed that someone, or a few "someones", was at work behind the scenes encouraging this version of the "Blue Flu" from the ranks of a previously well synchronized army of volunteers. In each case I saw the challenge as an opportunity to do something better, to broaden the resources from which we could draw in the future. It was indeed extra work, but I thought we were the better for it and less dependent on the same cadre of volunteers that had social connections with Lourdes.

We still received help from all parts of the area as was the tradition, but the organizing and promotion was now carried out by members of Grace Church. The "man in the pew" probably noticed no change – or perhaps an improvement. But I suspected that there were a few ghosts working in the background.

Lourdes, although having resigned from the planning group, none-the-less created some tension. Lourdes made it her business to request the usual church venue from the local pastor. In the guise of "doing me a favor" she made her point clear that access to this venue was through her intercession and she would be holding the church keys

Her email to me announcing this "favor" was far in advance of the usual time line, and her closing sentences had the tone with which I had become familiar, implying that she was in control of the venue.

> "…We have use of the church for our carol service courtesy of the Parish of St Roch en Piscenois and its present incumbent, Pere Jean Coste. It should not be seen as a certainty that he will always give his permission and, he is quite capable of changing his mind."

An attempt to meet with Lourdes to thank her for her good intentions and more importantly to set limits and avoid the tensions of 2007 and 2008 was first agreed to and then cancelled by her.

I followed up with the local pastor on my own to clarify that future requests would be made by Grace Church. I thanked him for his generous past offers and hoped that we could prevail upon him again in future years. Our relationship had become comfortable over the years and he could clearly see the signs of intramural conflicts. He was no stranger to church bickering and saw in my meeting with him what I hoped he would see.

A courtesy invitation was extended to Lourdes' husband to help with the refreshments as he had done in the past, but he declined saying that this year he and Lourdes would be out of town on the day of the Lessons and Carols service.

In our personal lives, Linda and I had made our research vacation to the Republic of Panamá and discovered that indeed we could consider Panamá as our next adventure. We had no firm time line, but I wanted to pass on this development to my bishop. The information was both in the interest of transparency and follow up to our earlier conversations about my intentions and I felt that if he knew that I was moving forward with my personal plans, he too would press on with the search for my replacement. From experience with the comings and goings in church leadership, I realized that an open-ended departure was often not a good idea. I was flexible but certain that a time-line should be developed for me to leave the congregation even if we did not move to Panamá immediately.

Just prior to the annual lessons and carols service I worked out a time-line with my bishop. I would stay on at Grace Church until the following Easter – April 2011- giving him four months to make his own plan for either a new vicar or an interim plan. He agreed. He, in turn, thought it best to inform the Bishop's Committee which was scheduled to meet the day following Lessons and Carols for a debriefing of the event and other regular business.

The bishop encouraged me to make my announcement to the Bishop's Committee. There were great sounds of silence as the inevitable met the incredible. The uncomfortable silence was followed by reassurances that care would be taken to follow through on current plans. Since the treasurer, Simon Peter, had called to absent himself from the meeting due to a family emergency, I made it my point to follow up with him personally the next day on both accounts.

At our kitchen table Simon Peter and I met briefly, and I told him of plans to make Easter my last official worship service as vicar for Grace Church. We rehearsed the current tentative plans for succession uncertain as they may be but with confidence that this was in the hands of the bishop. Simon Peter controlled his disappointment, but a bit of incredulity showed through. I could sense that he felt I had abandoned him in a battle that he was actually more aware of than I. Through his social contacts he was aware of something under foot.

At Christmas Eve services things seemed rather normal with a bit of the glow from Lessons and Carols hanging over us still. There were 35 in attendance. This was down from our December 2008, pre-conflict, attendance of 57people, but generally reflective of the previous year's attendance of 40 as our average Sunday attendance for 2010. As far as numbers were concerned this was actually encouraging, since this was the first year where the group who had separated from Grace Church were holding services on the same evening less than ten minutes away. The inevitable tug-of-war for church members was now in full swing.

Our Christmas letter 2010 attempted to bring friends and family up-to-date:

> Joyeux Noël et Bonne Année du petit jardin de l'âme. Meilleurs Vœux de Bonheur
>
> Each year at this time of year Linda and I have a tradition. The end of one year and beginning a new year has always been a time for us to do some life-planning. This year we have a goal for 2011; to begin (again) our retirement.

Sometime during 2011 (time yet to be determined) Linda and I will begin our next chapter of retirement in The Republic of Panamá. Our actual departure depends on the sale of our home, so it is difficult to say when exactly. We expect to be here through Easter, probably into June (perhaps longer). We experience a mix of uncertainty and excitement as we look ahead.

Ten years ago, our friends in the USA asked incredibly, "Why move to France?" We expect our friends here will again ask, incredibly" Why Panamá?" In part, the move is for us one of those freedoms of retirement we have decided to exercise. And after seven years of unfavorable exchange rates, Dollars-to-Euros, we look forward to a currency on par with the dollar.

It has become very expensive to live in Europe since about 2003 and with the economic crash of 2008. We could manage to stay here, but I find myself saying" Is life so good here that it is worth paying $7.00 a gallon for gas? Ironically, after several years of hoping in vain for at least "on par" euros-to-dollar exchange and seeing instead it has taken $1.30 to $1.40 (or more) dollars to buy one euro, we are ready to stretch our dollar a little further by moving to Panamá.

So, at this moment we hope for a continued weak dollar and strong euro until our house sells. This, according to Murphy's Law, will guarantee that the USA economy will experience a sudden surge to bring it "on par" with the euro and President Obama will thank us.

Our real estate taxes and health care are a real bargain here, so some of it balances out but, in general, I've come to the conclusion that we pay a lot for "ordinary". However, it may be difficult to find good wines in the "New World" at our Languedoc prices.

In general, financial benefit is one reason for moving to Panamá. Then there are the cumulative reasons that come with living 10 years here in France - We have "done France". Some disappointments and some high moments but the adventure is over here.

We thought we would like living village life - everything in walking distance - fresh green goods at the quaint greengrocer, and a little convenience grocery for things I've forgotten when preparing dinner Etc. While it is nice, on occasion, to run down the street for something I've forgotten - we now do most of our shopping at the big shopping centers. Frankly it's easier cheaper and more convenient. For starters, they are open at lunch time! After 10 years of immersion into local life as ex-pats, we are ready for a "gated community" – enough said here. You've read the book, so you know all that

When we moved to France, it was "forever". But we now realize that "forever" could be another 20+ years and we are not married to France. When we moved to France we chose to live in a "first world" country for the benefits of the 1st world. We found a few too many 3rd world elements. Linda and I still make bets on whether public WCs will have successfully assembled the basic necessities for the 21st century: plumbing that works, toilet paper, hot water, soap and something to dry your hands and a light so you can close the door and still see what you are doing! We can say "Thank You, France", the thought of living in a known 3rd world country (with a first world capital - in Panamá City) is not so daunting.

We have seen some great sights - but if I had it to do over again I'd visit them as a tourist - I'd go for breath, not depth - seeing a lot of things but not staying very long - never thought I'd say that. But I have found that the "soft lens" is more kind to old things (including us).
Linda could probably stay in France but even for her there is a sense that we started out on an adventure and now the adventure is over.

There will be some sadness in our departure. Both of us will miss our home - and the space we created here. And we must still address the issue of whether the Bunnies come with us or not. This is a tough one for us. We want to take them with us but need to consult with the Vet. It is a long transport and bunnies like predictability. An extended upset to their routine can be deadly. The trip may be too difficult for them.

We make this decision knowing that our choice also touches the lives of many in the little church that has grown up around us here in France. What began as a joy has turned into a full-time job and in the past two years a significant amount of emotional energy has gone into recovering from congregation conflict that began in 2008. I have come to the conclusion that it is actually necessary for me to leave in order for them to take their next steps and to raise up new leaders. The transition is planned and will extend well into 2011.

Panamá itself is probably too hot and too humid for either of us but the mountains nearby seem to offer moderate temperatures and spring like season all year. Altos del Maria, is our target, about 90 minutes from Panamá city. Personally, I really don't need hot summers – spring, most of the time, would be nice. While Panamá weather reports rain almost every day it is tropical short showers not day upon day of grey skies and rain. Our unremitting sun and long summers here have made us appreciate the relief of having a few clouds in the sky on occasion. Living now for nearly 10 years where we hardly see a drop of rain for months, then it comes all in November December and January I think everything needs a good "washing off" more often than that.

Who knows - God willing - in another ten years we might try something else different again. We are fortunate to have the resources to make this move. So, simply put, we are moving to Panamá because we can. No place (Panamá or elsewhere) will be perfect but we figure that we are on to another adventure - Stay tuned – watch this space!

Perhaps you will remember our Christmas Letter of 2000 when we left Chicago for France:

> *It is good for the soul that we be uprooted now and again ... transplanted, trimmed, and pruned. Twenty plus years ago, Linda and I each came to Chicago to grow a new life together. It's been hard work and wonderful. Now we're ready for the next great adventure at le petit jardin de l'âme.*

I think we will take the name of our home with us, to Panamá - *Le petit Jardin de L'âme - jardincito del alma* – little garden of the soul.

Chapter 20
2011 - Disturb Us Lord

Disturb us Lord,
When we are too well pleased with ourselves,
When our dreams have come true because we dreamed too little,
When we arrived safely because we sailed too close to the shore.

Disturb us, Lord
When, with the abundance of things we possess, we have lost our thirst for the waters of life,
When we have fallen in love with life, and have ceased to dream of eternity.
When in our efforts to build a new earth, we have allowed our vision of the new heaven to dim.

Disturb us Lord,
To dare more boldly, to venture on wider seas
Where storms will show your mastery;
Where losing sight of land, we shall find the stars.

We ask you, Lord, to push back the horizons of our hopes;
And to push us into the future, in strength, courage, hope and love.
Francis Drake, Explorer – 1577 Portsmouth, England

And yes, it was to be a disturbing year.

Before I continue; the prayer above, attributed to Francis Drake was meaningful to both Linda and me in several ways. The term "explorer" to describe Francis Drake is a bit of a euphemism. For me, the very image of Francis Drake is significant. In his place in history he is seen as a hero to the English and a Pirate to much of the rest of the world. He is to me a good example of how God can use all of us; our nobility and the not so noble, to inspire.

Literally the words fit our disposition at the time. But the words attributed to Francis Drake make that significant connection which reminded me at the time to keep some pastoral disposition even toward those who were pirating away with a treasure that had been built up with years of our work, not just mine, but the work of many in the congregation and the Episcopal Church Europe as well.

The year 2011 began as another hopeful year. However, the unresolved conflict and increasingly competitive undertones of the newly established Church of England congregation down the road made for uncertainty. I had, during 2009 and 2010 introduced alternative clergy to the congregation. One candidate seemed to me to be particularly promising as a successor. First, in his early 40's, he was young. He was also English. He was fluent in French. And he had the willingness to take on this part time paid position as vicar and work as a bi-vocational clergy teaching in Montpellier until such time as he could be fully supported by the congregation. As early as 2009 I had spoken with the bishop to ascertain if it was reasonable to encourage such a plan. The young English clergy had been well received by the congregation and it seemed that this would be a good fit. I had the impression that indeed it was. We were now at a point where hammering out the details was in order.

The congregation, being a mission church and considering the conflict, it was important to get some reading about how the congregation would accept a new vicar but there was no way in which they would hand pick a successor. Also, in Europe the options for clergy choices would be severely limited and there was no budget for a formal search process. These faults were built into the Church in Europe struggling with its own budget problems and priorities. I felt fortunate to have found a potential successor that appealed to the congregation, who wanted the job in spite of salary limitations and had an eagerness to prove he was up to the task. That he was English, was clearly a bonus.

I'll spare you the details of the new vicar's compensation package; In part, because this matter was between the bishop and the new clergy and was "a work in progress", changing along the way. I had done my best to initiate the transition from "free-retired" clergy to part-time paid clergy. The ground work had been laid with the congregation – those who remained at Grace Church. The specifics of the compensation package as a congregation with mission status were appropriate for the bishop to decide. I might add these decisions were also painful for him since there really was not sufficient money in the larger budget of the Episcopal Church Europe, to augment what the congregation could afford. Clearly the congregation could support some of the compensation but would need financial help from the bishop for a time.

More important or should I say more influential, there was a social dynamic underfoot that would undermine whatever compensation package, however it would be worked out – or not. Subterfuge was the prevailing determinant of what would happen in 2011. Yes, the discussion between the bishop and potential new vicar remained unresolved for too long but in the next few months events initiated by the new rival congregation were to overshadow any compensation discussion and plans for a new vicar.

Some basic church math may help to explain the situation. A small congregation, even of 40 people, with a financial commitment dedicated to the church of 2% of an average retirement income (both figures at the low end of a spectrum of possibilities) would more than supply a modest budget for part time clergy as had been described in Grace Church planning goals. This was not a financial endpoint but a financial beginning to grow from zero to part-time. The plan assumed continued growth which was reasonable given the history. Remaining united as one church was critical to the future of church growth.

I should note here that I refer to those who had broken away from Grace Church as "separated congregation" or "C of E congregation" because at this time they did not have an identified church name. This separated group eventually called themselves All Saints, an ironic choice, I thought.

In the early months of 2011 an English couple who had been attending Grace Church over the past two years became more active. I had seen them a few times while they were in the area, usually on vacation, as they approached their retirement. I now had the chance to get to know them more since they indicated that they had officially retired and were making their home permanently in the south of France. I was delighted to discover that the husband was a bi-vocational clergy like myself. He had just retired from his secular employment and he had, like me, been active and helpful as assisting clergy at church in his area near his home in England. I thought to myself, what a gift to us. When Linda and I met him and his wife I was clear that I was most happy to welcome him to celebrate Eucharist at Grace Church after he had some time to settle in. We had an open invitation for observers to attend any of the Bishop's committee meetings and his wife took us up on that, attending one of our routine meetings. I approached the bishop to encourage him to extend an offer to license him as clergy to officiate. And the young clergy candidate for new vicar did the same.

I also was candid about the recent past conflicts and the current division. He seemed no stranger to church conflict and indicated that he would do his best not to take a side. However, this proposed neutrality did not last and within four months he had been co-opted by the separated congregation as "their clergy".

Another English couple who had fist appeared on the scene in 2010 were among those who straddled the fence in this "tale of two churches". This couple were welcomed, as all were, but they played their cards close to the vest. Frankly, I became suspicious and early in 2011 my suspicions were confirmed. Julius and Ethel (not their real names) attended Grace Church but gradually were among those who attended both churches and then attended Grace church more for espionage purposes than for worship itself. They also lived in the same village as the newly retired bi-vocational clergy. In January of 2011 Julius and Ethel attended Grace Church but their real reason came clear after the service when they approached the Senior Warden of Grace Church and had an extended conversation. I was not privy to the conversation but noticed the involvement as I mingled with those attending the fellowship (coffee) hour. The attendance of Julius and Ethel and their conversation with the Senior Warden made more sense as events unfolded in the next few weeks.

Up to this point there had been considerable support for me by most of the members of Grace Church. People stepped up to fill vacancies and replace those who resigned in October 2009. Financial contributions increased to meet matching funds goals, and attendance levels recovered the losses of those few who left during the conflict. But in early 2011, with my departure on the Easter horizon, attacks from the separated group became more targeted and more personal. The uncertainties of future clergy leadership contributed to a decline in morale among the faithful. The voices of division became louder and more frequent from the group fostering division. It was amazing to me how successful an antagonist's strategy of repeating basic factual errors and unsubstantiated rumors could be on the morale of the faithful. It was as if things were said often enough they would become true.

Linda and I tried ostensibly to remain calm but frankly, we were on the alert in social settings. We were also aware that we would not let the social atmosphere shame us into seclusion. We were determined to maintain our social life unchanged. But at these events, it would be very much in character for someone to ask embarrassing or inappropriate questions at social events – the events were not necessarily church related but rather general social events attended by a mix of people that included members of both church congregations. We experienced a few cold shoulders and we admitted to each other that we would not be surprised to find our tires deflated or slashed when we returned to our parked car. I want to say that our car remained untouched, but the conversation was real between Linda and I. We lived sensing the possibility that the animosity could erupt in some petty crime, or aggression. It is the tone of the apprehension we lived with that I wish to convey. People were quite capable of being outright nasty in the most civilized of ways.

The spouse of the elderly retired clergy who had been a colleague to me for several years from the start up of the little congregation, was particularly vocal. On the surface she was a bit of a scatter-brain, but I came to realize that she was as sly as a fox. Wondering out-loud at one social event she recommended that I should move to England and take my ideas to one of their many struggling parishes if I wished to be paid and since I had lots of energy to develop a congregation she was sure that many a congregation would snap me up. Of course, she had completely over looked the fact that paying clergy was not a necessity for me but rather it was in the interest of the congregation's development - and basic fairness. However, said out-loud it would seem to any casual observer that I was the one seeking payment. Another person was to comment on how lovely our home was filled with beautiful antiques; and then go on to say that it was a clear sign that I did not need to be paid. Or, on two occasions of a meeting at a local side-walk café, persons with whom I was meeting expressed their concern, their voice rising above the ambient street noise, that my career would be ruined if I did not yield to the demands of this (separated) congregation. And, again returning to the elderly retired clergy's wife, on another occasion her husband stumbled at the curb as we left, she casually commented, "Well I suppose with a little nudge he could fall and break a hip… it would all be yours".

These nonchalant comments were like little trolls under the bridge at social gatherings by a few who had obviously honed their skills in this type of social sabotage. I had learned to let them roll off my back, but after a steady barrage they do take their toll.

I should say here that the most active in the subterfuge were but a handful. Most people were silent, and others shied away from the embarrassing moments. Some were openly supportive to me and Linda but not likely to confront their peers. But it was the vocal few who carried the day and the silent few would follow the most prominent voices under social pressure in the ex-pat group.

I attempted to stick to the facts; educate about the concordat, to urge unity to avoid the scandal to the larger community of separation and discord. In sermons where it was appropriate I pointed to illustrations in Acts of the Apostles and the Letters of Paul how conflict was inherent in the early church. Most of these were received silently and the behaviors did not change. I made an attempt to place facts before the congregation to counter the spread of innuendo or false accusation. But the conflict was not fact based.

I must admit that I began to have trouble making objective decisions. The effort was there but my ability to account for the outcome had been worn down. Try as I might, the strategy that assumed that people were interested in facts, in information, and objective data was losing ground to loud voices, baseless accusations and innuendo. At one point in a candid conversation with my bishop I expressed my exhaustion and said, "You know, after more than two years of managing this conflict, no matter how well or well-intended, one will eventually make a mistake. No one is infallible".

I present a few examples below as examples of this uncertainty. They were well intended. They might even have been advised in some situations, but I think they illustrate situations where an informed attempt to persuade people of the truth was clearly mismatched with their opposing strategy for which I had no name. To me it looked like tabloid journalism was winning the day. Facts no longer mattered. Emotions were high and exploited After January there was a rash of exaggerated reactions to three communiqués from me.

At one point there was a storm of emails. People had unfortunately now become accustomed to unauthorized use of the email distribution list for the congregation. There were numerous occasions where I tried simple short responses to outlandish accusations – noting for all that such emails were not being used appropriately, or in some cases trying to guide people to contact me personally, these often did not work. Longer emails which attempted to counter the errors point-by-point were also not very successful. In general, I find that dueling emails battle are seldom successful except for spreading mis-information to the masses most effectively and creating mounds of research to counter that information. In this case, I tried to use a prayer source, a favorite of mine from Compline, the church's official night prayer. It was my custom to use the prayer myself to remind me how evil cruises about seeking to destroy what is good. I sent it out to all in the group urging them to not be distracted, to stay focused on the good that we have. It was for me a way to offer a prayer that I often found helpful to regain equilibrium.

Le Petit Jardin de L'âme

The text of the prayer:

> *Be sober, be watchful. Your adversary the devil prowls around like a roaring lion, seeking someone to devour. Resist him steadfast, firm in your faith.*
> -From Peter chapter 5: 8-9a

To my surprise, one member, who had been attending Grace Church faithfully, had an unusual reaction. Like a thunder bolt he replied to my email, and added a copy to all from a source beyond my blind copy original, saying that I had identified him with Satan and he was deeply offended. Henceforth he would be taking his wife and daughter to attend the other church! Initially I was bewildered. I offered to meet with him and in that meeting discovered that he had a list of "grievances". Although he admitted that he himself had only been treated with kindness by me, but he had been fed stories of my offenses by someone from the other congregation. I spent my time responding to one absurdity after another but to no avail.

In February, the candidate for new vicar was scheduled to celebrate the Sunday Eucharist. This was all part of the preparation for normalizing his presence as part of the hoped-for plan. After looking at the scriptures appointed for the day, he suggested that I preach. I also thought it a good idea. The readings talked about the Law – Old law and New Commandment and the Spirit of the law: a common law, that if respected strengthens us – and makes us one - if ignored, separates us and pits us one against the other. To me it was an opportunity to apply these principles to our current conflict and specifically to respect the concordat which reflected how bishops of the world wide Anglican Communion had come, over time, to realize that competition between churches was not productive, and to my point, not how we should live out our Christian values. My hope was that perhaps we could have a cessation of hostilities and wait for the bishops to hand down a decision since it had been placed in their hands.

I reviewed the draft of the sermon with the candidate for vicar prior to the Sunday service. I was not asking for approval but rather for a second set of eyes to point out potential problems. He indicated that I was in a unique position to speak to the congregation because of my relationship with the congregation over the years. It would be difficult for him, as a new comer, to address these issues. And so, I believed that I was "cashing in" some of my relationship currency established over the years in the interest arming faithful members with some facts.

I include the text of this sermon in the appendix for your reference, gentle reader (Appendix VIII - Sermon 20 February 2011). It is not representative of my best, and perhaps I should not have even preached it. But I am certain that it was not offensive. It was specifically addressed to those who were still attending Grace Church but may find themselves faced with the dilemma caused by the separated congregation. It may have been something they did not want to hear, but it was not offensive. It was an attempt to make clear to all who might have heard differently, that there was a concordat between the Church of England and other parallel jurisdictions in Europe, and that the agreement was not being respected. More importantly there was a common law above all others that was not being followed. I wished to emphasize that the current efforts to divide this congregation was not only, not the solution, but left us all at the mercy of some "law of the Jungle". However, after that sermon I received two calls. Both used the content of that sermon – or what they thought they heard - as the reason they were going to leave Grace Church and join the separated church. I had, according to them, spoken unfairly about the other congregation. It seems that someone also contacted the bishop with their complaint. On one of his follow-up visits he asked me about the sermon. Fortunately, I had a complete document with the text to given him.

Another effort to place the facts in front of a growing line up of false accusations was to ask a colleague for his opinion. Was I (and was perhaps the bishop) misreading the intentions of the concordat? Since the C of E bishops seemed not to respect the agreement, was it unimportant? ... an inconvenience? Was there something else that I should know? ...some context that I had missed? My colleague's response was clear and firm. The actions of the separate group were a violation of the concordat. His response was succinct and helpful to me. So, I decided to copy its main points and distribute it to inform the larger congregation. It was clear that these were not my opinions alone. The response from one person was outrage. It was the type of Staged Rage described earlier, staged for an audience. The current Senior Warden who had last year stepped forward in support and positive leadership copied his response to all. He erroneously ascribed the content to the Bishop and accused me of being the bishop's pawn and that I am causing division. He was resigning!

What I did not realize at the time was that these responses were being choreographed from the sidelines. People were being goaded from behind the scenes, fed by a series of informal social gatherings. My eventual departure as it was known since my announcement in December was a form of license to some to use me for any reason that suited their purpose. A firm plan for succession had not been finalized, and members of the separated congregation were making the most of a perceived vacuum. In addition to some normal anger that comes from the anticipated loss of my departure, this had been stoked, inflamed and coached. Since I had announced my departure, any loyalty to me that had held people together had lost most of its effectiveness.

In February the bishop attended our annual meeting and the meeting agenda was modified to attempt to meet with the entire congregation of Grace Church and those who had separated. His hope, like mine, was to find some common ground to unify. He made several trips but one such meeting stands out. After an earlier overt rejection of his offer to meet, a few members of the other congregation decided to attend. This meeting was held in my home as the living room was large enough to hold all potential attendees. By now the usual complaints and rationale for the separation had been addressed more than once to no avail. At one point in the discussion Julius, identified as a member of the separated congregation stood up and asked to read a letter which he said represented the feelings of his congregation. After a perfunctory thank you to me for my service he segued into his main point. He proposed that Grace Church be shut down and that all who wished to attend church were welcomed to attend their newly established church. To my amazement, the senior Warden of Grace Church nodded his head in agreement!

This was a sample of the audacity of group but was it also a shift in strategy. This was no longer a small group of disaffected people who had a beef with the vicar (me) and wanted a different style of churchmanship or leadership. There was no effort to resolve or unite. They were intent by their strife to destroy the original church. In retrospect I think it not too much of a leap to understand what that conversation was about in January. Julius and Ethel, while attending Grace Church Sunday worship in January, used the time to call the Grace Church Senior Warden aside and discuss plans of subversion. No longer was the separated congregation satisfied to set up a separate congregation. They were now on course to desolate Grace Church.

In some attempt to intellectualize this experience and distance myself from the experience, the mimetic theory of René Girad came to mind and the theology of scapegoating. But in this I would be swimming alone and in a stream of thought that was beyond many even in the best of circumstances. Applicable as this view was, it was too far removed, too academic. People had proven themselves unmoved by facts, and theoretical analysis was too far removed for this situation and these people. This battle was to be fought on the field of expediency, following rules of engagement learned in school yard skirmishes.

The outspoken wife of the elderly retired Church of England clergy commented, that if Grace Church was uncomfortable with the proximity of the newly establish (separated) congregation, then it was Grace Church that should move, perhaps to Montpellier (about 50kms away)

It must be said that the intensities noted above were the expressions still of a few. What was noticeable was that the outbursts were evidence of conversations and activities that were happening informally and had the effect of stirring people up. The vocal few were growing – one here, one there. But more important those who wished for the conflict to just go away were subjected to continuous upset. Growing in number were the silent members, many English expats, under the pressure of social conformity to change sides and some just stopped going to any church.

At this time my mind had moved to the tasks of closure of ministry and administration related to Grace Church. My departure date had been set as Easter. So, there were worship services to prepare through that date. Resting more heavily on my mind was the passing on of administration related to the Association Loi, for which, as president, I was responsible and needed to make a transition of those legal responsibilities as required by the Récépissé de Declaration de Modification of the Association Loi. Happily, someone again stepped forward since both the Senior Warden and the treasurer, Simon Peter, now decided to join their English expats at the other church.

We created a plan with the Bishop as president, and a faithful Grace Church member as treasurer and secretary and one more member to make the minimum requirement. In my penchant for informed and smooth transitions there were documents to download and files to be updated, and then passed on along with my availability for consultation as needed for a few months.

The plate of troubles at Grace Church was not yet full enough – that another event came to disturb us. On 31 March, about two weeks before Palm Sunday, I received a call from the pastor of the Roman Catholic Church responsible for parishes in the area. He was calling to tell me that three teen vandals have broken into the little church at Conas that our congregation had been using for Sunday worship. A fire had been set and the church was not usable. The pastor and Archbishop assured me that they would find an alternative church for our use as soon as possible. Holy week, one of the busiest times of the year as quickly approaching but they were successful in providing a nearby church for our use.

Le Petit Jardin de L'âme

In spite of the shuffling about and the changes required for advance publicity of the re-located church service, the intended new vicar celebrated the Palm Sunday services to a good attendance (39). Six members of the separated congregation attended, perhaps out of curiosity and an additional three members from the local village who had generously offered their church for our use after the theft and fire at the little church in Conas.

I celebrated the remaining worship services for Holy Week and Easter, and to the untrained eye it all looked much like previous years. Attendance was near normal-attendance. Maundy Thursday, and Good Friday attendance was sparse but that too was normal. And Easter Sunday was 40; perhaps a few more I lost track.

I created these services still thinking that the plans for my successor would be worked out. In fact, so sure we were of his eventual arrival that we discussed receiving his moving boxes temporarily at our home and then making a move to his eventual apartment in Montpellier.

In early May I was told that a group (from both church congregations) wished to host a "farewell luncheon". I dreaded it. I am not good at these affairs but most of all I dreaded having to come face to face with the hypocrisy of some of the instigators of the conflict. Although promoted as an action from both congregations, it was in fact some vague attempt at atonement by those who had now joined the separatist group but felt a bit guilty. Some key members of Grace church faithful were not in attendance, not because they did not wish me well, but because they could see through the hypocrisy. Certainly, there were some unsuspecting souls for whom this luncheon would be a gesture of goodwill and bon-voyage, so I focused on those. But through the fond farewell gestures, and the going away gift, it was hard not to feel that some had come only to be certain that I was in fact leaving.

It is difficult in these situations to look out over the gathering and realize the diversity of intentions of those attending. There were some genuinely grateful, and there were those saddened that the conflict had taken its toll, there were also Pharisees in the crowd.

I must admit that since I felt obliged to attend I decided I would make it an opportunity for one more clarification. At the time of my brief "Thank You" speech I made it clear that while I had retired as vicar of Grace Church, plans had already begun in preparation for the Annual Lessons and Carols service scheduled for December. I explained that this was because it would be difficult for a yet unnamed replacement to take up this task on short notice. That was one part of the reality. A second unspoken reality was that I could sense the separated congregation chomping at the bit to take over this aspect of local church life as well and claim it as its own.

In fact, I had already contacted the organist, since Christmas was a busy time of year for her, to assure her that she would be needed and that although there would be a new celebrant, I assured her that she would be paid. I had already been approached by a second choral group and wished to find a way to include them but not step on the original choral group's toes. And because of the loss of some of the members of the planning group to the separated church I had searched out replacements. The role of celebrant usually taken by me could be turned over relatively easily, but the planning was more complicated and time consuming.

In the months that followed Easter, an extensive dossier was prepared by the bishop's staff with my assistance to document the "Tale of Two Churches" the separation of one church (since March 2010) from the original Grace Church. It would be clear from routine documentation that the various arguments given by the separated group for their actions had no basis in fact. But it would be a difficult, that is, sensitive document to write.

Some people had justified the coup on ground that it was necessary to rescue the congregation from a "Control Freak", an autocrat, who was telling them how much they needed to give.

The documentation would show that this view was not a reflection of the style of leadership they actually experienced but rather the style of choice of those leading the coup.

Let us ignore for the moment the fact that if such a "rescue "were necessary in the Anglican /Episcopal Canons and mission congregations, would be the prerogative of the bishop not individuals of the congregation.

Some objected that "Too much money was spent on the Order of Worship". The same worship and general format that attracted many, had become intolerable precisely because more kept coming. The liturgy that fostered growth became a target because it was the source (along with the clergy's style) of growth when the original few members saw their influence shrinking – diluted by new members. The actual cost of the worship was irrelevant (although it did grow some through cost for materials) it became a smaller and smaller percentage of the larger budget. The format of the printed worship booklet was the target of criticism – for printing of music and congregational participation which some found to "be the same from one month to the next", when in fact seasonal changes and printed texts were printed so that anyone attending for the first time would find it easy to follow and the rhythm of the worship would not be sacrificed to page flipping or searching for different books in the pew. Comments of quality of the worship far outweighed criticism. Often people were positively affected by the way the liturgy was organized and presented in ways which were subtle and often subconscious.

Some put forward that they felt "Coercion" about "making them Episcopalians" but the documentation would show that the identity of the congregation, indicated by its name was as Anglican and Episcopal, evolved over time. The identity of this congregation was shaped through information and education – not coerced – into a reflection of the larger Anglican Tradition – not specifically Episcopalian. Intentionally sources were used from the Episcopal Church USA, Anglican Church of Canada, Church of England and broader Anglican Churches in Wales, Ireland and Scotland. The churchmanship was decidedly Anglican in a broad sense. That it was not Church of England in its narrow sense was seen by some as problematic.

The supposed desire of the separated group to be Church of England was pretentious. Originally the group did not want to belong to any larger church. The C of E connection was now simply a convenient connection because the clergy in the wings were CofE and would not have been able to function if they in fact were not affiliated with the CofE. The Attachment to the CofE became a necessity by the separated group rather than a reflection of their identity.

But the most convincing argument was the one which would have to be approached most delicately. Having done the ground work and growing a successful congregation from nothing, having shown what could be done, the English members of the congregation wanted this with a C of E label on it. They were not satisfied with the broader identification of members of the Worldwide Anglican Communion, it had to be English. While there were a number of English members of the original congregation, not all were C of E and there were other English-speaking church backgrounds represented in the original congregation. Grace Church was not simply an English Church lead by and American.

In fact, in the initial stages of establishing their own identity and creation of their web page, the separated congregation called themselves The English Church.

Val J. Littman

The leaders of separation were an extension of some desperate, perhaps unconscious, grasp of imperialism in an age where England was no longer the great Empire and was itself becoming "little England" not Great Britannia. Related to this sensitive issue was a mind-set that England had a right to be on the Continent (Specifically France) and the USA, and any other country, were simply interlopers. Grace Church as an Anglican Episcopal Church in the Herault was not sufficient for them. Like an outdated form of colonialism, the hard work had now been done, labor and financial resources and resources of support were given by the Episcopal Church in Europe and now that the field had been cleared and plowed and the crop planted, the C of E wanted the harvest.

It was an extensive document which clearly showed the evolution of a small informal house church into a moderate sized congregation and the development of local governance according to church canons with the involvement of lay leadership and Episcopal oversight. It showed the education and discernment process guided by the local clergy and the involvement of laity through meetings, discussions and documented their vote to request mission church status in the Episcopal Church. It also documented the violation of the COABICE Concordat (The College of Anglican Bishops in Continental Europe) and resolution 63 of 1968 Lambeth. The dossier included many of the records of the conflict extending from late 2009, 2010 and early 2011. Original documents, Email correspondence and meetings of preparation and the signed petitions of the congregation to become a mission church etc were readily available in the church files as well as copies of email subterfuge of attempts to resolve the conflict.

I am certain that the dossier in its final form, created by the bishop's staff was worded as diplomatically as possible. But I am also confident because of the process of our work together that the issues described above were represented and presented to the Presiding Bishop of the Episcopal Church (In July, I believe). It was intended to shape discussion between the Presiding Bishop and the Archbishop of Canterbury.

I did not see the completed dossier, but I believe the bishop's office when I was told it was given to the presiding bishop. Nothing happened as far as I know. In some ways I was surprised to think that this local squabble was to find its way to their desks. But it was the logical chain of authority given that my bishop had not found satisfaction from the bishop of the C of E.

While the decision remained in the hands of the bishops, Sunday services continued through a series of supply clergy. Linda and I did not attend

Le Petit Jardin de L'âme

Sunday services at Grace Church because we felt it was important that I be truly "gone". Although our home had been placed on the real estate market, we did not have a firm departure date for the Republic of Panamá until we had an offer to buy our home in France. It was generally agreed by me, the Bishop and his staff that a planned absence might help the transition process. It also removed me as the target of criticism by the separated Congregation. Linda and I continued to support Grace Church financially and "behind the scenes" I worked in cooperation with the new lay leader, walking her through FAQs and administration details.

In early August I received a letter from a self-appointed committee of "The Fontès Carol Service" this new committee had changed the name from the traditional Festival of Nine Lessons and Carols. This change in itself was a message that Lourdes was involved. After an opening expression of gratitude for leadership and services for the past nine years, the newly formed "committee" announced that they were taking over control of the Traditional Service of Lessons and Carols held at Fontès. Like other decisions there had been no previous consultation on this matter, either with me or with the new leadership of Grace church. And no acknowledgement that the usual preliminary plans for organizing the service may have already been made. Clergy aligned with the separated church were conspicuously absent from the signatures.

The Bishop came to Grace Church to celebrate the 3rd Sunday of August and assess the situation, including the possibility of expanding Grace church to include development of a congregation in Montpellier. By now everyone was exhausted of this conflict. In response to my assertions that there were reasons for Grace Church to maintain its place as the organizing group for the Lessons and Carols service, the bishop advised me "just let it go". I did. It was for me the moment when I let the feelings of defeat enter in. The names of the new committee members read like a list of enemies that I had collected over the years, having one-by-one assembled themselves into a vengeful cohort of retribution.

I had not – until now - allowed myself to feel that this conflict was some win / loose battle. It was for me a resolvable challenge, and a positive outcome surely would be negotiated. I had not seen this in terms of the victorious and the defeated. And I certainly had not - until now - felt defeated. Until now, so much of this was text book organizational development and community organization. It was difficult yes, and frustrating and depressing but somehow it was on the sad end of a "normal" continuum of pastoral shepherding But now, there it was. They were announcing their victory and the traditional lessons and Carols service (now called Fontes Carols service – eliminating the links to the historic tradition from its name) would be their victory dance.

In October, the long tentative plan to make the young bi-vocational clergy, Vicar of Grace church began to materialize. Plans were for him to begin in November. The budget was thin and, worst case scenario, the budget may last only six months. But the bishop continued to seek funding for Mission development in general and the plan is for Grace to be the immediate beneficiary of that funding at this time.

As late as November the presumptive new vicar was apartment hunting in Montpellier, and scheduled his first worship service for the third Sunday of November at the new location in Nezignan l'Eveque on loan to us after the vandalism and fire at the original church building in nearby Conas. The vicar's initial contacts with the newly retired clergy who had sided with the separated church indicated that he planned to invite him to participate in the Lessons and Carols service at Fontes. And that there was a hope expressed by the newly retired clergy that the separated congregation would not schedule competing Christmas Eve services this year at the same time as Grace church - as they had done last year.

So, we thought we were to end the year with an "up-hill financial battle", an unresolved cross-jurisdictional battle in the hands of the bishops, and still a glimmer of hope for Grace Church.

This cautiously optimistic scenario changed considerably as a result of a meeting between the bishop, his staff and the prospective new vicar. It now appeared that he would not be coming to Grace church as vicar after all. At the late date of 13 Nov 2011, it not only was uncertain who may come as vicar, but it remained uncertain as to whether there will be Grace church representation at the annual Lesson and Carols (Dec 11), or a Christmas eve service at Nezignan l'Eveque. I could have interjected myself into filling any of these roles, but having "let it go" at the bishop's request, I indeed did let it go.

This late change also made it difficult to change advance publication information about both the Lessons and Carols Service and Christmas Services. In the case of the former, others were now in charge and such details as date, place and time remained the same as in previous years. However, in the case of the later this uncertainty would impact potential attendance because of the change of location from previous years due to the fire. I was officially free of this management nightmare, but I could clearly see how it would send confusing messages to the larger community-

Le Petit Jardin de L'âme

all of which affected attendance and did not project confidence or consistency to the broader community.

A meeting was scheduled between my bishop and the bishop representing the Church of England in the region for 05 December. The topic was to be "The Tale of Two Churches" as it had come to be called; Grace Church and the newly separated church at the village of St Pargoire here in the Hérault. It also was to include discussion of another area where a Church of England congregation near Brussels wished to change its jurisdictional alignment from C of E to the Episcopal Church. In this later case it seems that the Church near Brussels was following a protocol for making this change and had not split apart by conflict. In recent years, in that situation, the Episcopal Church had provided clergy to this Belgian congregation, in the absence of C of E clergy. That congregation had begun a process of inquiry and discernment about their future and decided to make the change. Their orderly process only made it clearer to me how destructive the approach of the separated church group was in our local situation, and how complicit the bishop of the C of E was in their action that was to tear apart Grace Church.

It comes to light that on the jurisdictional chess board the story of "The Tale of Two Churches" was not just a story of two churches in the South of France. It was not unique. It was, as it turns out, a story of how overlapping church jurisdictions in the Anglican Communion affect the local church. There was an orderly way to do things and a destructive way. Grace Church was suffering through the destructive format. In the bigger picture, both scenarios confirm that maintaining overlapping church jurisdictions – that archived church documents have advised against since the late 1800's - lives on to impair the contemporary church and its congregations.

This history above has attempted a certain objectivity and recording events as a participant-observer. I cannot say that I have been 100% successful. I did live through it and was involved in this history as a founder and vicar of Grace church. I do believe that an attempt at a certain objectivity makes this history useful and not overly (or uselessly) subjective. But in fact, in the lives of the congregation and the life of the larger community who observed this breech it is ultimately subjective, each taking away the affects of the conflict on their lives. It is my hope that I have been able to document what happened in the life of one mission congregation that began as a result of responding to those who asked for worship services in English. Together we built a lively mission congregation – with Sunday services, charity outreach, Adult Education, Training of lay worship leaders, a prayer group and an average Sunday attendance of 33 until the time of Easter 2011. I lived to see the congregation enjoy the luxury of conflict, to see ecclesial authorities themselves undercut one another, and enable a destructive process; to see persons' best of intentions out-witted by lies, errors and ignorance.

I learned of the deceptions that led to the founding of a separated congregation. And I have experienced the futility of, reason and fact as an effective response to these deceptions. I do feel that I "hung in there" long past my "expiration date". Is persistent hope a close relative to destructive enablement?

No matter, in the end there would be two struggling congregations in the south of France. One of these congregations may eventually out-grow the deception that was at its foundation. Perhaps in time a new generation of that congregation will come who were not part of the coup. What will they learn of the foundations of their church? There is always the possibility that the history of their founding will be re-written in some alternative truth. It is a somehow necessary for survival to create a history that is palatable.

It is necessary to look at these events with some touch of divine vision; deep, and broad; allowing for time and wisdom to put them into new perspective. But, telling the story like it is (or was, in its time) is an important part of telling the long-term truth. Because all things will evolve, it is important to get the facts as best we can capture them in their present moments.

During the writing of this work, I happened upon a video of President Obama's speech at the Journalism Awards Dinner of March 2016 here is what I heard. ... *"When our elected officials and our political campaigns become entirely untethered to reason and facts and analysis, when it doesn't matter what's true and what's not, that makes it all but impossible for us to make good decisions on behalf of future generations,..."*. I heard in his words, an undeniable truth about our experience in France.

The rise of "Fake News," "Alternative facts" and faux logic to replace inconvenient truths has given me a new set of descriptors for the events we experienced before these terms were so fashionable.

Grace Church did re-locate to the metropolitan area of Montpellier and start again with a token membership and determined spirit. Although the move to Montpellier echoed the wishes of the wife of the elder retired C of E clergyman, it was a practical decision and not one following her dictates. The strongest members of the remnant church lived in Montpellier, and the city offered demographics which favored long term growth. Eventually it was self-evident that the move to Montpellier was a practical move. I sometimes wonder what form that history will take. It could be important to include these early chapters in their collective memory, for there will be future conflicts rest assured.

Chapter 21
Moments of reflection and perspective

There may be those among you, gentle readers, who have found my concern about a divided congregation to be misplaced, or exaggerated. After all, why cannot a group of people with a different set of opinions just go and set up another church to their liking down the road. There are a number of churches co-existing in cities and villages in many places. No big deal. In fact, there were two other church groups developed in the area during the time frame covered in this book. One was comprised of a small group of people who wished for no denomination affiliation, no formal liturgical structure and no ordained clergy. Another had the support of an international organization with an evangelical "free church" style. Both churches were English-speaking, and had members who attended Grace Church regularly and leadership with whom I met on occasion. Both of these churches maintained their congregations without diminishing Grace Church. They were of different denominations, had different theologies, different church traditions. We lived in mutual respect.

So, there are occasions where establishing a second church in close proximity might make sense; In the case of different denominations. Other situations, perhaps those with varied and abundant demographics would pose a good argument for a variety of churches. Some, from the separated church, to bolster their argument, even argued that this is a common practice in the UK. But the separation of this congregation was not due to any of these. And as we now have seen, establishing a second church down the road is considerably different when it is coupled with the overt call to close the original church.

The Church of England and The Episcopal Church are part of the same Anglican Communion. With the limited demographics of this expat congregation it was certain that if two of the same churches co-existed both would struggle financially, and compete for members. More importantly, this separation is a testament to unresolved conflict. The separation is also a witness to disregard for an official church agreement. And in this case the establishment of the separated congregation was made possible by distortion and deception. This is a scandal to the larger community.

If I were a younger clergy, dependent on a congregation for my income this situation would have been devastating to me personally. As it was the loss of a financial base sabotaged the three-year goals and plans for growth for Grace Church, it also significantly affected plans for future clergy, but it made no difference in my ability to earn a living since I was retired.

I am reminded again of the metaphor from Jonathan Haidt's book <u>The Happiness Hypothesis</u> mentioned in my earlier chapter on The State of Depression and The State of France. Here I was again riding that elephant. No matter how skilled the rider, me in this incident, or bishops in their respective sees, the basic reality of unresolved problems of the church structure in Europe has a life of its own. While there remain two competing church jurisdictions the life of the church in Europe will suffer. When a second church is established in this instance it is not a witness to the growth of the Gospel, it is a shame. The rider can ride the course as skillfully as possible but ultimately the course is determined by the elephant. I was fortunate to be able to dis-mount.

The above does not adequately considered the impact of the separation on morale and spiritual life of the congregation. Separated jurisdictions imply unresolved differences; an inability to come together as one. In simple terms the separated congregation soothed itself with an image that all from the original congregation would be served by the new church. But, it left a path of destruction behind it. I know of people who stopped attending church because of the unresolved conflict. I do not mention those who might have come as visitors (as many did in the earlier years) but were turned off by the scandal and "bad vibes" sensed in the larger community. Or simply did not know where to go because the familiar forms of publicity just stopped. Some others attended the local Roman Catholic Church, some attended one of the two churches mentioned above. A few continued to hobble along and took the significantly reduced church to the large metropolitan area of Montpellier (45 minutes drive) in the hope of reviving the church with new blood from the metropolitan area.

My greatest sadness was not whatever people may have said or thought about me – although it hurt. I was reasonably confident that I had done my best. My great sadness was to witness a willfulness, a spitefulness that was set on destruction, much like I imagine a parent who sees their adolescent heading down a destructive path and sensing their shrinking parental limitations can only watch as the elephant choses to go on a path of danger.

Still, thank God, we had some friends. Our closest friends who were not church-goers kept a diplomatic silence about church affairs. In our relationship with two couples, a bit older than ourselves, we found an oasis. Interesting to me, neither couple found traditional religion a satisfactory expression for their view, but all were spiritual persons each in different ways. They shared a rich spiritual outlook on life but were not traditional "church-goers". It was with these two couples in France that we shared our special moments. Linda and I chose from the beginning not to debrief or process the affairs of Church life. For me it was both an embarrassment that people were behaving the way they were but more importantly there was no need to scandalize our best friends with the behaviors of church-folk.

Thanksgiving Dinner with friends, 2011, was a little window into our life:

> I begin this little note on the eve of Thanksgiving 2011. Because of Linda's eye doctor appointment tomorrow (one she has waited for, for six months we decided to hold Thanksgiving on the Eve of Thanksgiving Day with our close friends.
>
> As we prepare and eat our Thanksgiving dinner I was taken by the amount of "tradition" that is present and unspoken in our dinnerware. It is a lovely passing of tradition from times past to times present and I write this so that perhaps it might pass to some future time, eventually.
>
> I write this note as we have finished the clean up after the big meal. It makes me so aware of so many things and people for which to give thanks.
>
> For many years my mother had a prayer framed above her kitchen sink. It read:
>
> *Thank God for dirty dishes;*
> *They have a tale to tell.*
> *While others may go hungry,*
> *We're eating very well*
> *With home and health, and happiness,*
> *I shouldn't want to fuss;*
> *For by this stack of evidence,*
> *God's been very good to us.*
>
> By local standards ours is an elegant table setting.
>
> Our elegant table setting is a collection of gifts from friends and family along the way and over thirty years of marriage. As such it represents something of our life. It also reminds us to be careful stewards of what has been given to us.

This evening we were among friends and at ease. It makes the use of these family heirlooms easy and comfortable, and all the more they are in their rightful place to serve their original purpose and make a joyful ambiance.

The aperos (or aperitif): The Champaign glasses we used are crystal that we acquired during our "' Chicago days" Yes, the crystal makes a nice ringing tone as they "clink". They are not extraordinary, but they look very classy. The tray of hors d'oeuvres looks wonderful: a rectangular silver plate on copper and purchased during our Chicago period from an antique warehouse, again lovely when polished for special occasions but not "museum quality". It holds a bright assortment of treats: large green olives stuffed with manchego cheese, others stuffed with tiny rolled smoked ham, radishes carefully cut by Linda into little flowers, and cocktail tomatoes. There is nothing too exotic, but it shows care and an eye to color and presentation.

When we move to the table, it is filled with memories even before we begin the meal:

The table is set with silver ware from our Chicago life a pattern "coronation" that Linda likes, and was purchased from an estate sale in Chicago.

On the table are two footed, over-sized glass goblets with broad gold trim. These are inherited from my aunt by way of my mom. I believe they are actually "grapefruit" goblets. But this evening they serve to hold the cranberry compote – one for each end of the table since the compote has proven to be a very tasty and popular dish.

Wine and water glasses are a mix of Bohemian crystal – some a gift from my old Roman Catholic days at Our Lady of Victory Basilica, Lackawanna (Buffalo) from the organist and housekeeper at Our Lady of Victory in Lackawanna, NY. Actually, the house keeper / organist and I were arch-rivals at times in the area of music and liturgy (she very traditional and I was, at the time rather contemporary – well for the 1970's) but we respected each other's territory and got along. Even our stem ware tells a story. Additionally, an assortment of stem ware; some Fostoria inherited from mom, some purchase just because it looked pretty, all come together as pleasing to the eye.

The Turkey is served on a platter, which we purchased at Pier One in Chicago. The platter was big and cheap and has served us very well over many years. It also reminds me of our earlier years when our pocket-book was a little shallow. It looks much more impressive than its price would indicate.

Next to it, sits a covered compote which is expensive, and holds the vegetables. The covered compote is a lovely Limoges dish – a gift from friends many Christmases ago. It is a classic. And the antique silver serving spoon from my mom is both functional and elegant. We had the spoon re-plated when we were in Chicago it is a stunning piece and makes serving vegetables a sensational delight – the handle just feels good and it works so well for the task for which it was created.

Over the years we have acquired more than enough silver serving pieces, our favorite carving set was purchased in Paris at an antique silver store on rue des Francs-Bourgeois, just outside la Place des Vosges. I am always a little afraid that someday the bone handles on the knife and fork will break, but it has the best carving blade I have ever used   A second set of silver plate purchased here in France is from the early 1900's. Its lines are simple, but it is large in size and weighty.

Our plates are again a collection of gifts from friends and our own purchases over the years: The Killmans gave us the Haviland Limoges French dinner plates for Christmas one year, the square Long Champ side plates from Colmar France are signed and purchased locally in Pézenas, salad plates look lovely but are of unknown origin from a local flea market.

Not all of our treasures can be displayed on a single occasion. But even those closeted in the armoire remind us of their beauty as we set the table or tidy-up afterward. We have not used our most expensive Theodore Haviland Limoges oyster plates, but they are lovely to look at and testify to a mix-and-match kind of diversity which tells something of ourselves as well the table setting. We have an abundance of miscellaneous crystal cut glass serving dishes, and painted porcelain china. Each has a memory to call to mind as well as a practical function to fulfill.

All this is to say that beyond the menu itself we enjoy the feast for the eyes that a lovely table setting provides. Our friends seem to enjoy the experience. Since living in France, we have learned to be a bit more discrete about those whom we invite. It is a shame that the sting from those who used generous hospitality against us raises its head once in awhile like and annoying bug bite at a picnic. But I am aware that most people, most of the time, respond to generosity with thankfulness.

As December rolled around it was clear that we would not be attending the annual Lessons and Carols Service. I decorated the house for Christmas since we did not yet have a buyer and besides imparting some holiday spirit for us I thought the house decorated for Christmas might be even that much more attractive for prospective buyers if they came looking. But it would seem strange not to attend service at Christmas (or Christmas eve).

I knew that we would be most welcome at Grace Church, in its temporary location since the fire of March. I did not want to confuse matters by offering to be the celebrant although I did not know if one had been found. The new lay leader of Grace Church contacted me to say, "Thank You" for our offering to cover the costs of a professional organist for the service and to confirm that Bishop Mutigawa (retired Bishop from Rwanda currently living in Strasburg) was to be the celebrant. Linda and I offered to provide some Mulled wine for refreshments after the service and we planned to attend as members of the congregation.

Finding temporary clergy for Grace Church was to be a month-to-month task for the lay leader. I remember upon hearing that Bishop Mutigawa would be the celebrant at worship for Christmas, I thought it was such a fitting choice. Perhaps the fitness of the choice would go unappreciated by those who did not know his background, and even I was not sure that I understood fully his history but what I knew (or thought I knew) was so right for this remnant congregation.

Briefly: The Rt Reverend Venutse Mutigawa as Bishop of Rwanda was one a few African bishops of the Province of Anglican Church of Rwanda who chose to attend the Lambeth Conference of 2008. His attendance was part political and part theological since most of the bishops from his province were to boycott Lambeth 2008 as part of the dispute between the Global South Anglican Theological Realignment, and the larger Anglican Communion regarding issues to be discussed at the Lambeth Conference. In part, the area of dispute was the area of sexuality; ordination of an openly gay man as bishop in the USA, and church jurisdiction issues;

intrusions of bishops from the Global South into areas of The Episcopal Church USA. The cross jurisdictional issues of the Global South in the Episcopal Church USA were, on a grand scale, much like the cross-jurisdictional issues that have impacted our little congregation in the South of France. The intrusion of the Global South into areas of Episcopal Church USA gave Episcopal Church congregations a choice to divide and set up competing churches rather than work through these disagreements to come together.

Bishop Mutigawa returned from the Lambeth Conference, a causality of this dispute, to discover that he was being "retired". In his retirement Bishop Mutigawa came to France and supported himself by taking up a janitorial position in Strasburg.

I cannot claim that this brief biographic snapshot does the story 100% justice since the technicalities of the political and theological disagreement would require much more elaboration beyond the scope of this book. However, they are accurate enough to convey how I came to feel that Bishop Mutigawa was so appropriate as a celebrant for this congregation on this special night. To me, here was a man who chose to show his solidarity with the larger Anglican Communion of Churches, rather than to choose separation. Here was a man who came from another area of the World Wide Anglican Communion where cross jurisdictional issues have caused great pain for the church as a whole. Here was a humble man come to celebrate a humble birth.

Attendance at the Christmas eve service was around 20 as I remember. Music from the organ filled the church even if the people did not. But more disappointing than low turnout was the presence of one couple, Ethel and Julius, referred to in the Chapter above; 2011 - Disturb Us Lord. In my heart I tried to interpret their attendance as positive, perhaps they came in support, but in my head, I knew that they were attending to "snoop" and report to the separated group. Julius' reading of the letter at the February meeting in which he requested the closing of Grace Church stuck in my head. They were but a moment's distraction as I turned to listen to the reading of the Gospel.

Bishop Mutigawa's reading of the gospel was touching. His English was heavy with a Rwandan-French accent. His slight body was a bit frail and cautious-looking. As he read the scripture narrative about the birth of Jesus and the shepherds he was more telling of the story from memory than reading it. And as the shepherds approached the manger so did he walk up the center aisle and approach the Christmas crèche. It was simply beautiful and sincere. And it was perhaps a good way for 2011 to come to an end — with a small hope and much humility.

Chapter 22
2012

"All changes, even the most longed for, have their melancholy;
for what we leave behind us is a part of ourselves;
we must die to one life before we can enter another."
-Anatole France - Crime of Sylvestre Bonnard 1881

It would be nearly a full year before we would actually move From France to Panama. During that year I maintained my relationship with The Episcopal Church Europe. I completed my term on the Council of Advice, worked with the bishop's staff to create a mission congregation festival in Baden Baden for small churches of the Convocation of Episcopal Churches in Europe, and presented a closing report of my observations as Chair of Mission Congregations on the state of our Mission Churches. Linda and I attended the Annual Convention of The Episcopal Church Europe held in Florence Italy in 2012. It was good for me to see the new lay leadership of the embattled Grace Church feel comfortable and conscientiously work at establishing new relationships in the larger Church community. I was hopeful. In addition to words of thanks from the President of the Council of Advice, I received a Bishop's Award for service. There were a few tears and lots of joy and The Bishop himself presented the award with an impromptu chorus of the 1980's Van Halen's "Panama". And afterwards at our table he admitted an oversight; that perhaps the award should have gone to both Linda and I, knowing well the value of a clergy spouse.

We were not unsettled by the length of time it would take to sell our home here in France. It gave us time to visit Paris once again, Bruxelles for the first time, and entertain a few guests that had fallen off our social network during the busy and tense past two years of conflict between Grace church and the splinter group at St Pargoire.

Time also gave us some space to heal from the sniper attacks and the assaults and the lies that came with the struggle of what I have come to call "the remnants of English imperialism". We appreciated the recovery time and time to enjoy our home in peace and quiet.

Some days the "ghosts" of France past come to me as sound-bites. They rear their heads unbidden in my mind. It is difficult, for example to consider our next purchase and the inevitable renovation/ decoration projects without thinking of the earliest chicanery we experienced in our first years of life in France. How will we be able to avoid being taken advantage of as foreigners once again in our new adopted home? And then there are thorns that stick in my craw, from hateful comments during the church conflict. We had joyfully opened our home and our lives to a group of people for meals, for worship, for education events, for planning meetings, many of which we enjoyed fully. But a cacophony of catty comments rises up sometimes like nails scraping across a chalk-board. Their social sniping and staged outrage echoes in my brain. I know that such things fade away in time. But like stubborn stains of wine on white linen, efforts to remove repeated stains result in some deterioration of the basic fabric, wearing away at the woof and warp.

The quiet in our home was a good place to recover, and re-align with each other. During this time-in-between we make the internal adjustments necessary to move on.

On, 23 July, we had two showings scheduled – one from the realtor we had contracted with nearly a year and half ago and another one with a new realtor with whom we signed a contract only days before (a common practice since there is no cooperative multiple listing service). For a brief moment I entertained the hope that we might at last have two interested parties bidding for the house – Now wouldn't that have made it worth the wait?

It seems a couple from Norway had done preliminary research months ago and came expecting to like what they had seen on the web. We met only briefly as we let them in to be shown the house by our realtor while we went for a walk around the village of Florensac to give them private time. Upon our return after a bit more than 30 minutes they were still inside talking – so we took another tour and made our selves scarce to let them enjoy the house longer.

When at last, from our park bench, we could see that they had left the house we started to return. Our hearts dropped momentarily when we saw them meet a different realtor (as is often the case in France) who was taking them to another house for sale in the village.

It was only little more than an hour later that our realtor called to say that the couple did not care for the second house they saw but that they had fallen in love with our house and were considering an offer. We spent the day and the next day doing some "back-and–forth" to settle on the specifics of a contract. The buyer's offer was a solid one – but we countered to see if we could get closer to our asking price. They met our counter-offer at a half way point and we were pleased with the outcome. The realtor also reduced his commission a bit so that we could reach our financial desired outcome.

Then the interminable waiting begins. Even though the principles have all agreed verbally – on price terms and commissions for realtors the document must be drawn up, then translated into their first language, and then signed by them and then sent to us for signatures. Even after signatures there is a seven-day waiting period in which they might reconsider. That is the place where we are at the moment. I wait for the ink to dry and for the "fat lady to sing."

We signed the compromis de vente – the promise to purchase. The terms seemed normal with no special liens or requirements. The down payment arrived 01 September and we could feel that we have a commitment secured. Linda and I began our plans for a House search of our own in Panama. And the gradual process of letting people know that we have a buyer and a closing date (set for 27 November) The pace of activity directed to the move picked up and we have an end point – a target to reach. Search for a new home! Purchase it! Sort and pack! Make the necessary adjustment to documents! Move all of our worldly goods! All in the next four months.

Meanwhile, I see that both Linda and I are still processing the healing and pain of the past. We both avoid thinking or saying outright that, at times, we feel as though we have been forced to leave – ostracized by a group of the English ex-pat community here in the south of France. But we also feel that we had a choice: to continue to live with this tension, avoid the unpleasant ones and stay, or to move on. We want to own our own decision to move on. It is our choice under these circumstances, and we are thankful that we have the financial resources (and personal stamina) to move away from this unpleasant chapter of our life, and more importantly – to start over.

Along the way we had a joyful event of celebration of a good friend's 80th birthday. We anticipated that we would probably run into a few people at the party that we would have otherwise avoided. And so, it was; there were many in our social network that we knew and could socialize with comfortably. But persons who we would have wished to avoid, were there to meet face to face. The internal question is, do I continue the hypocrisy of "How nice to see you!" Do I say what is on my mind (probably not)? Or do I take some sort of tone of limiting the damages as much as possible – being civil but not encouraging etc. This was largely done by focusing on those people we wished to spend some time with and making a casual but non-engaging passing "hello". I was aware that in one case when a person approached with the, now grating, enthusiastic greeting + smile + south of France kiss-kiss-kiss, I deliberately adopted a tone of annoyed tolerance and cut the conversation short. Such things I cannot avoid processing in my head, and in my guts, as I still suffer from gastro-intestinal problems that surfaced over the past two years. I literally can feel in my gut how destructive this interaction is.

Even, five days later, Linda and I were still processing the "what to do – if there is a next time" I asked instead, is there something I could do – or not do – that would change the spirit from the divisive conflict to cooperation and unification. My internal answer is "nothing can be done for a relationship in which the other has decided on separation and division as their solution". There is nothing positive to be gained in that relationship by running after them seeking to resolve what they do not wish to resolve. No, I would say that the gospel imperative is to be open to their return but not encourage the current behaviors which are hypocritical. Perhaps strategic use of momentary interactions to neutralize further destructive behaviors is the best to hope for. They have chosen separation, so separate we will be until they show some inclination to return. I think this will not happen in our time remaining in France. I thank many years of working with Alcoholic and recovering alcoholics, which have taught me a tough love approach: To love the individual but not to approve of the behavior. It is best to kick the dust from my feet and move on to another town.

But now back to more pleasant things.

The buyers have contacted us with their wishes to purchase some of the house items which are for sale. We are delighted in many ways. It indicated their moving forward on the purchase. But for us there is an added enjoyment of leaving a few of our well-chosen antiques in their home space. A chandelier in the dining room, admired by both Linda and me on one of our last vacations, before moving to France, was purchased by Linda as a special birthday present to me. It is a lovely piece and was meant for the dining room. Reluctantly I must admit that it is best to leave it here where it truly belongs since we are not likely to have a more suitable space in the future. It is just right and adds character to the house. I am happy that the new buyers admire it also and wish to keep it in its home. They also choose the same for some of our beautifully framed prints. Other items will be put into a Fête du déménagement – moving day – house sale.
As if by providence, the November 17-23, 2012 edition of the Economist featured a cover and article "The Time-bomb at the heart of Europe" Inside articles comprised a 14-page special report- the general theme of

which was "Why France could become the biggest danger to Europe's survival". The article was mostly financial in its focus, but it included the impact of a social and political path that France has been on for many years; the lack of enterprise, general distrust, persistent political discord, and France's loss of sparkle etc. A confirmation of my disenchantment with idealized France, once again, showed up in an independent source.

And a story right to the end:

We were pleased with the sale of our home, and especially pleased to sell it to a Norwegian couple who fell in love with it; a creation made of hard work over several years, with attention to details and quality work. It was a joy to see that it would be loved as we had grown to love le petit jardin de l'ame. We had worked in the past with the Notaire in nearby Marseillan and were comfortable with him. We met in advance (in September) before our last research vacation to Panama so that he would have a sense of our timing and our intention to buy in Panama, and specifically to get a "time-line" on the transfer of monies from the sale into our account. Reassured that the money would be electronically transferred into our account in 24 hours we began putting together a "time-line" of financial commitments in Panama for a time soon after our scheduled real estate sale at the end of November in France.

The day of the closing came one day in advance of the original schedule, which was fortunate for us. Were were happy to move the closing to Monday 26 Nov - giving us one more day of grace for transactions. My last question to the Notaire as we stood up to leave his office was to ask when this money would show up in our bank account in France - so that we could then disperse it to areas where we had made financial commitments in Panama which were to come due in the week. The Notaire assured us "Tomorrow, next day at the latest." (that would make it Tuesday or Wednesday at the latest) We left his office confirmed that the appointment we had scheduled for Wednesday afternoon to transfer money from our account in France to accounts in Panama and the USA was perfectly timed. And since Linda herself had experience in making electronic transfers over time for smaller amounts, she knew the process and how quickly it could happen. Because the up-coming transfers were large amounts we had been told that we needed to appear in the Montpellier bank in person for these wire transfers, so a *rendez-vous* (RDV) was made.

Tuesday came and went but no sign of the transfer appeared in our Montpellier account, Wednesday morning - still no sign of the transfer from the sale of the house on Monday morning. Wednesday afternoon's RDV was cancelled and a call made to the Notaire's office, they would check ("no, it had not yet been sent") It needed the Notaire's approval before being sent. Persistent telephone follow-up in the afternoon until after 6pm that evening finally assured us that the transfer, promised on Monday had finally been sent Wednesday evening.

On Thursday morning a check on the Internet indicated that the money had arrived. This could have all been accomplished two days earlier had the Notaire been attentive to our very clear requests and reminders and his own assurance on Monday. While the administrative staff at the Notaire's office get special thanks for being pleasant during this time-delay, there was never a word of sorry or acknowledgment that this was causing an inconvenience to us - not even a "desole"

Immediately on Thursday we "hop-footed" it off to Montpellier but even if we were to leave immediately we would not arrive in time to reach the bank before the sacrosanct lunch time. So, when in Rome - or France in this case, do what the French do - go to lunch. Mind you the destination banks for these wire transfers were not at lunch nor was much of the rest of the world which was apparently being serviced by this international banking system - but nonetheless France was "out to lunch".

Because of the French mandated Lunch period we were not able to begin the process until after lunch, so the electronic transfer comedy of errors did not happen until 2 pm. It took two hours-plus to arrange for three transfers of significant amounts to Panama and to the USA accounts.

I should say that the "comedy" part of the errors was lost to us - and especially Linda who, in spite of giving printed details for the bank transfer to the clerk, found errors in the electronic transfer information. Each of the three transfers had to be done and re-done because of typing errors on the part of the bank clerks - not one mistake, but several - which would have resulted in wrong amounts going to wrong accounts or being rejected. Linda caught most of them. We left amazed that there was such a high degree of error when transferring hundreds of thousands of Euros to foreign accounts, but for the moment we were under the impression that we had accomplished the task only one day late and the proper amounts would show up in their respective places the next day. We were fortunate that we had allowed a couple extra days for just such fumbling about.

Since our home office had already been packed up and on its way to Panama, we went to some dear friends and made copies of all the transfers and scanned them in to send to the respective recipients confirming that the money promised was "on the way". It was at that time that Linda found one more error, then during, a sleepless, night she found another error. One of the errors might have not have affected the transfer process but the second discovery meant that more than two hundred thousand dollars would either go to the wrong bank or be returned to France because the SWIFT code was incorrect.

The next morning was already booked with a rendezvous to sell our car but we managed to conclude the sale and paperwork to arrive at the bank at 11:30. and Linda had managed to announce the problem via email. So, people were alerted to the problem. Our usual bank contact was not at work on Friday but had alerted a colleague who was very attentive. Eventually we were directed to the office of M. Patrick Clanet, judging by the position and size of his office, a senior executive at the bank. By now, the fact that this transaction would be conducted totally in French was not a surprise to us and we felt up to the task. However, one would think that a transaction of several hundred thousand dollars might elicit some English for the client's behalf. I suspect it was well within his abilities.

I should stop here to say that we were assured that the error had been Intercepted before it left France (meaning that the request from Montpellier had to go through Paris and M. Clanet was able to contact Paris and annul the two transfers that had errors in them (the third was let go to follow its normal path). But this end result was not achieved easily. Fortunately, we - although tired and worried - had now, after 12 years in France - summoned up a bit of Gaullist gall ourselves.

When the first error was pointed out to M. Clanet, his immediate response was to point to the signature at the bottom of the page, indicating that certainly this was our fault for signing a document that we should have made sure was correct. Allowing that the French are still learning the word "client service" we'll pass over this insult for a moment. In theory I do not disagree with M. Clanet. But instead of responding in defense with the fact that Linda had already corrected three earlier errors made by his staff, on that same page, she responded in French; Je compris que je travaillais avec des services professionnels, je lui donnais des informations correctes et pensais que ce serait correct. ("I understood that I was working with a professional, I gave him correct information and expected it to be correct"). M Clanet backed off a bit, although visibly perturbed - it was not clear whether he was irritated with us as clients or with his staff - or perhaps he sensed lunch time was approaching and we had just handed him something other than his first course.

Le Petit Jardin de L'âme

His original proposal was delivered with rapid-fire-French. We have learned in our 12 years of French life that this blast of French is not actually meant to be understood - it was not the words, but rather the tone, that was sufficiently clear, cool and crisp. Basically, it was explained that our money had, rather efficiently, already left the bank in Montpellier. The two transfers with errors would go through the normal process, the error would be discovered, and the transfers would, in time, be sent back to Montpellier and replaced into our account. At which point we could begin the process all over again! This was not so reassuring for us since were leaving France in less than three days, not to mention the implied delays in payment for this process to happen all over again a second time even If we were still in France. Assuming that the second go-round would be done correct - not really an assumption we were read to make.

At this point summoning calm from somewhere, I said, in measured French, that it was important that M. Clanet understand that we would not be in France to repeat this process a second time. We were - as the documents indicated buying a house and moving to Panama, we were leaving on Monday (a 24 hours fib, but what the hey!) We could not even let him think we had an extra day for this to work out. It was necessary to find a resolution today.

To his credit, M. Clanet got on the phone to Paris and, after a few call transfers, connected with someone who could identify the information sent by fax last night from Montpellier, arrived in Paris that morning, and was able to annul the two erroneous transfers and instructed that they be re-done and sent again.
The information was then corrected on the documents at M. Clanet's desk and they were prepared again for our signatures to the transfer the money. Exercising a bit of restrained self-righteousness, oh so delicious, Linda noticed that the newly corrected documents awaiting our signatures had yet a new error! No words were necessary as she pointed it out. And they were sent back to be done again. In the end, since it was now 12:38, they were corrected, signed and left on M. Clanet's desk to be sent out later that day by him personally.

It would have been more reassuring if the fax was send immediately but we felt that we had pushed our luck well into Lunch time. M. Clanet had looked at this watch three or four times in the last hour. I said to Linda that I originally felt annoyed by the gesture and then thought perhaps he was (in our interest) calculating how much time he actually had to catch any of his colleagues at their desks to be of service. Whatever it was, we were escorted to the already locked door and let out of the bank which had closed for lunch. As we left we still did not know whether the money would actually arrive or when, but we felt that at least we were able to abort the error of the day before. And M. Clanet did say that the money would arrive sometime in the coming week - what day he would not commit. We hoped that after his lunch he remembered the morning's mission and completed the process.

We left France enroute to Panama with the hope - not the fact - that our money would arrive where it was intended in a time frame that would comply with the contract we had in Panama. You will understand that hope actually runs a little thin at this point. And since the plane was not likely to wait for us, we left France much in the way we had lived in France, realizing that reality was likely to fall short of the promise. Our departure from France was much like our previous 12 years: filled with the uncertainties of life and a glimmer of hope.

The final passage of the French satire *Candide* describes it well as Pangloss attempts to put an optimistic spin on his travails and Candide offers up a practical metaphor of the garden as life:

> *You are perfectly right, said Pangloss; for when man was put into the garden of Eden, he was put there ut operaretur eum, so that he should work it; All events are linked together in the best of possible worlds; for, after all, if you had not been driven from a fine castle by being kicked in the backside for love of Miss Cunégonde, if you hadn't been sent before the Inquisition, if you hadn't traveled across America on foot, if you hadn't given a good sword thrust to the baron, if you hadn't lost all your sheep from the good land of Eldorado, you wouldn't be sitting here eating candied citron and pistachios.*
>
> *That is very well put, said Candide, but we must go and work our garden.*
> *-Final passage from* **Voltaire's 1759 novel, Candide, ou l'Optimisme**

Linda and I have acquired many life skills through an interesting life. On occasion we are called on to use them to survive, perhaps even to grown, through life's twists and turns. More simply, we tend to our little garden of the soul making the best of the corner of the world given us by a divine master gardener.

Chapter 23
In the New World
Touch-down, Terra Firma, Panamá

Linda's emails to our personal banker in Panama had gone unanswered, before our departure from France and upon arrival in Panama contact with a new personal banker did not hold out much promise, but we had been forewarned in Panama banks simply do not provide client service. So we started with lower expectations. Our connection with the bank (which was literally just down the street from our hotel) during our first four days began to reflect these lowered expectations. Our first days in Panama City were fruitful in other areas - Like picking up our new car, and establishing mobile phone connections, and meeting with an architect. However, meeting with the bank did not happen while we were in the city and a stone's throw from the bank.

So we moved on to Altos del Maria, and to a little rental house where we would live for a couple months until the purchase of our new home was completed. Linda tried the HSBC international banking contact who had set up the original Panama connection, once again. At that time, she was told that it was imperative that we go to the bank and meet with the personal banker to finalize the account or else (in four days) the money transfer would be returned to France and the account in Panama closed. There were several things upsetting in this scenario. Not the least of which was that the 181 thousand dollars which seemed somewhere in cyberspace was the bulk of what remained after the purchase of our Panama home. Also, if the account in Panama were closed it would un-do a process that we had worked on since August to set up from France so that we would have a bank account in Panama.

As it turned out, with the help of telephone assistance from HSBC International an appointment was scheduled with a Personal banker for the next day. Linda specifically asked if we needed to call to confirm - " No that would not be necessary." We drove the 90 minutes into the city for the appointment only to be told that the person no longer worked at that location but was transferred to another location. The person whose name had been given to us as fall-back, an assurance that someone would help us, was on vacation.

But the clerk at reception was resourceful and left her post and found someone to meet with us. This person was pleasant, spoke English and was very helpful for more than two hours during which we re-established that the original documents were correct, that the money had been transferred. She advised us on how to divide up the 181 thousand in ways that would make some cash fluid and other cash would earn a bit of interest. We were happy to discover that this person would be our personal contact with HSBC in Panama. I should say that she even anticipated our difficulties with registering for on line banking. Although the process was in English it posed some challenges filling in the form, from the keyboard which only looked like a qwerty keyboard. Getting to "@" for example had its own Spanish route not familiar to me and although the person on the phone spoke English it was not her first language so at one point we were all searching for a dictionary to understand what she meant. Regardless, we were now happy and satisfied that the account that we had been trying to establish for the past five months was indeed set up and the money from the sale of our home had at last made it to all its designated locations.

During the first four to six months in Panama, Linda's Dell Notebook was our life line to the world for news and Email and essential correspondence. Linda's note to her sister on 20 December 2012 sheds some light on our new context:

.

> Thanks for your Christmas letter. We always love an update.
>
> I'm sitting here at 10:21 am. It's quiet except for the cicadas-like insect sound from the dense tropical forest. At first, we thought it was the sound of distant weed-whackers, but no. On one of my walks I discovered that in fact the sound was coming from areas of forest with no one around. Every day is a new discovery. Every day is the blue morpho butterfly and his friends. At first, I was tempted to write each day with an update and then I realized it would be so tedious for my friends to be inundated daily with the beauties that surround us. But the other night we had an experience that I can't pass up trying to describe. We had gone to Panama City and stayed two nights in the hotel we like on the Panama Canal. We had several appointments there and wanted to avoid the trip back and forth so stayed in town. On our last evening about 6pm --now dark-- we hailed a taxi after getting our new license plate and meeting with our architect. A mature English speaking Panamanian and his woman friend picked us up for what, when there is no traffic, would be about a 10-minute ride--it took an hour-- there was mucho tranque--LOTS of traffic. The streets were parking lots. After several minutes of small talk about who we all were etc, we fell into silence snugly in our taxi pod watching the congested

world around us and listing to Latin music. After awhile, with our limited Spanish, we realized that the vocals we were listening to were hymns though none of the melodies were familiar to us, and our driver and his friend were sweetly singing along as he adjusted the AC and struggled to control the steaming windows inside and condensing windows outside our safe quiet pod. It was truly a special moment where our souls met in silence and we wished each other good-by and Merry Christmas.

Lots of love to you both,

Linda

In this first month in Panama everything is new; sometimes wonderfully new sometimes frighteningly new at other times. All happens in the context of a temporary living situation - in a rental house, and without the support of our accustomed belongings. We live our lives with what could be packed in two suitcases, until we rest in our house and our belongings arrive safely. Later we will begin the process of living in Panama - settling in to life in Panama. During this "interim time" we are able to take care of many of the necessary administrative items for setting up life in a new land: registering our passports, updating our pensionado visas, registering our new car, getting our drivers' licences, setting up the bank account, establishing new wills, getting health insurance, and the list goes on. There is much to do to keep us busy while we wait to move into our house.

During this time our first Christmas would be celebrated much differently than when we were in France or when we were in Chicago. My expectations for the first holidays in a new land are set rather low. We were without familiar traditions and friends. We had no time yet to make new ones. It was just us and our suitcases.

We discovered that our postal mail started to arrive. A pleasant surprise since it happened just as planned - at Mailboxes Etc. based in nearby Coronado. We contracted for this service because, each person we consulted during our preliminary research-vacations to Panama, described the postal system as inefficient, or unreliable. We were doubly surprised at the number of friends sending us Christmas cards and emails and e-cards, many in response to the early Thanksgiving letter that I sent out just before we left France.

We celebrated Christmas Eve by driving to a neighboring village of El Valle to visit the orchid preservatory / museum and for Lunch at a lovely

Restaurant Casa de Lourdes. We learned a bit about the orchids in Panama and we captured a moment of Europe in Panama at Lourdes with familiar surroundings of Mediterranean architecture, French specialties on the menu with a Panamanian touch, a bottle of Cote du Rhone and a waiter who spoke English and helped us with an informal Spanish lesson. On the drive back to Altos del Maria we crossed the continental divide, and climbed steep curved roads testing the new four-wheel drive car and our own nerves in a few places along the way.

Christmas Day, we celebrated with a picnic lunch on the covered terrace of our soon-to-be-home at 314 Toscana II. Since we had not technically closed on the real estate sale we did not have the key, but we were able to lunch al fresco and envision the future renovations. The view is panoramic, the potential excites us. No doubt, at some later time, we will experience the inevitable frustrations that come with remodeling and construction but for now we dream.

Among our holiday surprises and the welcome to Panama are Linda's morning walks and discoveries of flora and fauna. Her Christmas present for herself (and us) was the purchase of seven rain forest publications on Panama's birds, butterflies, trees, reptiles, fruits and flowers.

The mountain climate is very agreeable. There are Spring-like days with gentle breezes and the occasional brief showers with mostly blue skies behind the passing rain cloud. We hear it rain most nights. With the windows open, we hear the approaching rain come and go, and the croaking of frogs and beetles and rainforest nightlife. We are awakened by the song of birds, one of which I dubbed "Frere Jacques" because his song mimics the first four notes of the children's song. We enjoy the flutter of blue butterflies at breakfast, and Linda has sighted some Amazon Parrots in the tree down the road. We enjoy road side stands of bananas, mangoes, papaya, and pineapple. I gradually come to the realization that we have probably seen our last raspberry for a long time.

There are some new behaviors in a new land. Two new behaviors we encountered are the use of umbrellas and tipping. Obviously, both are not totally new but have new contexts. We are discovering that having an umbrella at hand most of the time is really an asset. Umbrellas here serve two purposes, as a parapluie for protection from a surprise, thought brief, rain shower and perhaps more important as a parasol for protection from the sun. It is not unusual to see locals walking with a parasol or when waiting for a bus. With my fair skin, I find that it is very useful in its capacity as a parasol. The second cultural shift is "tipping". While tipping is not new to us we had grown accustomed in Europe to the tip being included in the bill - with a tax of 19.6% most French gave no tip at all and some gave a token "small change" tip as an extra. Panama's sales tax ITBMS on most items is, between 5-7% and does not include a tip. So, this must be figured in to the final cost. Some restaurants make it really easy for you. At the bottom of the credit card invoice - before you sign it - is a suggested range, with the tip figured at 10% and 15% and 20 % with the corresponding amounts listed.

But another aspect of tipping not often discussed is the myriad of service people who pop out of nowhere to carry your bags, to hail you a taxi, to package your groceries and many other tasks that one could very well do themselves but having a bit of local knowledge they often find ways to do it quicker and "know the ropes" and are often Helping you before you know it. I begin to think that they often work in tandem - one "scout" offering the service and guiding you to a waiting taxi, that in all likelihood his friend is driving. I find that I walk around with a small roll of single dollar bills readily at hand. Actually, I would prefer to use small change but find that it is scarce and even small bills are hard to keep in supply.

One example of the culture change regarding everyday tipping is the grocery store. In Europe (and a practice that was growing in popularity when we left the USA many years ago) when checking out and paying at the grocery store, one brings their own bags, packs their own bags and wheels them out of the store to their car on their own. In Panama, not only has the custom of bag-boys remained, the store and the grocery carts are actually organized so that you must leave your emptied grocery cart in the store where you have unloaded your food onto the check-out conveyor belt. In one store recently, we actually noticed that the aisle parallel to the cashier was intentionally narrow - too narrow for the shopping cart to pass through. So, you unload your groceries on to the conveyor belt at one end and leave the cart behind. (Presumably there is someone who comes to remove the collection of shopping carts since there seems to be no obstruction at the entrance to the cashier. There is a bag-boy (or two - sometimes three), waiting at the end of the conveyor belt ready to pack your groceries into a mile-high pile of plastic bags. Actually, comparing my memory of bag-boys in Chicago to these fellas, they actually think when packing your food: They wrap glass bottles with a layer of newspaper. They do put like-things together; frozen foods all together, heavy items in the bottom, fragile foods on top etc. Then with your goods piled in neatly packaged plastic sacks enough to build your own land fill, they wheel up a trolley of a different style and push it to your car and load the bags into the trunk. A tip is appreciated of course!

Initially I resisted tipping for something that I could easily do myself (and often, from past experiences, I know I can do it better). But I learned that they actually do a reasonably good job, and my tip is an important part of the local economy. My dilemma is how to manage this process when there is not one but sometimes three bag-boys doing this job. Three packers and one of them who usually wheels the cart to the car. Who to tip? and how much to each one? Perhaps a little more to the fella (they are most often young boys) who gives up his position to walk to the car? It took us a couple trips to the local supermarket and some behavioral observations to figure out the system and I am sure in the process of trial and error, I alienated a few bag-boys, violated store policies and on occasion was overly generous. But in the end, we discover that that is the way it is done in Panama.

This morning Linda called to me, "Come quick!", to see a small herd of cattle walking down the road followed by one of the local people, who live in the small mountain villages, riding a horse behind them. They were headed for an area at the end of the road that, to us, goes nowhere. But I am sure they know exactly where they are going. Yesterday there was an email on the Altos del Maria group web site with the subject line: "Watch out!" One of the residents was alerting the rest to a half-dozen cows that were "occupying" a plot of land near her home. The cows here usually look a bit like the "Brahman" variety that I associate with India (white or grey, with a hump and floppy ears).

We have yet to figure out the relationship between this 7-thousand-acre mountain development and the locals who live in little villages scattered throughout the same mountains. But it is not unusual to see gardeners, and cleaning people literally come out of the woods. Many are employed by individual homeowners and some by the development of Altos Del Maria itself. Then there are these other surprises like cows grazing "free-range", horses actually used for basic transportation and little men armed with machetes carrying rudimentary baskets on their backs going to and from work, appearing and disappearing in the blink of an eye into the forest on paths known only to them.

We made it! And we are on to a new adventure. A friend, more travelled than we shared an insight with us from her many international moves. "The best thing about an international move is that each time you get to start over again". And that we will – start over.

*It is good for the soul that we be uprooted now and again;
transplanted, trimmed, and pruned, to grow to new life.
The work is a wonderful part of God's creation.*

*Now we're ready for the next great adventure
at le petit jardin de lame… jardincito del alma*
-Val Littman

Epilogue

To become a spectator of one's own life is to escape the suffering of life.
-Oscar Wilde – From *The Picture Of Dorian Gray* -

Some interpret Wilde's comment in his novel to make the same observation as Plato; that sometimes life can best be viewed from the outside. I believe the quote is also a comment on Wilde's story-telling, for which he was famous. Stories were, a bit of himself; more than autobiographical they were therapeutic. I think this may apply to other autobiographers, memoirists and to myself. Writing is often therapeutic as well as an opportunity for insight into one's own life.

I realize that it is possible that you have read this book and think that after this experience, I might have something against "The French" or France, "The English" or England. I hope that I have conveyed that both good and bad happened to us during our 12 years of life in France. In the end French, France, English, England are just descriptors which help to put our experience into the context in which it was lived. I believe that the French and English are just "everyman" and in all of us. My experiences happened to have been with the French and the English and, so they have that flavor. But everyman's experience can be in any country around the world. It is in this way that our story is a universal story.

> *Folk wisdom a-plenty, philosophical insight, psychological theory, learned texts and many scriptures holy, tell of an original goodness placed in our hearts at creation. Yet each tradition allows that from that interior garden also springs bitterness, brambles and suffering. And like the one in whose image we are made, it is for us to determine what are the fruits of such a garden.*
> -Val Littman, personal meditation

All experience does occur within a social environment. Each society sanctions certain behaviors by its laws and customs and everyday practices that bring out the best or less than the best in the experiences we share. Each society has the ability to encourage or discourage certain behaviors and thus creates men and women that live from day to day with the effects of its laws, social norms and many unspoken influences.

Perhaps a further illustration will help. During the time of writing this book I was drawn to read *The Ghosts of Europe* by Anna Porter. At the end of her book she reflects on the moral shift in life in Central Europe between 1946 and 1989, although geographically this could be another land and another time. Her work focuses on the struggle to Democracy in Central Europe and the lives of the people who lived through these years; how social structures can influence and allow evil to happen and good to be destroyed or to inspire the best in people.

Our experience in France was not the life shattering experience of the men and women in Anna Porter's book: But she points to the same universality; that people, some willing, others unwitting, are the tools of the social structures in which they live their lives. What we experienced in our microcosm of life in France shared the same dynamics in a most mundane way. There were times in our life in France that I clearly felt that we were living in a world where the level of deception tolerated was more than a few steps beyond my personal value and moral comfort level – and perhaps I needed to adjust. And to some extent I did adjust. I found ways to live with what I sensed around me. But what was it around me?

> *"… No society… can function without a moral foundation,*
> *without conviction that has nothing to do*
> *with opportunism, circumstances and expected advantage.*
> *Man does not define morality*
> *according to the caprice*
> *of his needs wishes, tendencies and cravings;*
> *it is morality that defines man."*
> -Jan Patočka - Translation from Rupnk, *The Other Europe*.

A part of my experience in France was to realize that I was living with evil around me, close to me, in a way I had not experienced before. Evil, not in some apocalyptical sense as it is often used today – extreme, catastrophic, ominous, end-of-the-world sense. But more accurately in the traditional sense, life in France was a revelation and insight - into evil. Most people reserve the term "evil" for the extreme end of a spectrum. But in my life in France I came to know evil in its banality, its mundane, everyday life form. The chinks of those little falsehoods, exaggerations, and deceptions, innuendo, when supported by a level of acceptability and unspoken social norms, become an environment in which "staged outrage", false accusation, faux logic, and some good old-fashioned scapegoating creates a sink-hole which pulls the rug - or foundation - out from under good. Evil in this form springs up with the goodness in the garden of life and has the ability to eat away the garden.

As a pastor to a small church community, not only was I saddened to witness this disintegration of something good in the small church, I also realized that the time spent in conflict was also time spent in a distraction from what we could have been to the larger community and for our own spiritual development. Conflict, unresolved conflict, eats away at the gospel that could instead be lived out in that community.

Evil may be too strong a term for some, gentle reader, but it is this term which helps to explain the sowing and the fostering of enmity, the breakdown of trust and the eventual tearing apart of a church community. For me this happened in an ex-pat community, a small church group, in the South of France but it could be anywhere. Evil comes into our lives in the most banal of ways. Sometimes, seemingly, in such insignificant ways that we hesitate to name it for what it is and give it some less offensive euphemism.

It is my hope that this universality has come through my story. In our twelve years of *La vie Française* we discovered that while living in 21st Century France we were also living with people, their personal history, their behaviors and the accumulated affects of social norms and sanctions that allowed behavior that was destructive. The ghosts of World War II, the Vichy regime, the shadows of England's faded imperialism still live on. And in spite of the official ecclesiastical rhetoric in its Concordats, the World Wide Anglican Communion is lived out in real time, at the local level, for better or worse in the lives of real people influenced by these ghosts.

We happened to have encountered some very destructive behaviors during our time in France. We also found some notable exceptions that enriched our life. I hope I have been able to communicate this sufficiently in this book so as not to alienate everyone French or English from my life. The nastiness, and the goodness, happened. And it happens in France, received from both French and English. That is the context and the truth is universal.

We still keep in touch with those who enriched our life in France. These friends are English and French, Belgian and Dutch; a few Americans, a few Canadians. They are from Grace Church and the Episcopal Church Europe, and a few from our broader social life in France. Their good will, then as now, is the stuff of which we hope the garden of life is made – and that we will cultivate and nurture and grow.

Matthew 13 - New International Version - The Parable of the Weeds

> [24] *Jesus told them another parable: "The kingdom of heaven is like a man who sowed good seed in his field.* [25] *But while everyone was sleeping, his enemy came*

and sowed weeds among the wheat, and went away. ²⁶ When the wheat sprouted and formed heads, then the weeds also appeared.

²⁷ "The owner's servants came to him and said, 'Sir, didn't you sow good seed in your field? Where then did the weeds come from?'

²⁸ "'An enemy did this,' he replied.

"The servants asked him, 'Do you want us to go and pull them up?'

²⁹ "'No,' he answered, 'because while you are pulling the weeds, you may uproot the wheat with them. ³⁰ Let both grow together until the harvest.'"

When we first came to retire in France in 2001, it was not unusual to hear people say things like" you are too young to be retired" or "you don't look old enough to be retired" and indeed we were, at 53 younger than most retirees. Time passes, and we seem to have lost our youthful edge. Somewhere during the years of "la vie en France", the strains of "you look too young to be retired" faded like and echo in a canyon and, it seems, for better or for worse we fully fit the look of retirement age. At 53 we looked younger than our age, by 64 we were clearly looking very much like most "60-something" retirees. Much of that had to do with emotional and physical wear and tear; a worn out, worn down look. Our smiles had faded, and the joy was gone. Perhaps these important markers and behavioral foundations of a fountain of youth – no matter what age – can be recovered in a new land with new air and new dreams?

An Introduction to the Appendices

There are several documents listed in this appendix section. They all refer to the congregational life portion of the book.

To those gentle readers who think that these documents may be "dry" and cold institutional documents, be assured that they can be skipped or skimmed and scanned, only to read what interests you. The story has been told, I hope that you have found reading this far rewarding – perhaps you are done – And that is OK!

For others there may be some interest in searching the appendices in an attempt to make better sense of some of the details in the life of the congregation or understand some of the church practices mentioned in the book.

In writing the book I sometimes vacillated between <u>telling</u> the story and <u>documenting</u> the story. The addition of these appendices is an attempt give the reader the documentation they may wish to explore without interrupting the flow of the story itself.

Appendix I
October 2009 Letter from the president of the association

l'Association Anglican/Episcopal Church in the Hérault

Important Notice

For members of the Association and friends

I have decided that the meeting called for 21st October 2009 should be cancelled. The run-up to this meeting has caused considerable unpleasantness and unhappiness, and I would like to see an end to this. But my reason for cancelling the meeting is that its purpose was to decide upon the budget, while the basis for our divisions is mainly the split between those who support the move to an Episcopal Mission, and those who are against this move and would prefer to continue more or less as before. The reasons for and against have been extensively discussed. **The budget can be decided when the future of the congregation is clearer.**

To help clarify the future of the congregation, I have asked ▮▮▮▮ to act as a focus for those who are against the move to an Episcopal Mission. **So if you intend to support the Episcopal Mission, please get in touch with Val. If you do not, please get in touch with Mike.** We can then move forward with a better understanding of what you want to do.

If most of the congregation choose to support one way forward or the other, the future is clear. But if you split down the middle, then we may end up with two congregations. This would be regrettable; however, it would be better that the two groups separate than that there is one group which continues to be riven by dissention, or gradually disintegrates.

The Association is needed by the Episcopal Mission, but not otherwise. I shall call a management meeting to accept the resignation of those members who are against the Mission, and to appoint new members who support it. I shall stand down at the meeting.

▮▮▮▮
President

4th October 2009
Marseillan

Contact information:

Appendix II
Annual Meeting January 2010, after group resignations.

Anglican Episcopal Church
www.gracechurchherault.org

General Meeting of Grace Church

The following document was prepared at the suggestion of those attending the General Meeting of 21 January. It is hoped that the following pages will help to explain the period of transition at an important time in the history of the congregation between October 2009 and January 2010, as we move on the future.

Here follows the announcement of the general meeting of January 2010: (Names blackened for this publication)

Notice of General meeting: This notice was sent to all via email on 15 December as part of general announcements in advance of the 20 Dec Eucharist. Also printed in the Christmas Eve Order of Service and Announcements used at worship, was sent again to all on 05 January via email in advance of the 17 January Eucharist and was printed in the Order of Service and Announcements for worship on 17 January

A general meeting of the congregation of Grace Church, is scheduled for 21 January 2010 – beginning 6:30 PM
at Le Petit Jardin De L'âme, 10 rue Molière Florensac.
All those who wish to participate in the congregation are invited

The agenda: General Introduction
Appointment of members of Association & Bishop's Committee
Amendment of Rules of Association
Constitution & Bylaws
Treasurers Report
Future plans
Other Business

Val J. Littman

An RSVP will help to approximate the number who plan to attend. Telephone: 04 67 00 1495 or mail@petitjardin.com

If you have questions, or have items to propose for the agenda, please, contact either the Secretary of the Bishop's Committee: Sally John, or Bishop's Committee Chair: Val Littman before Sunday 17 January. 2010

Please note: This meeting is a part of our system of communication with the congregation. This meeting is based on reports. Not all future meetings will be like this. It just happens that way now as we take steps to re-organize our common life.

On the evening of the General meeting an annotated agenda – expanding on the original announcement - was provided to those attending along with hymns and prayers for the evening

Annotated Agenda for the evening:
Opening Prayer/ Hymn
General Introduction – ■
Transition and re-organizing our common life after 21 October
Appointment of members of Association
Following the example of other churches in The Convocation
Establishing an acting Bishop's Committee
Q&As

What the meetings of 30 October and 11 December were like – Bryan
Q&As

Amendment of Rules of Association - ■
Q&As

Statues & Bylaws (Church Canons) – ■
Bishop's committee
Governance according to Church canons
Membership roll
Q&As

Treasurers Report – ■
Budget 2010 – copies available
Report of Income and Expenses – copies available
Q&As

Le Petit Jardin de L'âme

Future plans
Reviving Charity Outreach - ▮
A time for setting congregation priorities
Lay Delegate for Convention – October 14-17, Nice
Children's Program
Increasing our visibility in the community

And a longer list of "to –dos" for bishop's committee + Congregation

Other Business? (Ask about creation of "Fact Sheets" for Congregation)

Closing Prayer / Hymn

A glass of wine and a few snacks follow for further informal discussion

Appendix III
Minutes Annual Meeting

What follows is, the general summary (minutes) of the meeting (one page) with additional documents attached. The additional documents contain the notes used by each speaker during their presentation.

Report on General Meeting of the Congregation of Grace Church 21/1/2010

Present:

Apologies for Absence:

General Introduction

Val gave an account of the developments in the organization of the church since 21 October. (see document VALCOM.doc – General Introductory Remarks)

Report on meetings of 30 October and 11 December

Bryan gave a summary of these meetings.

30 October: ▓▓▓ and ▓▓▓ were co-opted onto the management committee, and committee duties were agreed. It was agreed that the *Association Loi* would deal only with financial matters, and that all other matters should be dealt with by the Bishop's Committee.

11 December: The *Association Loi* rules were agreed. The Bishop's Committee agreed on the proposed Constitution and Bylaws. Alan presented an interim financial report.

Rules of the Association

Alan explained how the rules of the Association had been changed so that it dealt only with finance, and the members were limited to the Bishop's Committee. (see document: General meeting rules of Association)

Statutes and Bylaws

Val explained our current status, as a mission. The Bishop's Committee is appointed by the Bishop (so is currently provisional). Normally after a few years a congregation becomes a parish, with a vestry (equivalent to a PCC) elected by the congregation.

Voting Membership of the congregation is generally similar to being on the electoral roll of a Church of England church. (see document VALCOM.doc - Regarding Statutes and Bylaws)

Treasurer's Report

████ presented his report of income and expenditure, and a budget for 2010. (see Document – Treasurer's Report)

Charity Outreach

████ spoke on this subject. (See document Charity Outreach Report)

Other Business

It was agreed that the reports and minutes of the general meeting would be put into a form of "fact sheets" or information documents prepared for members of the congregation.

Val J. Littman

General Introductory remarks: Val
Brief History of the Transition period after ▓▓▓ called for the cancellation of the general meeting of 21 October and resignations were tendered from ▓▓▓, ▓▓▓ and ▓▓▓

After resignations were accepted the remnant members of the association management committee (▓▓▓, ▓▓▓ and ▓▓▓) met with prospective new candidates for the management committee (▓▓▓, & ▓▓▓) and Appointed them to serve the balance of the term for those who resigned in October.

A meeting of 30 October was called – new management committee was formed consisting of Val Littman, ▓▓▓ continuing as Treasurer, and ▓▓▓ continuing as Secretary. New management committee members ▓▓▓ and ▓▓▓ were appointed.

Val Littman was selected by the new management committee as president.

At this 30 October meeting it was noted that:
Membership fees / annual subscriptions for membership were last collected between September and November 2008.

The first membership meeting was held on 16 November 2008
And original election of management committee with terms of one year began 16 Nov 2008.

Since all previous memberships were expired, we therefore that these events actually gave us a clean slate to start over.

The management committee renewed its membership at the meeting to allow the association to continue into the new year in the form of the five members of the management committee.

The new management committee ▓▓, ▓▓, ▓▓, ▓▓ and ▓▓ meet first time on 30 October– see minutes for the 30 October Meeting - and scheduled second meeting for 27 November 2009
(re-scheduled to 11 December)

A revision of association bylaws – were drafted to be submitted to the *sous prefecture* for approval. These new by laws were to reflect changes necessary to reflect the new status of the congregation as a Specialized Mission of the Convocation of Episcopal Churches in Europe

Le Petit Jardin de L'âme

A modification to the Old Association rules were to be made to allow the Congregation to be governed by the Canons of the Church. (In April 2009, the congregation had petitioned to be received as a Specialized Mission and had now formally been accepted as a Specialized Mission at the 18 October Annual Convention)

The effect of the revisions:
At this time – and according to revised association bylaws, the five members of the management committee are the association.

In the future: The governance of the congregation of Grace Church will follow the church canons as do other congregations in the Convocation of Episcopal churches in Europe.

General membership for the congregation of Grace Church, will be according to church canons and bylaws. An annual meeting of the congregation will be held according to church canons.

Future meetings of the Association Loi 1901 will be held according to revised association bylaws. Members of the association are the five members of the management committee.

Amendment to the Rules of Association – Report

Before dealing with this subject I thought it would be helpful to provide a simple overview of our current organization, why we have Rules of Association and what they mean for you as a member of our church community in the Hérault.

The way the Church is run is simple. In the Anglican Tradition the church is organized following the order of Bishops Priests and Congregation, each order making decisions in collaboration with each other. Locally, we have the Priest in Charge and the congregation. Any communication and decisions should be between the Priest and the congregation. But as part of the larger Anglican Communion we depend on the Bishop's authority.

The congregation appoints officials to carry out certain functions such as Treasurer, Church Warden, assist the Priest etc. These elected officials form what is called the Bishop's Committee. Locally we choose, who we wish to serve in these roles and the Bishop Appoints them to act in his name.

Formal procedures have been evolved to assist this process and these are known as the Constitution & By- laws of our Church.

Val J. Littman

Because we are subject to French Law a further device is necessary. This is called an Association of loi, a loose set of legal guidelines for running any association in France. We need this legal framework to, for example, open a Bank account. It is unnecessary for the Association to have any further involvement with Church life. Indeed, the only activity of our Association is the Bank account.

Our Association must be registered at the Sous-Prefecture and a set of Rules of the Association must be submitted also for approval. Thus, we continue to need a set of rules despite being governed by Church rules.

Once our revised rules have been approved a copy will be available to all members and / or interested parties.
Considering this framework, we have sought to simplify our organisation. The five members of the Bishops committee are the del facto members of the Association. No other members are necessary. Members of the congregation continue to have all previous advantages but as members of the congregation. This structure will prevent a re-occurrence of the problems seen this year.

So, what has changed?

* The official base to be Florensac.
* Membership of the Association reflect the criteria for membership of the Congregation.
* Membership records are confidential
* membership is restricted to members of the Bishops Committee.

All other rules remain unchanged.

I will now take questions.

Le Petit Jardin de L'âme

Notes for presentation at the meeting
Remarks regarding the Statutes & Bylaws (Church Canons). – ▮
Going forward the Congregation of Grace Church as s Specialized Mission of the Convocation of Episcopal churches in Europe will govern itself according to the Canons of the Church.

This is a work in progress. We have consulted with the Bishop and have received a Model of Mission Bylaws from him. We have consulted with other churches in the Convocation (most notably Christ Church Clermont Ferrand) to pattern our Statues and Bylaws after their example.

This document has been reviewed by our local Acting Bishop's Committee (Myself, ▮, ▮, ▮ and ▮) and as of today is now signed to be sent to the Bishop for his approval. (Approval comes from the Bishop and from his council of Advice) for the Convocation of Episcopal Churches in Europe. We anticipate that this document will meet with their approval.

After approved, the Status and bylaws will be available to those who wish to receive them.

If necessary in the future, they can be amended according to the process outlined in the document for amendments

Membership in Grace Church will be determined by the Statues and bylaws (according to Church Canons) Technically all baptized person are members of the church. However, **membership on the Electoral Rolls** of the local church will be determined by church canons for the purposes of eligibility for voting and holding office.

This is a form of church governance used throughout the Anglican Communion. While some details vary from one national church to another the governance is similar in many ways throughout churches of the Anglican Communion.

Val J. Littman

Treasurers Report – █████████

Income & Expenditure Statement for the year ending 31st December 2009

Future Budget Forecasts

Ladies & Gentlemen,

The Income & Expenditure Statement, which you have before you are the first such document to cover a full calendar year. The reason is to bring our bookkeeping & accounting records in line with the Church in Europe. As the old accounting year ran to September I have had to reflect several subscriptions received late in the 2009 accounting year. Most of the subscription income was received in the year ending 2008.

Overall, our financial position is sound even though we show a small excess of expenditure over income. This is due to the re-organisation of our finances.

It is not our intention to record such a large surplus every year. In this year it has happened more by accident than design. Your future especially charitable giving may well impact on year end balances.

A summary of Charitable Giving is included in the notes to the accounts. In future such income will be paid to the Treasurer, with proper records maintained and monies directed to whatever charity fits your charitable objectives.

The budget projections reflect modest plans in financial terms for a growing Church. Some of these figures will change as we, for example, develop such items as Lay Worship Training, confirmation classes and general educational events for the congregation. And work toward a goal of part time clergy compensation.

Finally, I should say a word about income. We have reorganized our means of financing considering past difficulties & concerns with the objective of ensuring each member of the congregation can freely give in accordance with their means.

We shall continue to depend upon collections; we shall introduce planned giving for those who wish it and provide opportunity for donations from others.

Le Petit Jardin de L'âme

In summary therefore, and with your continued support, I am in no doubt we shall achieve all our plans in the coming year.

May I take this opportunity to thank you all for your support. It is your church and now you should be very proud to be part of the foundation of a new, growing church in Herault.

If you have any questions I am now at your disposal.

New Church Warden's report:

Report for General Meeting of Grace Church – 21st January 2010

6.30 p.m. at Le Petit Jardin de l'Âme, Florensac
Future Plans (reviving charity Outreach and much more)–

Much of what I have to say is to do with future planning. Alongside joining the Convocation of Episcopal Churches in Europe, both continuity and change have gone hand in hand.

Continuity because Education within the congregation and fund-raising for Charity are ongoing projects. Change because we are moving forward into a new phase of development, with a new committee and some changes in our constitution and by-laws.

We have to define roles and 'jobs' within our Bp committee and amongst our lay membership. Education must be continued and developed. Small Group meetings have to be reviewed and developed, eg. We have a new Prayer Group, which meets once a month, and we may begin a Bible Study Group in the near future depending on demand. What we have to bear in mind in all of these things is that geographically we are spread far and wide as a congregation. It's not like being members of a village church.

We will have to identify priorities with regard to stewardship, charity outreach and the creation of a website to put us on the 'map' for community awareness.

As well as Education in the general sense, we will be considering children's needs specifically, and at this point I'd like to mention YAE (Youth Across Europe) which is as its name suggests a Europe-wide organisation run by the Convocation specifically for teenagers and young adults. They run residential educational and sport-oriented courses and holidays so that young people can meet with their peers from other areas and church communities.

We will be considering Space needs, eg. Space for children's learning programs, WC needs (quite important when you have travelled a distance for the service), and the need for some kind of heating in the winter months.

My main concern at the moment is to revise and plan our Charity Outreach program. From very early on in our church life at our home Eucharist group and continuing into the period when we started at St Martin's, Conas, we have always been a group which donates part of our income to Charity, and we have held fund-raising events for organisations like Restos du Coeur and Water Aid. My task will be to review, revise and set goals and priorities for future fund-raising, both for our church running costs and for charity giving.

I think we are all reeling after seeing the most poignant and devastating scenes on tv of the Haïti earthquake, and the tragedy that has brought to a very large proportion of the population of that country. It has been heartening to see the brief moments of joy and relief at the discovery of someone alive, be it child or adult, after up to a week, or more, of being trapped. Most people will have responded individually in some way to the Disaster Appeal, and our congregation received information on some of the ways to give at our last monthly Eucharist. We will be looking towards giving continued support to this cause. Incidentally we have received some information from members of the Convocation who live in Geneva about some of their relatives who were working in Haïti. One young woman has died, the daughter of the family in Geneva, some are still missing. Others we know are alive and well. We remembered these families in our prayers last Sunday and do so on an ongoing basis.

One of our on-going projects in the area of charity outreach is our Lenten lunches, and Jenny Morgan has again organised a rota for these this year, starting in February (information leaflets?). This is the third year that we have held these events. Again, one of our problems in this area is our geographical spread. But they have proved popular in past years, so we are hoping for a similar response this year.

As you can see we are as a new Mission of the Convocation moving forward one step at a time. There is a lot of planning ahead of us, and the work we are doing is a work in progress.

Appendix IV
Research: Patterns of Charity Giving and Church stewardship USA and UK

USA

http://findarticles.com/p/articles/mi_m4021/is_11_24/ai_95309979/

It's true that the wealthier the individual, the greater the amount they are likely to donate to charity. On average, people whose household income is $100,000 or more donate about $4,000 a year to philanthropic causes, compared with about $600 per household for those earning less than $25,000; the national average is $1,600. Arguably, lower-income earners are the more altruistic group, as they tend to give away a greater share of their income. People earning less than $25,000 contribute an average of 4.2 percent of their household income to charitable groups, while those making $100,000 or more shell out an average of 2.7 percent of earnings. This trend has been a consistent finding of Washington, D.C.-based Independent Sector, a nonprofit organization that has been tracking charitable giving since 1987.

UK

http://www.churchtimes.co.uk/content.asp?id=77982   Church Times July 2009
Since 1978 the Synod of Church of England has set a goal of 5% of net income to and through the church in 2009 that was reconsidered to recommend giving and additional 5% to giving to other charity as part of stewardship

It (National Stewardship Committee) had been asked time and again to retain the initial giving target of five per cent of net income given to and through the Church. This it was glad to restate, since it had been set forth in the report A Resourceful Church (1978), and through subsequent reports this basic premise had never changed. Today presented the first opportunity in nine years to debate that policy.

Thirty-one years on, in no diocese had that target been met. But there had been consistent growth, and church members now gave more than £600 million a year, more than half the total income of the Church of England. A sense of urgency was needed, however, because if the average of five per cent was reached, it would create "an additional £300 million".

The Bishop of Ripon & Leeds, the Rt Revd. John Packer, said that the latest figures (2007) showed a rise from 3.2 per cent to 3.4 per cent, but it was still only two-thirds of the persistent call to the Church from the Synod.

http://answers.google.com/answers/threadview/id/433612.html

Subject: **Percentage of personal salary to give to charity (UK)**
Category: Business and Money > Economics
Asked by: **jamessiddle-ga**
My question has two parts:

1) What is the average percentage of personal salary (or income) given to charity in the UK?

2) What percentage(s) of personal salary is it recommended to give to charity in the UK by the key charitable organisations / bodies?

I'm trying to work out how much people give to charity, on average, in the UK, as well as to work out how much it is recommended that you should give to charity.

The short answers are:

1) About 0.8% of income.

2) The Chief Executive of the Charities Aid Foundation, the Institute of Philanthropy and The Giving Campaign have suggested giving 1.5% of one's income to charity.

You'll see the information I've collected below. When you've had a chance to look through the material, please don't hesitate to ask if anything is unclear.

Best wishes - Leli

Mean weekly income in the UK in 2003/4 was 408 = 21216 p.a.
(Page 11)
http://www.dwp.gov.uk/asd/hbai/hbai2004/pdf_files/chapters/chapter_2_hbai05.pdf

The CAF (Charities Aid Foundation) says, "The average annual donation per UK adult for 2004/05 was 170.02."

Le Petit Jardin de L'âme

This suggests an average donation of about 0.8% of annual income.

It isn't ideal using figures from different years, but I don't think the Department of Work and Pensions have published income statistics yet for 2004/5. If the annual increase in income was the same as between 2002/3 and 2003/4 this might change the figure from 0.8% to 0.78%.

" . . . amongst households who donate, the poorest fifth, who cannot really afford it, give on average 3% of their household expenditure while the richest 20%, who can afford it, give only 0.7%.

(From page 33 of? A Lot of Give?? trends in charitable giving for the 21st century? written by Catherine Walker & Cathy Pharoah, published by Hodder and Stoughton, 2002)"
http://www.givingcampaign.org.uk/images/uploaded/blueprint_for_giving.pdf

The Institute of Philanthropy uses 0.7% in its "giving calculator".
http://www.instituteforphilanthropy.org.uk/home.html

For example, it says:

"The average person in Britain, on an income of 30,000, donates 210.00 a year (0.7% of their income).

If you were to give away 1.5% of your income, as suggested by The Giving Campaign, then you could donate 450.00 each year."

This suggested figure of 1.5% of income is sometimes increased for those on 100,000 or more. The Giving Campaign suggests 2% for people at this level, and 3% for people with an annual income of 500,000.

"We suggest a benchmark for giving of 1.5% of income on average with the percentage for the better-off going upwards according to their income and wealth and going down for those who cannot afford it."

See "A Blueprint for Giving":
http://www.givingcampaign.org.uk/images/uploaded/blueprint_for_giving.pdf

Val J. Littman

("The Giving Campaign (July 2001 - June 2004) was an independent, National campaign supported by the voluntary sector and the Government.") http://www.givingcampaign.org.uk/

"I think it is realistic for us in the UK for donors to aspire to contribute 1.5% of average income to charity." Stephen Ainger, Chief Executive of CAF
http://www.cafonline.org/conference/speech03_ainger.cfm

"People belonging to faith groups are able to base their giving around a norm well understood in their community. For example, the Church of England recommends that its congregation tithe, giving 5% of their income to the Church and 5% to other good causes.

Secular society does not provide a norm and it is clear that many donors wishing to give have no idea of what is a reasonable amount to give. What wealthy people in particular tend to do is to apply absolute amounts when giving, rather than relate their donations to their income and wealth. As a result, they are normally far less generous than poorer people when their giving is expressed as a percentage of their income."
http://www.givingcampaign.org.uk/images/uploaded/blueprint_for_giving.pdf

The CAF say individual donations to charity represent 0.9% of GDP.

http://www.cafonline.org/downloads/UKGiving2004-05.pdf

"The percentage of individual giving to GDP is more than double in the US compared to the UK? in the US, $183.7bn (104.6bn) was donated in 2002, 1.75% of GDP compared to 7.3bn, or 0.76% of GDP in the UK."
http://www.financialdirector.co.uk/accountancyage/features/2144706/cause

"The average American gives 3.2 per cent of his or her income to charity? here, the average is 0.7 per cent."
http://www.thetablet.co.uk/cgi-bin/archive_db.cgi/tablet-01060

Survey of charitable giving 2004/5:
    ... around three-fifths of the population [give] to charity per month, and the value of donations [is] 0.9% of GDP . . .? The average annual donation per UK adult for 2004/05 was 170.02.?

But not everyone gives to charity: the average amount donated by each person who gave was 297.10.? In 2004/05 57.2% of UK adults gave to charity in an average month.

? The average monthly amount given per person was 14.17.
This equates to 24.97 per donor.
http://www.cafonline.org/downloads/UKGiving2004-05.pdf

Val J. Littman

Appendix V
Stewardship Reflection

(a Stewardship Sermon, if you will) July 2009 – Preached, printed & distributed in paper copy, and lastly sent by email)

Email text followed by stewardship Reflection
By now you should have received emails from ▮▮, ▮▮, and ▮▮. ▮▮ described the choices that are before us as a group. ▮▮ described the budget implications for the next few years. And the questionnaire from ▮▮ begins to link our financial decisions to programs and services in the life of the local church for 2010 and beyond. (If you have not received these three pieces of information please let me know at ▮▮ or telephone ▮▮ or ▮▮ at ▮▮)

What I would like to do at this time is to put the talk of budget in the context of our spiritual life – usually called Stewardship – reflecting the parable of Matthew 25:14 (or Luke 19:12). It is important that our financial life be a reflection of the Gospel. As a church, if we miss the connection between what we do and what we believe we have missed the boat. My contribution, as clergy, is to make this connection. It also falls to the clergy as pastor to "show the way"; to give a path to accomplishing what may seem at first impossible.

Although I am personally reluctant to use quotes from scripture to justify one position or another, I will, at the end of this reflection, give you passages to look up, to read and reflect on, to pray over and make your own interpretation, as you consider how you will support the church that we have come to know, here, in our community? At this point I will stay with a more general reflection and application of the Gospel to our lives. **This, I hope, will help you to make a financial contribution that reflects the spirit of the Gospel.**

There has been talk, and worry about growth (in numbers) about what that will do, or has done, to the little home church that began at *le petit jardin de l'âme* on 19 October 2003. I too have fond memories of those Home Eucharists. There were no committees, there were no conflicts, and there was, in fact, no collection as we began. My life was simpler – and there was more time for prayer. And if the group should choose the option to disband (mentioned in the Association Newsletter written by the association president) rather than take steps to invest in the future, my life will be simpler again.

I am willing to do the work of building a church, though I did not come here to build one. This is a very real change for me, and Linda, in how we live our life in retirement. But I am (we are) willing to do it.

The need for an active church has been demonstrated not only by growth in numbers (average attendance is nearly four times the size of when we began) but also in the growing requests for programs and services beyond and in between Sunday Worship, and the attendant people-management, administration and documentation that comes with increased size. Over six years I have responded to requests, to a spirit of enthusiasm from people who appreciate a place and space to grow their spiritual life. We have a special character to our worship that attracts people. And so, we experience that it is the nature of the Gospel to grow and to stretch us past our individual comfort zones.

If we are to live out the Gospel we cannot go back to the beginning any more than we can regain our youth. There are those who may wish to try, but the Gospel requires us to grow into the future. Having enjoyed our past with a grateful heart for what we have been given, **we are called to be good stewards, to grow the treasure entrusted to us.**

Your financial contribution is meant to reflect your gratitude for what you have been given. Whatever you decide to give, regardless of the amount, if it reflects the Gospel mandate to grow in the life of Christ, it will be a stretch. It is not meant to be comfortable.

Thirty + years ago, the parish priest who helped Linda and me prepare for marriage said to us that most people think of the biblical tithe of 10% as beyond their means. But he encouraged us to make it a life goal; to strive year by year, so that at some point in our life, we would, in fact, reach that 10 % tithe. He stressed that the church did not need to receive all of that 10% but no doubt would benefit from a few of those percentage points, as well as the generous spirit and the discipline that were necessary to achieve the tithe. Even if we began with one percent of whatever little we had, we were to make a start; and we did.

Even at poverty level income (in France, calculated at 10,370 euros per year) **everyone, of whatever means, can have a tithing goal and can begin somewhere – 1%, 2%, 3%.** For those more comfortable with a UK or Church of England reference, The Church's General Synod considers we should give 5% of take home pay to the church.

Val J. Littman

According to various statistics on average UK pension incomes, as a congregation with many retirees, we are not likely to become a wealthy congregation. But you do the math for your household, and see if your income is at poverty level, or, as the statistics indicate, most incomes for the households in the congregation will be above that poverty level. Consider a starting percent of your income to the church and work toward the tithe. Set your own goal, but know what it is, and what your contribution amount reflects of your over all good fortune.

There is an instinctive reflex action when people look at budgets – they are all too big – and seem impossible. The budget presented to you is very conservative since it still assumes many "freebies" which, in time we should pay for, but do not and will not need to pay for a few more years to come. Clergy compensation at 40 % time is a token – beginning at a portion of poverty level income, and over three years, rising nearly to 40% of the current minimum clergy stipend in the UK. (Without any of the usual costs of clergy housing, utilities, pension, healthcare etc). Additionally, this conservative budget assumes reception of a three-year annual matching funds grant of 2500 € each year from The Convocation. The current congregation assessment is 0% (zero) paid to the Convocation. Also, the financial support for clergy to attend two events each year; one for retreat and one for professional development, is provided by The Convocation not the congregation. And because of our good fortune we have virtually no building and maintenance costs typical of other church budgets. **All this, to say that even with the budget increase, as a congregation, we remain the recipients of others generosity and have much to be grateful for.**

Generally, the seemingly impossible – if broken down into manageable steps - becomes possible. In the correspondences up to now the focus has been on giving and receiving information. I would like to give you hope. **No one has talked about a way to accomplish what at first seems impossible. It is, in fact, attainable. A particular gift of English Spirituality is a keen ability to make a practical application of the abstracts of spirituality.** In ascetical theology studies, this characteristic is called *The Homeliness of English Spirituality*, in its best sense of the wisdom from the hearth. We could use some homely spirituality at this time.

There have been references to big increases in the budget. Yes, any increase from the current average of € 1.08 per person, per week may be viewed as big. At the risk of limiting some people's more generous contributions, **I want to give you some very homey examples of what this big increase would be for you as your investment in the future.**

A € 5 contribution per week multiplied by 26 people from the congregation would meet the budget goal in both 2010 and again for 2011. Yes, there would probably be a need for an increase to reach the goal of 2012. A contribution of one Euro per day multiplied by 30 people would more than meet the budget goal for 2012. For heaven's sake, put a mite box in the kitchen and, each adult member, as a part of a morning prayer of thanksgiving, drop in 1€ every day, and get on with it.

I do not know what the future will bring. Obviously, from experience I am a poor judge of what would become of a few people gathered for Home Eucharists hosted by the earliest church members. But I do know that it is the Gospel to grow and to stretch us to grow.

And yes, there will also be opportunities to give other gifts of time and talent in addition to financial resources. The Gospel is a tough taskmaster. We are still looking for an organizer of children's activities on Sunday mornings. We will be calling for volunteers to take positions on the Bishop's Committee and The Association Management Committee. It is likely that we will be searching for a fund-raiser for Charity Outreach. The gospel demand never ends. And there is never ending divine assurance that we will not be asked for more than we are truly able to give. But we will always be stretched beyond our level of comfort.

Well, enough from me. I now turn this over to a "higher power".
Val

Please, Read Study and Pray – then Give accordingly:

Link to Bible Gate way - http://www.biblegateway.com
You can search these passages on your own and choose your own translation, and reflect.

- Parable of the Talents: Matt 25:14 or Luke 19:12
- Widows mite - give not from our surplus but from all that we have: Luke 21:1, or Mark 12:41
- The mustard seed: Matt 13:31, or Mark 4:30, or Luke 13:18
- For the measure you measure will be measured back to you: Luke 6:36
- To whom much has been given much will be required: Luke 12:41 - 48
- About the collection for God's People: 1 Corinthians 16:1

- Sow sparingly, and you will reap sparingly, sow bountifully, reap bountifully: 2 Corinthians 9:6

Grant that we may in such wise hear them, read, mark, learn, and inwardly digest them, that by patience, and comfort of thy holy Word, we may embrace, and ever hold fast the blessed hope of everlasting life, which thou hast given us in our Saviour Jesus Christ. (Book of Common Prayer.)

Appendix VI
More research on stewardship practices

Name removed

U.K.
Available

Response from online expert
I hope to answer questions on the theology, history, and constitution (there isn't one!) of the Church of England (but not necessarily on the wider Anglican Communion)
Experience in the area
A priest in the Church of England for over 30 years, with some specialist knowledge of the 19th century
I hold a Master's degree in Applied Theology
Publications
Church Times; Church of England Newspaper; Lion Encyclopedia of the Bible

You are here: Experts > Homework Help > Christianity - General > Anglicans > Tithing

Anglicans – Tithing

Expert: Name deleted for publication – 5/23/2005

Question
Are Anglicans required to tithe, i.e. giving back 10% of income to the Church? What is the Anglican Church's teaching on tithing?

Answer
Very few denominations "require" tithing.

Two centuries ago, the Church of England would have distinguished itself from "voluntary" (dissenting) churches because the cost of its ministry was met, as an established church, from ancient endowments, out of church rates (a levy on businesses) and out of agricultural tithes (a legal obligation on farmers) and also (according to critics) out of taxation.

In the nineteenth century, people objected to paying both church rates and tithes - especially if they were dissenters and had to pay involuntarily to support the Vicar, as well as voluntarily to support their own minister and church.

At the same time, the Church of England started raising subscriptions to build new churches in urban areas, and by the end of the century it was quite normal to take collections in Anglican churches (though it is unlikely that the level of giving was anything like one tenth of income, and many continued to give nothing). There are still ministers and congregations who do not take giving seriously, and their viability is increasingly questioned.

Many biblically-minded ministers would now preach tithing, but the general "expected" level of giving is five per cent of disposable income (i.e. after tax and housing costs).

Without the background of historic endowments, Anglican churches abroad have always been more likely to expect their members to pay their way.

It would be fair to say that Church of England congregations have in recent years met the challenge well of increasing their giving despite falling numbers attending worship.
http://www.independent.co.uk/news/uk/the-church-of-englands-general-synod-carey-suggests-10-tithe-from-rich-anglicans-1533072.html
The Church of England's General Synod: Carey suggests 10% tithe from rich Anglicans
Named deleted for publication, Tuesday, 14 July 1992

Sir Douglas Lovelock, the First Church Estates Commissioner. ...On the commissioners' own figures, average giving from parishioners need rise the real target would be a level of 5 per cent of net pay,

http://www.thetablet.co.uk/pdf/3212
THE TABLET | 18 July 2009
■■■■■■■■■■■■■ - **is a freelance writer on religious affairs.**

Return of the tithe
Last week's gathering of the Church of England's General Synod was forced to face the sobering fact that it is failing to balance its books. However unpalatable, the Church has to make cuts and to find ways of persuading its members to give more

http://www.cofe.anglican.org/info/funding/stewardship.html

Unless our money gift has cost us something, it is not really a thanksgiving but more like a tip. And one of the tensions in our discipleship lies in whether we live our life and give to God the odd crumb, or whether we give to God first, and then manage the rest. If the Christian disciple does the first, he will never be satisfied: If he does the second, he will always have enough.

http://www.churchtimes.co.uk/content.asp?id=77982   CHURCH TIMES 17 July 2009

A NEW DRIVE to increase stewardship giving was launched by the General Synod last weekend. It endorsed a new booklet aimed at raising average giving to ten per cent after tax — **five per cent to and through the Church, and five per cent directly to other work that "helps to build God's kingdom"**. ….

It had been asked time and again to retain the initial giving target of five per cent of net income given to and through the Church. This it was glad to restate, since it had been set out in the report A Resourceful Church (**1978**), A further five-per-cent target was set for giving for "other work that helps to play our part in building God's Kingdom". This point was implicit in the report First to the Lord (**2000**), but had not been in the Synod's motion at that time. Today, Mr. Slater believed that the Synod would want to take away any doubt about this. …The Bishop of Ripon & Leeds, the Rt Revd. John Packer, said that the latest figures (2007) showed a rise from 3.2 per cent to 3.4 per cent, but it was still only two-thirds of the persistent call to the Church from the Synod.

BBC NEWS Tuesday, 14 July 2009 12:39 UK

The average Anglican now donates more than 3.5% of take-home pay to the Church, supplying half of its income.

Val J. Littman

Appendix VII
Becoming a Mission and applying for a grant

This document is included in the list of Appendices because it helps illustrate the step by step process taken in the development of congregational life. The development was multidimensional; including growth in numbers of members, growth in interpersonal congregational relationships, development of lay leadership positions, formal organizational and legal processes required by the state and by the church. While this happened under the shepherding of a pastor, it could not be forced and certainly not accomplished by simple autocratic cohersion as was accused during the height of congregation conflict in 2010 and 2011.

Petition to: Bishop Pierre W. Whalon
　　　　　　The Council of Advice
　　　　　　Committee on Mission Congregations

Date:　　　　Easter, 12 April 2009
Regarding:　Application for Special Mission Status
　　　　　　　　as a member of the Convocation of American Churches in Europe

A brief description of the nature, scope, organizational structure and leadership:

Beginning in October 2003 a small group of local expatriates, living in the Languedoc-Rousillon; wished to worship in English. The Rev Val J. Littman responded to requests and volunteered pastoral leadership.

Since 2003 we have met monthly for Eucharist and our congregational life has grown to include increased numbers of retirees and a few younger families with children. We also have become more visible in the larger community as an English--speaking church group.

In 2008 we formed an Association Loi 1901 and an honorary lay leadership group. We identify ourselves as both Anglican and Episcopal but to date we have no official standing with either group.

It now seems right for us to establish our connection with the larger church through this petition for Special Mission Status to The Convocation.

Therefore:

1. We, the undersigned, make this application for Specialized Mission status in The Convocation as provided in Canon 20, section 2 of the Constitutions and Canons of The Convocation.
2. We seek this status because membership in The Convocation gives us participation in the larger Anglican Communion.
3. We believe that membership in The Convocation and the larger Anglican Communion is consistent with our worship tradition, based on the Book of Common Prayer.
4. We recognize now that we may not yet meet all standards of practice of The Convocation, but we have the desire to comply with those standards and practices.
5. We will, as a Specialized Mission, strive to bring the ordering of our common life - our worship, our local governance and our finances – to the standards of practice of The Convocation.
6. We request that after a period of no more than three years our status as Specialized Mission be reviewed to consider Organized Mission status subject to the General Canons, Title I, Canon 15

Evidence that work may continue without interference with existing cures:

To the best of our knowledge there are no other cures of The Convocation proximate to our geographic location; none in the department Hérault (34). The closest English speaking congregations being a congregation established in October 2006 by the Diocese in Europe between Alés and Anduze (the Gard department 30). A Protestant Evangelical Methodist Church in Narbonne (the Aude, department 11), and an International Chapel of Montpellier, an evangelical Protestant Church (Hérault).

Signatures below are those of members of this congregation, of persons at least eighteen years old, who wish to establish and continue the work of a Specialized Mission.

NOTE PLEASE: Signatures are gathered on **TWO documents**
The petition for mission status is printed on "ivory stationary" - to distinguish it from **the petition for a financial grant (printed on white stationary)**

If you make your decision to sign, please consider signing both petitions.

Author's note: The names of the signatures have been removed for this publication. However, they remain in the official church records. The respective petitions garnered 36 signatures requesting Mission status in the Episcopal Church and 33 signatures for the petition for Matching Funds grant. These signatures are out of a possible 39 total signatures of members of the congregation.

A modest plan to grow the financial base to eventually compensate part time paid clergy.

SOME PLACE TO BEGIN: A comparison of minimum clergy compensation from a variety of standards:

The graph below compares minimum compensation from four sources (below first column in the graph)

Church Pension Fund USA: Minimum clergy compensation for actuarial purposes at the Church Pension Group Episcopal Church USA (2008) = $ 18,200 (Euros 14,400)
Actual minimum clergy salaries set by the executive council of the national church, established the 2009 minimal salary for clergy with less than a year experience at $38,442. (€30,227). I have not used the national church standard because it seems too out of our reach.

The **Council of the North,** National Executive Council, General Synod of the **Anglican** Church of Canada. **The minimum stipend for C of N, or mission dioceses, is Canadian $24,051.** (€14,745) After 13 years that increases

---

A Matching Grant Proposal for years 2010, 11, 12 assume receipt of a three year matching funds grant from the Convocation.

In Year 2010 the Convocation gives 2 Euros for every 1 Euros pledged by the Congregation for clergy compensation, up to a max from The Convocation of 2500.

Therefore, in 2010 The Convocation gives 2500 and the congregation gives 1250, for a total of 3750 compensation in 2010.

Year 2011 the ratio is 1 to 1, Convocation gives a max of 2500 if the congregation pledges 2500 resulting in € 5000 clergy compensation.

Year 2012 the ratio is the reverse of year 2010. Where The Convocation gives 1 euro for every 2 euros pledged by the congregation up to max of 2500. If the congregation pledges 5000 euros the convocation will contribute € 2500 for a total compensation of €7250.

to Canadian $26,451 and the maximum for 25 years of service is Canadian $29,051 yearly.

C of E Sept 2001, recommended raising the minimum stipend from £16,900 to about £20,000 which, when housing benefits are added, is about 80 per cent of the salary of a primary school headteacher. Pay for **curates and licensed lay workers was to increase to a national minimum of £18,200** (€ 20,132)

In France current median income (all incomes not just clergy) is listed as 20,440 Euros. **Poverty level is determined at 50% of the median income (€10,220).** If we base clergy compensation on poverty level income, a 40%-part time position - current time required for our congregation - would amount to a minimum of 4,080 Euros.

Note: clergy compensation figures normally include a basic salary as above + housing + utilities + benefits such as health care and in some cases partial payment of taxes. For our purposes here, all the above noted ONLY THE CLERGY MINIMUM SALARY with no other parts of the compensation package.

The second group of "bars" marks 40%-part time compensation if the various church standards were applied to our local situation.

Some Minimum Clergy Compensation Standards and French poverty level income. As objective guides for beginning some clergy compensation

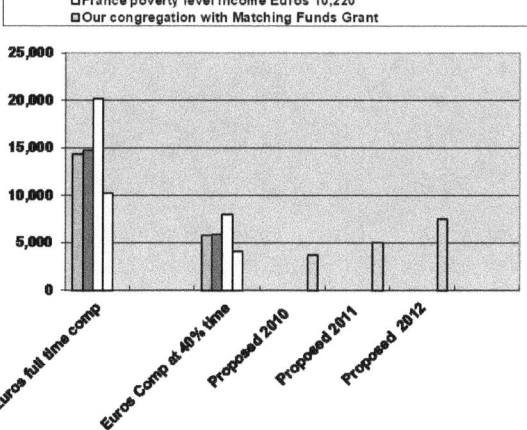

Val J. Littman

According to this plan, in year 2011, part time (40%) clergy compensation rises to slightly above 40% of the French poverty level income based on current data. **Poverty level income cannot be a long-term goal. However, it is a place to start since we are currently at zero.**

Le Petit Jardin de L'âme

Val J. Littman & Linda S. Korolewski
10 rue Molière, Florensac 34510 France
Téléphone: France (0)4 67 00 14 95
Email: mail@petitjardin.com
www.petitjardin.com

The Right Reverend Pierre W. Whalon
Bishop in Charge
Convocation of American Churches in Europe
23 Ave George V
Paris 75008

21 April 2009

Dear Bishop Whalon and members of the Convocation of American Churches in Europe

Below you will find a grant request for your consideration. It is a request for "seed money" to develop the worshiping community here in the south of France as a specialized Mission of The Convocation.

Since I have not found updated forms for 2010 grant requests yet available from the new online handbook on the convocation web site, I am using an older form and revising dates on the original form. I have updated the dates in the form to reflect a grant request to be dispersed in 2010, which, I believe is the soonest possible deadline that we can make given the grant request time line. It seems the requests need to be made no later than end of May 2009.

If this form is no longer sufficient, please advise me and I will re-submit on the preferred form if necessary.

I am making this request under the provisions for **Special Grant Categories, Item number 7** the Rowthorn Fund as a new mission project and **item number 3 of the General Grant Categories**; a Multiyear grant to provide seed money for a new mission.

Thank you, in advance for your consideration

Val J. Littman

Val J. Littman

PS - As you may remember a similar grant request was made for 2009. At that time, it was premature, in the view of some of the congregation to make a petition to join the convocation as a mission. We have since April 2009, following the Bishop's advice, petitioned the Bishop and council of Advice to be received as a Specialized Mission of The Convocation.

Proposal and grant request attached
Signatures of 33 members of the congregation attached

Le Petit Jardin de L'âme

CONVOCATION GRANT REQUEST FORM
FOR GRANTS TO BE DISBURSED IN 2010
(In €)

Grant requests must be submitted to the Convocation Office using this Grant Request Form. To be considered in the Convocation's budget for 2010 this form must be received no later than May 30, 2009.

Financial statements of 2007, 2008 and year-to-date 2009 of the entity requesting the grant must be sent together with this request. If not available, please explain.

Explanation: Beginning in September 2005 we have an annual accounting of our free will offerings and our expenses, but this is not in any way a formal budget. The accounting is for free will offerings collected. Our current operating year is determined by our first service in September and the last service in June. I have attached the statement for 2007 / 2008 which is available. A statement of our collection and expenses for Sept 2008 to March 2009 (year to date) is also attached.

We have only recently, since February 2009, organized into a French Association Loi, and even more recently, April 2009, requested special mission status as a member of The Convocation. Our financial accounting is simple and is linked to our current worship schedule (September to June) rather than to a fiscal year. This could be changed in the future to be in line with the usual and customary calendar of the convocation.

Object of the grant request:

This church community developing in the south of France now has a five-year history. It began as an informal gathering of English speaking Christians. To date, The Rev. Val J. Littman, volunteering his time and talent, has provided services. (See background below) This request is made, as part of regularizing our status as a new mission, and introducing a time of transition from an informal congregation into (eventually) an Organized Mission.

The step to Specialized Mission allows the congregation some time to adjust its organization and finances and congregation life to meet standards of the convocation. If the request is granted the funds will help the congregation begin to include clergy compensation in its budget.

Val J. Littman

The Objective of the grant is to use a "matching funds" formula to challenge the congregation to match funds received from the convocation to reach a modest clergy compensation goal. It is intended to use different levels of matching funds ratios, over a three-year period so that the congregation will take on progressively more financial responsibility. The grant would allow Rev. Littman, who has been donating his time for the past five years, to receive an honorarium. Realistically, it is unlikely that the end financial result will meet current clergy compensation standards. But this would be a major step for the congregation to increase from zero compensation to something that approaches minimum clergy compensation.

Amount requested: €2,500. or € 3,000 if available.

Expected date(s) of related expenditures: Calendar year 2010, first year of a multi-year grant (three years)

Please provide a brief statement of reasons for which Convocation funding is required; ex. What other funding sources have been considered or approached, what are expectations about being able to continue this activity in following years without Convocation financial support (if applicable), etc.

Reasons why Funding is necessary: Current funding is limited by the demographics of the congregation: mostly British retirees currently feeling the impact of the decrease in the value of their pensions. Donations of regular members who attend the services meet basic costs of our informal budget to print worship service booklets, to support charitable outreach, and a token contribution for a church building we are permitted to use by the Roman Catholic Archbishop of Montpellier.

Initially clergy financial support was not thought necessary since it involved less than one day a week. With the growth of the congregation clergy time commitment has grown from less that one day a week to over two days per week to support the congregation life. The clergy time commitment is now equal to a 40%-part time position, requiring some financial compensation.

Other sources of Funding considered:

Since most of the congregation is British, there is a considerable cultural gap to cross regarding clergy compensation. Most of the congregation fully expect that for a congregation of this size (in Britain) the clergy salary would be provided from the national church.

Le Petit Jardin de L'âme

In March 2009, the treasurer submitted a paper concerning likely future levels of church expenses. There was considerable resistance to the proposal. However, it was accepted that total expenditure (excluding charity outreach) in the region of euros 1500-2000 would be tolerated - a threefold increase over the previous year. This increase is much too small to support clergy compensation but is a big step forward in what will be a continuing process. Other steps to raise the level of income will be explored, such as fund-raising events.

The Plan for funds if granted: The attached document <u>A place to Start: A chart to compare minimum clergy compensation</u> was used when meeting with the lay leadership. In addition to providing some objective and varied standards of minimum clergy compensation, it outlines the basic grant proposal based on a matching funds scheme. Year one, The Convocation would match funds on a two for one basis; The Convocation giving two euros (up to the grant limit of €2500) for each euro raised by the congregation. Year two the convocation would match funds on a one to one basis; The Convocation giving one euro (up to the grant limit of €2500) for each euro raised by the congregation. Year three, The Convocation would match finds on a one to two basis (up to the grant limit of €2500); giving one euro for each two euros raised by the congregation. While the grant proposal assumes the same amount from the convocation in each year, this amount is used to triple the amount raised by the congregation over the three-year period.

Assuming maximum contributions from both the convocation and congregation this raises clergy compensation from its present state of zero, to French poverty level income (a rather modest goal), and then to an amount only a little short of the church pension fund minimum. These are all very modest goals but a significant improvement from where we are now. The most important development would be the development of the congregation's ownership of the responsibility for clergy compensation. – a significant asset if we are to move eventually to Organized Mission status. Expectations for continuing after the funding period: The grant itself is a vehicle for acculturation of the current congregation to the Episcopal Church. Simultaneous with the grant we will also be setting in order a Bishop's Committee, training Lay Worship Leaders and gradually organizing our common life in conformity with convocation standards.

Background: Since October of 2003 regular monthly Eucharists have been celebrated in the region surrounding Pezenas (Dept. 34, Herault, France) in response to requests from a small English-speaking community in search of occasional worship services in English.

- During the past five years, the community has grown in numbers attending. We began on average as 17 attending once a month home eucharists. We now average 40 attending each month and have moved into a church building we are permitted to use thanks to the Roman Catholic Archbishop of Montpellier.

- The number of services and public events has grown. We began with 10 monthly services, held in people's homes from September through June. In addition, to monthly Eucharists, other tradition parish services have developed: Holy Week and Easter services, one or two education events each year, blessings of marriages, a baptism, a funeral and a "first communion" for our two youngest members. Training for Lay Worship Leaders is also in progress. Clergy and members of the congregations make a significant contribution to a Lessons and Carols service in December each year. The visibility of the English-speaking congregation has grown. Val Littman is an occasional contributor to two of the regional English/French news magazines {"Blablablah", and "The Languedoc Sun"). We have public service announcements in these publications. The English worship community volunteers as a group to support the local Restos du Coeur charity, and as "The Vicar of Blah" (Val Littman's "byline" in his writing for the magazine Blablablah), is sometime a celebrity at local fundraisers with his Orgue de Barbarie.

To date Church services, relationship development, and community involvement have been led by (The Rev.) Val J. Littman. Val's time has been donated, costs for materials are supported by donations from the members of the developing congregation to cover an informal "budget "of three items, Worship, Education and Charity Outreach. There is potential for development of a mission congregation. But there is significant cross-cultural work to be done before the congregation is ready to take ownership of its responsibility to pay for its clergy. The object of the Grant request is to provide some compensation in the form of a token salary. The grant would help to establish the congregation's responsibility to pay for its clergy.

Please provide the name, telephone number, and email of contact person who can discuss this grant application with a member of the Council of Advice during July and August 2009

The Rev. Val J. Littman
Telephone: County code France = 33
              (0) 4 67 00 14 95
Email = mail@petitjardin.com

Attached: Four documents
1. Financial statement - summary for 2007 / 2008
2. September 2008 to March 2009 - year to date financial statements
3. One-page Summary - **A Place to Start**: Chart to compare minimum Clergy compensation – used to describe the Matching Funds concept to the congregation
4. Signatures from 33 members of the congregation who wish to join in this petition and commit to the Matching Funds strategy

The accounts are drawn up to cover the period 1 st August to 31st July following; this coincides with the activities of the year and the annual summer break.

Donations to Resto du Coeur, and the contribution to expenses at Canas, are shown against the period to which they relate; the actual date on which the funds were withdrawn is shown in column 3.

Val J. Littman

	Receipts Euros	Outgoings Eures
Brought forward from 200617		
Cash in hand 1st August 2007	609.07	
Receipts during 2007/8		
Annual Subsonptions	775.00	
Offerings	389.42	
Total Available	1,773.49	
Expenditures during 200il8 relating to 200617		
Donation to Resto du Coeur		400.00 9.10.2007
Contribution to Conas expenses		100.00 9.10.2007
Funds avaifable for 2007/8	1.273.49	
Expenditures during 2007/8		
Materials for service sheets		132.44
License for use of music		14.69
Pascal candle		96.30
Total outgoings for 2007/8		243.43
Balance taken forward to 2008/9	1.030.06	
Planned expenditure in 2008/9 relating to 2007/8		
Donation to Resto du Coeur		400
Contribution to Conas expenses		100
Balance available for other uses	530.06	

Accounting records

In French law, the Group is an 'association non déclaré' - perfectly legal, but lacking a legal identity and so unable to have a bank account in its own name.
To avoid confusion, and to keep the accounting as simple as possible, funds are held in cash <in the red tin box). It is therefore preferable if all subscriptions and donations are made in cash.
Separate records are maintained for receipts and payments, and the books are reconciled with the actual cash position monthly. When a cheque is

required the treasurer pays a cheque out of his personal account and and is reimbursed in cash.
It is of course our intention to become an Association Cultuelle as soon as we can organise arrangements with
the Sous-Prefeeture. We have prepared all the necessary papers for Submission.
RSF 31.09.2008

Val J. Littman

L'Association Anglican/Episcopal Church in the Hérault

		Accounts
	Euro	
Recettes		*Receipts*
Cotisations	1,025.00	Subscriptions
Offrandes	433.87	Offerings
Collecte de Fonds	0.00	Fund-raising
	1,458.87	
Dépenses		*Expenditure*
Matériel des feuilles de culte	238.25	Service sheets
Autres frais de culte	0.00	Other costs of worship
Formation	125.57	Education
Frais de voyage	0.00	Travel expenses e.g. Convention
Autres frais	0.00	Other costs
	363.82	
Dons		*Donations*
Restos du Coeur	400.00	
Conas	100.00	
Burkina Faso barrage	100.00	
	600.00	
Excédent/ Déficit	495.05	*Surplus/deficit*
Liquide		Cash Position
Reporter de 2007/8	1,030.06	Brought forward from 2007/8

Le Petit Jardin de L'âme

Disponible 31.03.09	1,525.11	In hand at 31.3.09
Constitué en	-	Represented by
Especes	855.01	Cash
Compte	670.00	Bank Account

███████, trésorier
Marseillan, le 2 avril 2009

Val J. Littman

**L'Association
Anglican/Episcopal
Church in the
Herault**

Accounts for the period 27th September 2008 until 31st March 2009

Notes

1. These accounts are drawn up from the date on which the Association was gazetted until a date just before the transfer of the role of Treasurer from Robin Field to Alan Morgan
2. The opening balance was transferred from the Home Eucharist Group, an 'Association Non-declaree', which preceded this Association
3. The Association is an Association Culturelle according to the Loi 1901 gazetted on 27th September 2008
4. The accounts are drawn up on the basis of income and expenditure during the period. There are no assets, debtors or liabilities at 31st March 2009
5. The payments to Restos du Coeur and for the use of Conas were budgeted during the previous year but not paid until after the transfer of funds to this Association and so appear in these accounts
6. Funds raised from charitable events which were not passed through the accounts are not included in these figures, but may be included in the year end accounts
7. The bank account was opened after much delay with the Banque Postale. No cheque book has yet been received
8. The accounts have not been audited but the books are available for inspection to any member of the Association by arrangement
9. I believe that the accounts are an accurate record of our finances.

SOME PLACE TO BEGIN: A comparison of minimum clergy compensation from a variety of standards:
The graph below compares minimum compensation from four sources (below first column in the graph)

Church Pension Fund USA: Minimum clergy compensation for actuarial purposes at the Church Pension Group Episcopal Church USA (2008) = $ 18,200 (Euros 14,400) Actual minimum clergy salaries set by the executive council of the national church, established the 2009 minimal salary for clergy with less than a year experience at $38,442. (€30,227). I have not used the national church standard because it seems too out of our reach.

The **Council of the North,** National Executive **Council,** General Synod of the **Anglican** Church of Canada. **The minimum stipend for C of N, or mission dioceses, is Canadian $24,051**. (€14,745) After 13 years that increases to Canadian $26,451 and the maximum for 25 years of service is Canadian $29,051 yearly.

C of E Sept 2001, recommended raising the minimum stipend from £16,900 to about £20,000 which, when housing benefits are added, is about 80 per cent of the salary of a primary school headteacher. Pay for **curates and licensed lay workers was to increase to a national minimum of £18,200** (€ 20,132)

In France current median income (all incomes not just clergy) is listed as 20,440 Euros. **Poverty level is determined at 50% of the median income (€10,220).** If we base clergy compensation on poverty level income, a 40%-part time position - current time required for our congregation - would amount to 4,080 Euros.

A Matching Grant Proposal for years 2010, 11, 12 assume receipt of a three year matching funds grant from the Convocation.

In Year 2010 the Convocation gives 2 Euros for every 1 Euros pledged by the Congregation for clergy compensation, up to a max from The Convocation of 2500.

Therefore, in 2010 The Convocation gives 2500 and the congregation gives 1250, for a total of 3750 compensation in 2010.

Year 2011 the ratio is 1 to 1, Convocation gives a max of 2500 if the congregation pledges 2500 resulting in € 5000 clergy compensation.

Year 2012 the ratio is the reverse of year 2010. Where The Convocation gives 1 euro for every 2 euros pledged by the congregation up to max of 2500. If the congregation pledges 5000 euros, the convocation will contribute € 2500 for a total compensation of €7250.

Val J. Littman

Note: clergy compensation figures normally include a basic salary as above + housing + utilities + benefits such as health care and in some cases partial payment of taxes. For our purposes here, all the above noted ONLY THE CLERGY MINIMUM STIPEND with no other parts of the compensation package.

The second group of "bars" marks 40%-part time compensation if the various church standards were applied to our local situation.

Some Minimum Clergy Compensation Standards and French poverty level income. As objective guides for beginning some clergy compensation

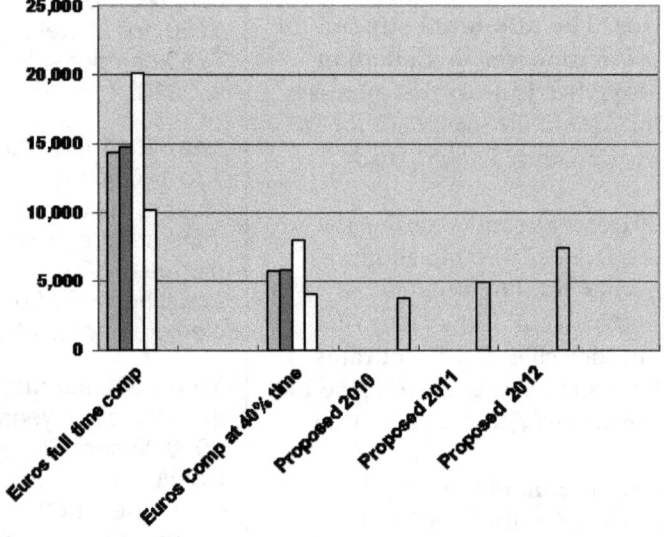

According to this plan, in year 2011, part time (40%) clergy compensation rises to slightly above 40% of the French poverty level income based on current data. **Poverty level income cannot be a long-term goal. However, it is a place to start since we are currently at zero.**

Appendix VIII
Sermon 20, February 2011

B4 The Service Reflection for 20 February 2011

A Before the Service Reflection was routinely used to help the congregation be prepared to listen to the scripture for the day. This one is a departure since it helps to prepare the congregation for listening to the sermon of the day.

It seems at first glance that both the Old Testament reading, and Gospel focus on "Commandments". But let's take a closer look and reflect on them in their different contexts.

I chose the 1648 tableaux, at the left, of Moses and the 10 Commandments by Philippe De Champaigne to move our reflection from the obvious to the less obvious. That is, it is probably safe to say that Moses did not receive the 10 Commandments from God, in French as depicted by M. De Champaigne.

There are a few points that I would like to make to put today's sermon in context:
- You know that I do not often preach a traditional sermon – except perhaps at Lessons and Carols.
- And I apologize now to those who come this morning to hear comforting words. I hope you will remember seven years of "sermons" that typically were silent reflections B4 the service.
- With the scripture readings appointed for this morning I cannot ignore the elephant in the living room; the conflict between two churches within the same Anglican communion.
- I am also most aware that often the people who most need to hear this sermon, may not actually be here and I "preach to the choir" so to speak.
- I hope you will hear this as my prayerful and considered thoughts on the scriptures. I did not choose them, they are given to us now for our hearing.
- So I asked myself what can I give to you who are here to better understand the scriptures and perhaps to better understand the difficulties we have all suffered through in this past year. As we live under the cloud of conflict.

Val J. Littman

The Prepared Sermon text:

Were you surprised to find what we commonly call the 10 Commandments are read from Leviticus? Leviticus 19:1-2,9-18, Surely those famous 10 Commandments were given on Sinai in the desert as in the Book of Exodus, N'est pas?

There is more than one version of what we assume to be a single definitive version of The 10 Commandments: one in *Exodus 20:2–17*, another in *Deuteronomy 5:6–21* and the version we hear today in Leviticus 19:1-18.

Each is written in a different context and with a special purpose:
- One written in the context of a story of a long journey of formation of God's people,
- one written at a time political transitions, important crossroads in the life of God's People.
- And one is a "re-write" with its focus on worship.

All three versions are part of the five-part Torah which makes up Jewish law.

We even have a poetic version of the law, written in the form of Psalm 119 (a part of which you prayed today in Morning prayer)

The Psalm is organized in a style that was designed to help worshippers focus on the law of God and remember God's teaching. In the 176 verses of Psalm 119, the law of God is mentioned 169 times using one of ten synonymous terms that refer to God's law; *teachings, testimonies, instruction, precepts, statutes, commandments, ordinances, decrees, word, ways, paths, promises, and judgments, rulings*. The effect is a litany that provides the worshipper with a guide for living in peace with oneself, being at one with God and with one another.

The Law gives in whatever form it comes to us is given to us to give order to the life of God's people.

Yes, the essence of all in the passages appointed for today, is the statement, "to love God and to love your neighbor as yourself"

If the main point of God's Law is love of neighbor, why can't we just stick with today's gospel reading and Jesus' commandment for his followers (Matthew 22:34-36)?

Le Petit Jardin de L'âme

Because we hear God's Word, each with our own ears (with what else you might ask?) We also hear God's Word in the context in which we live and with our hearts.

It is important to see that the eternal changeless law, changes as it is lived out differently, because <u>we</u> have insight and clarity from time to time into God's Ways.

Each time we hear God's law, in whatever context, the law helps to put flesh on the bones of this eternal moral imperative. Love is not an abstract feeling or disposition toward another person; it is evident in standards for relationships, calling for truthful speech, for justice, patience, and an effort to keep our neighbor from going astray. Love is embodied in our lives and actions.

For the Old Testament people one understanding of their God was the *lex talionis* or the old law of retaliation.

This was an attempt to enact justice among the people of ancient Israel…"an eye for an eye". Among a primitive people this form of justice was important to keeping social order (often through fear)

Today we are horrified when we hear 21st century versions of this same sort of justice in some cultures today. Yet, if we scratch the surface of many interpersonal conflicts we will surely find the roots of lex talionis – to get even.

At different times, in different places and in a variety of different conditions of God's people, God's Love is manifest in different ways. And for Christians, God's Love is embodied in The Christ.

The Gospel for today Matthew 5:38-48 contains Jesus' "New Commandment". We are perhaps so overly–familiar that we miss just how many times this commandment is repeated and rephrased throughout the New Testament each with its special purpose. Jesus' new commandment is to overcome the humiliation of injustice, deceptions, and divisiveness, by drawing people back together.

Jesus comes and sees more clearly, just how limited "*lex talionis*" is. He has an alternative strategy for dealing with injustice and the harm we do to each other. His objective is to overcome sin and injustice with good. His action, which embodies the law of God is decidedly different. Extend a hand (don't separate it from the body), open the door (welcome instead of walking away) … the Law lived this way brings fullness of life.

The more serious challenge comes in the form of admonitions in which Jesus advocates a commitment to do good despite the suffering one endures. This is difficult: it knows that rumors and accusations cannot be contained, they are like feathers in the wind. Living out this law Jesus knows there will be sadness of division, betrayal and misinformation - Still the mandate is to do good; to respond to discouraging words with hope. This is a very vulnerable spot to be in. Who knows this better than Jesus.

This faith of Jesus is to live on in us. It is this foundation in Christ that Paul just cannot seem to get the Corinthians to understand. In Paul's Letter 1 Corinthians 3:10-11,16-23 he attempts to reconcile the various ways in which God's plan for life applies to these Christians in their time and place in history.

Paul writes to the Christians at Corinth to redirect their focus away from fractious divisions, to their foundation in Christ. The early church struggled with internal Conflict and Order from its beginnings, and has found the means to maintain it ever since. Order is how the fabric of the church is <u>held together</u>. This age-old dilemma is one, which I have taken care to point out when the letters of Paul are read at our Sunday services because we are not far from the 1st century Corinthians.

Like Paul, a friend reminded me recently that we must keep our eye on Christ, not the Christians.

The community at Corinth, was torn apart by arguments about Who to follow? Paul? / follow Cephas? follow Apollos? see 1: 12-13. and wrestling with questions about sexual morality (chapters 5 and 7), lawsuits (chapter 6), and the proper way to celebrate the Lord's Supper (chapter 11), among other things.

Paul is seeking to call this distracted church back to the essentials by reminding them, "There is one foundation, the one that has been laid by Jesus Christ" (3: 11).

Le Petit Jardin de L'âme

Let me be clear about our local version of this respect for order: Our churches in Europe have a concordat, an agreement of the heart.

Specifically this takes the form of not setting up churches of the same communion, on each other's door-steps. It was established in 1968, precisely because Bishops in consultation at Lambeth had experienced and could foresee the destruction and division that occurs when this happens. Locally this is not being respected. And now the people have run out of patience as the bishops try to sort out a very sticky wicket in a problem that is a concern in the larger church far beyond our little corner of France.

Walking away was not the proper solution a year ago and it is not the solution now. And while this drags on, the devil does his work of division and discontent – chipping away at the foundation.

The Law is the way – for the Jews it is in the Torah. For Jesus, the law is embodied in the way we act on our faith - extending a hand, welcoming not walking away, and being vulnerable to rejection, even powerless against what is said.

In times of conflict it is natural to search for a quick solution, <u>for relief</u> and ignore the law because we grow weary. And heaven knows it is sometimes inconvenient to wait for reconciliation – it takes faith to persevere and not rush into what seems an easy solution. With diligence, and carefulness and patience, and in an orderly way as we live out this Christianity of ours, we must keep our eye on The Christ not the Christians.

Long ago and before our current church conflicts – and I speak of those conflicts between churches, on a grand scale and in our local church. This dialogue (from "A Man for All Seasons") **- between Thomas More and his son-in-law William Roper - jumped from the stage and into my heart and it often comes to mind. (I was in my early twenties 20's when I heard it and a bit like Will, who begins the dialogue)**

(Man, For All Season's – Robert Bolt)

<u>William Roper</u>: So, now you give the Devil the benefit of law!

<u>Sir Thomas More</u>: Yes! What would you do? Cut a great road through the law to get after the Devil?

Val J. Littman

William Roper: Yes, I'd cut down every law in England to do that!

Sir Thomas More: Oh? And when the last law was down, and the Devil turned 'round on you, where would you hide, Roper, the laws all being flat? This country is planted thick with laws, from coast to coast, Man's laws, not God's! And if you cut them down, and you're just the man to do it, do you really think you could stand upright in the winds that would blow then? Yes, I'd give the Devil benefit of law, for my own safety's sake!

I wish to conclude by drawing your attention to two prayers: One, which takes the form of a hymn to be sung later in the service this morning. Our Communion Hymn today is a translation from the early 1st century teaching from the Didache: Perhaps you will remember a little bit of this sermon when we reach the communion table.

Father we thank thee who hast planted Thy holy name within our hearts.
Knowledge and faith and life immortal Jesus, Thy Son, to us imparts.
Thou, Lord, didst make all for Thy pleasure, Didst give us food for all our days,
Giving in Christ the Bread eternal; Thine is the pow'r, be Thine the praise.

Watch o'er Thy Church, O Lord, in mercy, save it from evil, guard it still,
Perfect it in Thy love, unite it, Cleansed and conformed unto Thy will.
As grain, once scattered on the hillsides, was in this broken bread made one, so from all lands Thy Church be gathered into thy kingdom by thy son.

The second and more immediate is an excerpt from a prayer that has come to mean much to me in my adult life because of conflicts great and small. And in some strange way I thank the conflicts in our little congregation for bringing it back to mind: William Laud Archbishop of Canterbury - was no stranger to division in the church of 17th Century England. After being tried, acquitted, and granted a royal pardon, parliament suspended both by an act of attainder and he was beheaded.

Join me in this prayer:
O merciful God, since you have created me to live in these times, in which the divisions of the church are grievous, I humbly beseech you to guide me, that the divisions of men; may not separate me from you

Le Petit Jardin de L'âme

my God,....
In the meantime bless, I beseech you, this Church in which I live, that in it I may honour and serve you all the days of my life, and after this be glorified by you, through Jesus Christ our Lord. Amen.

Val J. Littman

Appendix IX

Names and identifiers removed for publication

Letter from Simon Peter

Dear Val,

Private & Confidential

Two things said by ▮▮▮▮▮▮▮ on Thursday evening – 10 June (after the formal meeting) have prompted me to write to you now as I have suddenly realised I am in a unique position to make some sense of why we are where we are now. It may not do any good, but an overall view could be helpful to our cause.

Perhaps I should have done this earlier but, like completing a jigsaw puzzle suddenly one sees the picture after the last few pieces are added. Indeed you & others, in turn, may add to this picture as I am far from certain that every piece has been identified. Rising above events in which one is intimately involved, to seek the overview, is difficult, especially when one enters the age of the rot!!

History of the split in the Congregation.

Provide here the Attendance and History info about our beginnings in October 2003

The momentum to establish a formal church came from ▮▮▮▮▮▮▮, ▮▮▮▮▮, T▮▮▮ & other parties. They pressed you to form a church. At some point this core group, joined by ▮▮▮▮▮▮▮ and others (much later), felt that they were losing power, control and influence.

Gossip circulated cruising leadership, direction, consultation etc. After talking to others, I would date this dissatisfaction to the move to Conas Church & the discussion and establishment of a formal body, formal structures etc. From that time trouble gained momentum. At the beginning this was just gossip, mutual moaning but, at some point, ▮▮▮▮ and ▮▮▮▮▮▮▮ began, perhaps unconsciously, to discuss & plan for a different type of church to that seen by Val. They could not have their own way and sought to oust you from the church. I think the idea was slow to form but

Le Petit Jardin de L'âme

gained momentum with planning & action visible during 2008/2009 cumulating in a breakaway in 2010.

They attempted to do this in many ways.

Firstly, they deliberately ignored the Rules of Association of loi for Clermont Ferrand Church, provided to them, (the 1905 version which permits Clergy pay) and used the 1901 version (which does not allow clergy pay) to be the basis of the Association of loi. **This has only just come to light.**

Secondly, ███████ attempted to use the Budget figures as a pretext for a vote of no confidence (in Val) at the Annual General Meeting of the Association of loi. He canvassed votes directly through personal contact with the disaffected and by use of the church address book / e-mail contact. The planned intention was to ensure sufficient unhappy people voted against the budget forcing Val to resign. ███ planned to take over the association after your resignation and bring into being a congregational church.

Thirdly, he and others used the confidential e-mail list of the church to send messages to the general congregation to sow seeds of discontent, insecurity over money issues and garner support.

Fourthly covert, informal gatherings took place.

At that time, I was taking over the position of Treasurer from ████. Up until then I had heard gossip about personal dissatisfaction but had no direct knowledge of strategy and tactics. However once in the role of Treasurer I was invited to join this revolt. Most of my information came by e-mail but I learnt, after the event, of meetings taking place at ██████'s house, T███████'s house and even the █████ (? not certain – may have been a moaning session). I was not invited to any meeting as I was an unknown element.

████████ is correct in saying she and █████ did not attend any meetings. But she and █████ did host dinner parties (and she was in the gossip circle). I know because I was invited and heard the comments round the table. █████ said and did nothing, thus the ability to deny all). However, he was aware of the general direction this small group was taking.

████ was also fully aware that meetings had taken place. Her very fast response on Thursday, « I was in the UK at the time » was just too quick. I couldn't remember that long ago without pausing to think. She didn't pause. We now know that she was aware of ▮'s comment about resignation which implies she was informed by others.

▮▮▮▮▮▮ actively conspired, with others, during 2009 to establish a new church as he had been leading to believe that you Val would resign if the vote at the Annual General meeting went against you. (I use the word « conspire » in the sense that he secretly planned with others a harmful act)

My budget figures and comments were to be used as a pretext for the vote of no confidence. This was merely a ploy to convince others to join in. Question: Why did ▮▮▮▮ call off the meeting of October 2009? It was a strange move – and in the end, I think it may have inadvertently helped Grace church at the time.

Once I realised that ▮▮▮▮'s real intentions were the collapse of the plans for a church linked to Episcopal/ Anglican way and replacement with a wholly Anglican way, (pardon - pun not intended – but with hindsight too good to remove) I felt it impossible to have any further dealings with these people. I thought deeply about their tactics and sought a meeting with you Val to explain how all their plans would fail.

When ▮▮▮▮ made a tactical decision to postpone the AGM, and, in the process, upset ▮▮▮▮▮▮, I seized the opportunity to demand the resignations of ▮▮▮▮, ▮▮▮▮▮▮ and T▮▮▮▮▮ from the Management Committee, Bishops Committee and we formed a fresh committee. As Treasurer I felt it impossible to resign as well for the sake of continuity of the Bishops committee.
The core group split away forming their own « rival » church under the guidance of Richard ▮▮▮▮. (his word, rival) They justified their actions by saying, after the event: (letter to Bishop Pierre confirms)

> The affiliation to the Convocation was not fully discussed.
>
> The final decision to join had come as surprise.
>
> Trust had been broken.
>
> Concerns were expressed about the style of Leadership.

After listening to the views of others and examining the timeline of the troubles these points are excuses. Further evidence is the results of the

Le Petit Jardin de L'âme

survey carried out by ▓▓▓ ▓▓▓▓▓▓. There is very little in the way of complaints from most of the congregation. **What they do not say is just as important as what they do say.** Thus, I believe the true reasons for the breakaway were loss of power & influence by core group members.

It is worth noting that certain members of this core group immediately sought positions of influence within the new group without any formal electoral process. Thus, they reverted to their past ways of achieving status, control & influence.

A few of those attending on 10 June made this comment immediately after the meeting: -

there are a small number of key members (▓▓▓▓, ▓▓▓▓▓▓, ▓▓▓▓▓▓, ▓▓▓▓▓▓ and ▓▓▓▓) who lead dissent. Others may have been convinced or coerced in some way, few others recruited by the rationalizations, with euphemisms presented in the letters of ▓▓▓▓▓▓ ▓▓▓▓▓▓ and ▓▓▓▓▓▓.

It is these core couples (8 -10 people) which drove the split. Others who may worship at St Pargoire are more flexible.

With these comments in mind, it comes clearly into view that one of the areas of conflict is a difference in ecclesiology. The Power and Control issues surfaced using the payment of clergy and joining the convocation. They were an excuse perhaps not even consciously recognised by those involved. It was a clash between a hierarchical church and congregational church ecclesiologist (or perhaps more accurately some form of congregationalism). With some of the leading lay persons wanting power central to the laity - with clergy called upon simply to provide ritual worship.

Val's leadership style is predominately collaborative- (using the traditional roles of Laity, Bishops, Priest, Deacons). He is the priest in Charge and worship itself is realized by the extension of it into other areas of our congregational life.

▓▓▓▓▓▓ fits the needs of a "congregationalism" called for by the other congregation.

In this form it is possible to have the council run the parish and the priest shuffles in to "Say Mass" at their bequest for which they may or may not think to pay him because his "work" is seen to begin and end a few

minutes before and after the ritual service. All else is decided on by the council. Clergy do not need even attend the meeting.
Finally, I would add that as soon as their current positions are threatened by the actions or words of Bishop Pierre they will seek to blame you Val, and others for their loss of status!
Thus, the final proof will come through their actions & words.

Also, if they must surrender to a higher authority they will seek an alternative. Their membership is superficial.

Here ends my simplistic history. Please add to it where you wish. The more contributors the better the perspective.

Present Sense

I am regarded, so vividly described by ▮▮▮, as a turncoat. So perhaps you and I, Val share the position at the stake!! Ah honour to be beside a valiant pilgrim. For their hatred can only be directed at you and me!!

What has also prompted this letter was the other comment ▮▮▮ made to me; namely that you had indicated, at some point, that you would resign. I now realise could have given ▮▮▮ hope, purpose and opportunity. Have you ever considered that ▮▮▮ could be a manipulator who has used you??

(Subsequently, I have discovered an e-mail dated 19th March 2009 where ▮▮▮, in the final paragraph comments
« you regarded walking away from the situation as a possible route. »)

So, this stems from a meeting (?) in or prior to March 2009. This comment was broadcast to others because ▮▮▮, not only remembered it but mentioned it to me.

How interesting. If ▮▮▮ was so fully informed could ▮▮▮ remain unaware. - we now know he was aware because of his after-dinner comment to you. Also, she must have been involved in some way to have been a confidant of such information. The March 2009 e-mail also confirms the long-term nature of their dissatisfaction and discussions.

If there is anger within the St Pargoire congregation it can only be amongst this core group and the reason must be that, again they feel their positions are threatened. They can no longer use the four excuses listed above to justify their feelings. Isn't it interesting that T▮▮▮ always assumes the role of Churchwarden without any idea what the job is about!! She is an example of a person motivated by status and, once threatened, turns aggressively to protect her perceived position and seeks to blame others. Do you recall her husband, ▮, writing to the Bishops committee, after her resignation, (no mention that it was forced through her own machinations) complaining that we had not formally thanked her for everything she had done to help Grace Church!! They are truly divorced from reality!

I believe I was wrong to see this as a personal clash about Val's style of leadership. This analysis has revealed deeper reasons which would have arisen whosoever was in charge.

On a philosophical point Hegel comments that most people have no spirit of creation or invention. They know only what they already know. If you want to teach them something new you must mix what they know with what they don't know. Then they see vaguely in their fog something they recognise. In this case their idiosyncratic idealism failed to absorb the reality of a hierarchical church and reverted to what they knew already, indeed what they were comfortable with.

It was convenient to hide their true feelings, so the convenient problems became the truth. Any awkward efforts were avoided. There was no need to think as their excuse became a self-fulfilling act. Whatever contributed to their image became the truth? They were comfortable in their contented acceptance that they were, and will remain right.

These comments, perhaps, form the basis of forgiveness:

They know not what they do

May I conclude by saying this document can be a means to focus our thoughts on our mistakes and seek a sure foundation for the future. For if we do not learn from the past, we are likely to repeat it. Of course, it can be of help in many ways. **For example, explaining why you Val were not to blame in any way for this split.**

However, the bottom line must be that if our Bishop succeeds in interfering with their plans their anger will be directed outwards, in our direction. If we understand the nature of these people we can protect ourselves against the inevitable backlash.

Blessings,
(Simon Peter)

Val J. Littman

Appendix X
Letter to the congregation before departure

Each year now Linda and I have a tradition. The end of one year and beginning a new year has always been a time for us to do some life-planning. This year our goal for 2011 is to begin (again) our retirement. Sometime during 2011 (time yet to be determined) Linda and I will begin our next chapter of retirement in The Republic of Panama. Our actual departure depends on the sale of our home, so it is difficult to say when exactly. We expect to be here through Easter, probably into June (perhaps longer). We experience a mix of uncertainty and excitement as we look ahead.

Ten years ago, our friends in the USA asked incredibly, "Why move to France?" We expect our friends here will again ask," Why Panama?" In part, the move is for us one of those freedoms of retirement we have decided to exercise. And after five-plus years of unfavorable exchange rates, Dollars to Euros, we look forward to a currency on par with the dollar.

We make this decision knowing that our choice also touches the lives of many in the little church that has grown up around us here in France. How you receive this information is very much in our minds and hearts and in our prayers - and so, this letter.

On 13 December Bishop Pierre Whalon attended the meeting of the Bishop's Committee where I presented the news of our eventual re-location. This put the previous discussions of transition to new clergy leadership for Grace Church into a new perspective. During this first quarter of 2011 there will be a transition plan from Bishop Whalon and the Bishop's Committee, answering the Who? What? and When? questions. This plan will allow me to retire again.

As part of an orderly transition to new clergy, The Bishop's Committee will consider the practical adjustments necessary for the transition in consultation with Bishop Whalon. As we move forward you will be kept informed.

Transitions provide moments for growth. As the congregation moves from the first clergy (me) to the next in a long line of clergy and congregation members yet to come, this is an opportunity for new life. This is a normal part of church life

Thank you for eight years of unexpected ministry here in the Hérault together. We have seen the congregation that began as a once a month house-church in 2003, increase worship services, for Holy Week, Easter and Christmas and recently added the summer months. We anticipate experimenting with adding a second monthly service in May of 2011. We have education events, bible study, a prayer group and charity outreach. This year, two Lay Worship leaders completed training enabling them to lead Morning Prayer on occasion. And this year Grace Church was responsible for continuing the tradition of Lessons and Carols Service at Fontès (the largest attendance ever).

Our budget has stretched, and you have responded generously. We have exceeded the budget demands for 2010 and are in a good position for 2011. The Bishop's Committee has established good infrastructure for the future, in revising our Association Loi 1901 and 1905 and Mission bylaws. We are now able to offer a token clergy stipend to attract new clergy.

With 26 registered members of the congregation, and a core work group of about a dozen, we are the size of many small Anglican Congregations across the Worldwide Anglican Communion. Part of our service to the larger community is to provide a church "home-away-from-home" for many. Our revised address book is a list of 80+ visitors wishing to know more about our services. What a blessing, and good ground for continued ministry.

We tell you this knowing that changes are anxious times for all. And so, it will forever be; the edge of moments of great opportunity often looks like a chasm ready to devour us. We all have an opportunity to respond increasing our faith, to do the work that God has given us to do, and to Grow in Grace.

Our Best Wishes to you all, at the beginning of a New Year - Val and Linda

Val J. Littman

Bibliography for *Le Petit Jardin*

Some of the works below have been referenced in the chapters of Le Petit Jardin de L'âme. Others, not specifically mentioned in the text, have been an influence in my life, spiritual formation and professional experiences as a psychotherapist, organizational development and conflict management long before my experience of life in France.

A Brief Annotated Bibliography:

Curran, Charles A., PhD. A Need for Listeners. Windsor Ontario, Canada: Counseling Learning Institute, ©1970

Haidt, Jonathan. The Happiness Hypothesis Putting Ancient Wisdom and Philosophy to the Test of Modern Science. London: Arrow Books, Random House. © 2006.

Hastings, Max (23 November 2008 the Sunday Times Review). The Shameful Peace: How French Artists and Intellectuals Survived the Nazi Occupation, by Frederic Spotts. There is no need to punish or judge people for this act which they saw as necessary for survival. But we cannot deny that it has an impact on the way people live and think. There is a similar review in The Economist of Nov 22-26, 2008 entitled Smoke and Mirrors: France in the 2nd World War

Heim, Pat Ph. D and Murphy Susan A, PhD, MBA with Susan K. Galant. *In the Company of Women:* Indirect Aggression Among Women Why We Hurt Each Other And How to Stop. Jeremy P. Tarcher/Putnam a member of Penguin Group (USA) Inc. © 2011. The book was recommended by a dear friend in her attempt to understand dynamics between women in organizations. In my reading I also found it helpful to apply these observations to the Church as a "female" organization. Although ostensibly governed by a predominantly male hierarchy, and, composed obviously of men and women, the "Mother "church as an organization, in its raison d'etre has many female, nurturing, characteristics. And, within many congregations, women's prominence in roles of service in church activities. Also, the female archetype prevails as "mother church". The insights of this book apply well to the church to help us understand why we hurt each other and how to stop. ISBN 1-58542-223-1

Irving, W. George Washington: A Biography. Charles Neider (ed.) Garden City, New York: Doubleday 1976 (quote from letter to John Augustine) "I am embarked on a wide ocean, boundless in its prospects and, in which, perhaps, no safe harbor is to be found."

Joly, Julie. Cette méfiance qui tue la croissance . L'Express. September 20, 2007. Individualistes, corporatistes, les Français suspectent tout et tout le monde : voisins, patrons, justice, élus... Dans un ouvrage audacieux, deux chercheurs expliquent les effets ravageurs de cet état d'esprit – Chercheurs Pierre Cahuc et Yann Algan pour la recherche économique et ses applications

Kilvert, Robert Francis. Kilvert's Diary – See, The Kilvert Society
The ***English*** diarist Robert Francis Kilvert (1840–1879). His diaries reflect rural ***life*** in the ***1870s***, which were published over fifty years after his death. In 1937, the poet and novelist William Plomer made a momentous discovery in a pile of manuscripts at the offices of Jonathan Cape in Bedford Square, where he worked as a reader. Sadly, it's difficult to find copies of Kilvert in bookshops today. The one-volume abridgement, published by Penguin, and subsequently by Pimlico, has fallen out of print, while Plomer's three-volume edition has long been unavailable. I was fortunate to read the one-volume abridgement on loan to me from a dear friend

Kovess-Masfety V, Briffault X, Sapinho D. Survey in a large region of France between 1991 and 2005. Source : Université Paris Descartes (Equipe d'Accueil 4096), Fondation Mutuelle Générale de l'Education Nationale pour la Santé Publique, Paris, France. fsp@mgen.fr. The study compares the prevalence, risk factors, and use of care for depression between 2 periods, concerning changes in social factors and health care provision.

Maynard, Dennis R. *When Sheep Attack.* Booksurge Publishers, © 2010 Dennis R Maynard D.Min. This was a thoughtful -and very helpful - Christmas gift from my bishop in the midst of very difficult times. Written for clergy and the people they serve, it is anecdotal research and analysis of a painful dynamic in congregations. But could also be applied to many small successful volunteer organizations ISBN: 1-4515-1391-7

O'Donnell, Richard W. Do You Hear What I hear? The Story Behind The Song . Featured Article Saint Anthony's Messenger December 2007

Porter, Anna. The Ghosts of Europe. Vancouver / Toronto: Douglas & McIntyre, D & M Publishers Inc., © 2010 Anna Porter. The dynamics, of the countries of central Europe in the 20th and 21st century, described by the author are not to be limited to Central Europe alone. Throughout the book and especially in the pages of the "Afterward" reflects what I felt of the darker side of France (and of my contacts with the English in France). Beginning with the reference to George Soros on page 275 to the end quote of Jan Patocka at the end reflects the moral shift I experienced in life in Western Europe, although geographically another land "… NO society… can function without a moral foundation, without conviction that has nothing to do with opportunism, circumstances and expected advantage. Man does not define morality according to the caprice of his needs, wishes, tendencies and cravings; it is morality that defines man." Translation from Rupnk, *The Other Europe*.

Pritchard, John. The Life and Work of a Priest. London: Society for the Promotion of Christian Knowledge (SPCK). © 2007 John Pritchard. This book, also a gift from my bishop to his clergy, helped to give concise words to my approach to the representational ministry of all the baptized (Page 6), 'the priests role presiding at the Eucharist (chapter 2) and, in the last days, the question Where is God in all this? (Page 50ff)

Rachman, Gideon. (2009) Why are the French so depressed? October 14, 2009 12:47 pm, **The World** http://blogs.ft.com/the-world/2009/10/why-are-the-french-so-depressed/#ixzz1rpzVssaf and companion article from **The Economist**. Bonjour Tristesse, Suicide in France. Asks Why are the French so prone to Suicide? October 08, 2009 http://www.economist.com/node/14588104?story_id=14588104

Rooney, Andy. My War. New York: Public Affairs a member of Perseus Books Group. © 1995, 2000 by Essay Productions Inc.
I read this book in 2013, a few years after these events in France and after our settlement in The Republic of Panama. The style and candor of the book prompted me to continue to write of the years of 2004 to 2012. Although the conflict in the church in France could never be compared to WWII, Rooney's approach to the most serious of events with a sense of humor and candor inspired me. I borrowed his opening paragraphs on page three of the book direct into my writing – it was true for him and it is true for me.

Trivers, Robert. The Folly of Fools: The logic of Deceit and Self-Deception in Human Life. Basic Books a member of The Perseus Books Group. © 2011 by Robert Trivers.
This book is a bit of "slow going" at times with moments of spark and enlightening insight. Highlights for me were pages 67, 112 and Chapter 7, Chapter 10, and Chapter 13. It was the title that initially intrigued me as a possible way to make sense of two years of church struggle which involved copious self-deception, abusive relationships and rewrites of history. I quote from page 112 in Chapter 20 of the book.

Vanier, Jean. Becoming Human. New York: Paulist Press. © 1998 Jean Vanier and The Canadian Broadcasting Corporation – and - Community and Growth. London: Darton, Longman & Todd © 1979. Originale Publisher as la Communauté : Lieu des Pardon et de la Fête by Les Editions Fleurs, Paris and Les Editions Bellarmin, Montréal. Jean Vanier, Philosopher, Theologian, Humanist and founder of L' Arche. Vanier, presents in his writing, and in his life, the adventure of building community. His approach and insights into what is often perceived as weakness, vulnerability and evil, in the human condition has been very influential in my life and work in psychotherapy, community organization and the building of a church community.

Wiesel, Ellie. Night. New York: Hill and Wang, a division of Farrar, Strass and Giroux. © 1972, Translation copyright by Marion Wiesel 2006, Preface to the new translation © 2006 Ellie Wiesel.
I would not be so grand as to liken my experiences in France to those described in Night by Wiesel. But the re-reading of this book in its new translation in 2009 brought home to me how the dynamics of evil and deception have their effect on people in every age. The quote from the opening lines of his new preface made so much sense to explain my present at that time.

Le petit Jardin de L'âme –
About the Author: Val J. Littman:

After establishing careers in the church, in America's corporate-life, in Chicago Real Estate and after twenty-five years of marriage, Val Littman and his wife Linda Korolewski were ready for a change. They decided to exchange their accumulated Master's degrees in Divinity, Theology, Public Health and Clinical Social Work, along with their professional licenses, certifications, and their Chicago urban lifestyle for life in the south of France.

Formed by their experience in religious life, ministry, teaching, psychology and social work, Val and Linda bring to their new life and to this book a perceptive, prayerful, carefully considered, and often comical view of *la vie en France*.

Born in 1948 Linda and Val are among the Baby-Boomer generation that has often pushed the cultural envelope, crossing over to living their lives in new ways. Their early retirement at age 53 puts them at the edge of many in that generation who will be living out their own dreams of a good-life in the "The Third-Age", and the growing trend of international living.

Their first book; *A Bright Sun & Long Shadows* is a candid reflection on the glorious and gruesome realities of creating a new life in France. In this second book, *Le Petit Jardin de L'âme*, Val continues the story and opens to you, the reader, the heart of a struggle that affected, his life, their marriage, and the church congregation that grew up around them. Each book can be read separately or sequentially as a chronology of the twelve years of life in France.

www.ingramcontent.com/pod-product-compliance
Lightning Source LLC
Chambersburg PA
CBHW070534010526
44118CB00012B/1133